SIX PLAYS OF STRINDBERG

SIX PLAYS

of

STRINDBERG

in New Translations by

ELIZABETH SPRIGGE

Doubleday Anchor Books 1955

DOUBLEDAY & COMPANY, INC.
GARDEN CITY, N.Y.

ON STRINDBERG

By Eric Bentley

The lifework of August Strindberg (1849–1912) may be arranged in three concentric circles. Tangential to the outermost circle are his occasional works, translations, essays, and treatises; within it are the autobiographies, which are the raw material for Strindberg's art works; within the second circle are the novels, a very rough attempt, for the most part, to impose order upon the chaos of his experience; within the innermost circle, as Strindberg's central achievement, are his plays.

Reading through the dramatic *oeuvre*, we encounter a wide range of types. The polar extremes are both very simple, not to say simplistic forms: on the one hand, chronicle histories and, on the other, fairy plays. More important are Strindberg's deviations from the rival simplicities—namely, his quasi-tragic "naturalistic" dramas and his "expressionistic" fantasies.

In the present volume are three examples of Strindberg's "naturalism"—THE FATHER, 1887; MISS JULIE, 1888; THE STRONGER, 1890—and two of his "expressionism"—A DREAM PLAY, 1902, and THE GHOST SONATA, 1907; while EASTER derives its fascination from the fact that it eludes classification.

Included in the present volume are the Foreword to MISS JULIE and the program note on A DREAM PLAY—documents which give a rather explicit account of Strindberg's intentions in both groups of plays. Here, for their suggestive value, I will only give three comments on the first of the plays in the volume, THE FATHER:

1. THE FATHER is the realization of modern drama, and as such is something very curious. Very curious because the struggle takes place between souls. It is a battle of brains, not a dagger fight or a poisoning with raspberry

juice as in Schiller's *Robbers*. The French are still seeking the formula. . . .

2. Your play interests me very much. The philosophical idea is very daring, and the characters are boldly drawn. You have traced the doubt of paternity with a powerful and disquieting effect. Finally, your Laura is the true woman in the unconsciousness and the mystery of her qualities and faults . . . Your piece is one of the few dramatic works to have moved me profoundly.

3. I read your tragedy twice over with deep emotion; it has astonished me beyond all measure to come to know a work in which my own conception of love—with war as its means and the deathly hate of the sexes as its fundamental law—is expressed in such a splendid fashion.

The first comment is by Strindberg himself; the second by Emile Zola; the third by Friedrich Nietzsche.

CONTENTS

THE FATHER

A Tragedy in Three Acts
by

AUGUST STRINDBERG

INTRODUCTION

In the last half-century Strindberg has enjoyed a growing reputation both on the continent and, latterly, in
England, for the simple reason that of all nineteenth-
century dramatists, he is the least dated. He developed
at a time when theatre had begun to be a contemporary
affair, a platform for moral debate, an organ of modern
thought which influenced public opinion, thus changing
customs and even laws, and so the playwright had become
an important international figure.

Until Zola, in the 'seventies, made his dramatic assault
on the theatre, demanding the whole of life, by which he
meant the most crude and violent aspects of life upon
the stage, drama had, as usual, lagged behind the times.
Now, stripped of romanticism, refinement and rhetoric,
led by that pioneer of little theatre clubs, Antoine's
Théâtre Libre, it exploded into so-called Naturalism. In
came Ibsen with GHOSTS and the stage was set for THE
FATHER.

Yet to call THE FATHER a naturalist play is absurd. As
the Swedish authority Martin Lamm points out, Strindberg intended it to be the modern equivalent of AGAMEM-
NON, the Swedish captain like the Greek king victim of
woman's sex hatred and lust for power. OTHELLO, MACBETH
and KING LEAR were also in Strindberg's mind as he conceived THE FATHER, and he deliberately drew his hero
larger than life. The strength of the play can thus be said
to be due partly to the influence of Aeschylus; the plot is
stark, the construction economic, the pace swift and the
movement towards fatality inevitable. The Captain is a
giant who, like Strindberg himself, impresses us with his
size and shocks us with his clumsy weakness. In fact, in
this play Strindberg gives a penetrating diagnosis of his
state of mind at its most unhappy and it is his own hysteria
which prevents THE FATHER from being wholly great.

While the play grips us with its dramatic force, shatters
us with its brutality and leaves us admiring its craftsman-

ship, there is no aftermath of imagination, no echo of
beauty. In spite of the Captain's good points, the play
is consistently black, particularly when played, for it is
usually produced with unrelieved violence. This, to do
the author justice, was not his intention. In a letter to
Lundegård, the Swedish critic, at the time of the first
production in Copenhagen in 1887, Strindberg stated that
the Captain should be presented "as a normally robust
man with a taste for irony and self-mockery, and the
lightly sceptical tone of a man of the world." He also
directed that the part should be played "subtly, calmly,
resignedly," and described the Captain—here we see the
Greek influence—as "going to meet his fate almost light-
heartedly, wrapping himself in his winding-sheet of
spiders' webs, which the laws of nature will not permit
him to destroy." True, Strindberg declares elsewhere that
the protagonists in THE FATHER should be acted with complete abandon—consistency was not his bugbear—but certainly one cannot afford to miss one spark of the Captain's
humour. "By and large," Strindberg said, "he symbolises
a masculinity which society is trying to invalidate and
hand over to the third sex."

Laura is a more difficult character to analyse. Certainly
she symbolises a terrible femininity, and is Strindberg's
answer to Ibsen and women's emancipation. But she is
neither a blue-stocking nor a virago. It is her lack of
common-sense, not her lack of morals, that the Captain
criticises when he upbraids her for ruining his life. It is
only her brother who sees her as clever because of her
stubbornness in getting her own way. Her husband's attitude so riles her that her parting shot, before he throws
the lamp at her, is: ". . . now you have seen my wits are
as strong as my will."

The play falls to pieces if we cannot see Laura as an
ordinary, rather stupid, middle-class girl, brought up in
ignorance, and the Captain as an intelligent, ambitious
young man, walking in the springtime woods and falling
in love. Later, through sex difficulties and the sex conflict,
both of them are caught in a trap of domesticity and
debt and doubt—all of which were Strindberg's own unending problems.

A further problem for the producer is the child Bertha.
We are told that she is seventeen, but she behaves as if

she is seven—about the age of Strindberg's eldest daughter when he wrote the play after the frenzied break-up of his own marriage. Laura is a silly featureless little girl and the other minor characters, too, are merely sketches. "Ordinary people," Strindberg calls them in his preface to MISS JULIE, "as country pastors and provincial doctors usually are," but to us they seem extraordinary, and he mocks both church and medicine. Indeed, with his characteristic economy of words and the lack of stage directions—it is a matter of chance whether he even remembers to bring a character on or take him off again—Strindberg sets his readers and translators, producers and players, a hard task. Much is asked of an audience too, but the dramatic reward is unique and justifies the toil.

                                                      E. S.

Characters

THE CAPTAIN
LAURA, *his wife*
BERTHA, *their daughter*
DOCTOR ÖSTERMARK
THE PASTOR
THE NURSE
NÖJD
THE ORDERLY

*The whole play takes place in the central living-room of
the Captain's home. He is a cavalry officer in a remote
country district of Sweden.*

It is about 1886, shortly before Christmas.

*At the back of the room, towards the right, a door leads
to the hall. In the left wall there is a door to other rooms,
and in the right-hand corner another, smaller door, covered in the same wall-paper as the walls, opens on to a
staircase leading to the Captain's room above.*

*In the centre of the room stands a large round table on
which are newspapers, magazines, a big photograph
album and a lamp. On the right are a leather-covered
sofa, arm chairs and a smaller table. On the left is a
writing-bureau with a pendulum clock upon it. Arms, guns
and gun-bags hang on the walls, and military coats on
pegs by the door to the hall.*

ACT ONE

Early evening. The lamp on the table is lighted. The Captain and the Pastor are sitting on the sofa talking. The Captain is in undress uniform with riding-boots and spurs; the Pastor wears black, with a white cravat in place of his clerical collar, and is smoking a pipe.

The Captain rises and rings a bell. The Orderly enters from the hall.

ORDERLY. Yes, sir?

CAPTAIN. Is Nöjd there?

ORDERLY. Nöjd's in the kitchen, sir, waiting for orders.

CAPTAIN. In the kitchen again, is he? Send him here at once.

ORDERLY. Yes, sir.

Exit.

PASTOR. Why, what's the trouble?

CAPTAIN. Oh, the ruffian's been at his tricks again with one of the servant girls! He's a damn nuisance, that fellow!

PASTOR. Was it Nöjd you said? Didn't he give some trouble back in the spring?

CAPTAIN. Ah, you remember that, do you? Look here, you give him a bit of a talking to, there's a good chap. That might have some effect. I've sworn at him and thrashed him, without making the least impression.

PASTOR. So now you want me to preach to him. How much impression do you think God's word is likely to make on a trooper?

CAPTAIN. Well, my dear brother-in-law, it makes none at all on me, as you know, but . . .

PASTOR. As I know only too well.

CAPTAIN. But on him? Worth trying anyhow.

Enter NÖJD.

What have you been up to now, Nöjd?

NÖJD. God bless you, sir, I can't talk about that—not with Pastor here.

PASTOR. Don't mind me, my lad.

NÖJD. Well you see, sir, it was like this. We was at a dance at Gabriel's, and then, well then Ludwig said as . . .

CAPTAIN. What's Ludwig got to do with it? Stick to the point.

NÖJD. Well then Emma said as we should go in the barn.

CAPTAIN. I see. I suppose it was Emma who led you astray.

NÖJD. Well, not far from it. What I mean is if the girl's not game, nothing don't happen.

CAPTAIN. Once and for all—are you the child's father or are you not?

NÖJD. How's one to know?

CAPTAIN. What on earth do you mean? Don't you know?

NÖJD. No, you see, sir, that's what you never can know.

CAPTAIN. You mean you weren't the only man?

NÖJD. That time I was. But you can't tell if you've always been the only one.

CAPTAIN. Are you trying to put the blame on Ludwig? Is that the idea?

NÖJD. It's not easy to know who to put the blame on.

CAPTAIN. But, look here, you told Emma you would marry her.

NÖJD. Oh well, you always have to say that, you know.

CAPTAIN, *to the* PASTOR. This is atrocious.

PASTOR. It's the old story. Come now, Nöjd, surely you are man enough to know if you are the father.

NÖJD. Well, sir, it's true, I did go with her, but you know yourself, Pastor, that don't always lead to nothing.

PASTOR. Look here, my lad, it's you we are talking about. And you are not going to leave that girl destitute with a child.

You can't be forced to marry her, but you must make provision for the child. That you must do.

NÖJD. So must Ludwig then.

CAPTAIN. If that's how it is, the case will have to go before the Magistrate. I can't settle it, and it's really nothing to do with me. Dismiss!

PASTOR. One moment, Nöjd. Ahem. Don't you think it's rather a dirty trick to leave a girl destitute with a child like that? Don't you think so—eh?

NÖJD. Yes, if I knew I was the father, it would be, but I tell you, Pastor, you never can know that. And it wouldn't be much fun slaving all your life for another chap's brat. You and the Captain must see that for yourselves.

CAPTAIN. That will do, Nöjd.

NÖJD. Yes, sir, thank you, sir.

CAPTAIN. And keep out of the kitchen, you scoundrel!

Exit NÖJD.

Why didn't you haul him over the coals?

PASTOR. What do you mean? Didn't I?

CAPTAIN. No, you just sat there muttering to yourself.

PASTOR. As a matter of fact, I scarcely knew what to say to him. It's hard on the girl, of course, but it's hard on the boy too. Supposing he's not the father? The girl can nurse the baby for four months at the orphanage, and after that it will be taken care of for good. But the boy can't nurse the child, can he? Later on, the girl will get a good place in some respectable family, but if the boy is cashiered, his future may be ruined.

CAPTAIN. Upon my soul, I'd like to be the magistrate and judge this case! Maybe the boy is responsible—that's what you can't know. But one thing you *can* know—if anybody's guilty, the girl is.

PASTOR. Well, I never sit in judgment. Now what was it we were talking about when this blessed business interrupted us? Yes, Bertha and her confirmation, wasn't it?

CAPTAIN. It's not just a question of confirmation, but of her whole future. The house is full of women, all trying to mould this child of mine. My mother-in-law wants to turn her into a spiritualist; Laura wants her to be an artist; the governess would have her a Methodist, old Margaret a Baptist, and the servant girls a Salvation Army lass. You can't make a character out of patchwork. Meanwhile I . . . I, who have more right than all the rest to guide her, am opposed at every turn. So I must send her away.

PASTOR. You have too many women running your house.

CAPTAIN. You're right there. It's like going into a cage of tigers. They'd soon tear me to pieces, if I didn't hold a red-hot poker under their noses. It's all very well for you to laugh, you blackguard. It wasn't enough that I married your sister; you had to palm off your old stepmother on me too.

PASTOR. Well, good Lord, one can't have stepmothers in one's house!

CAPTAIN. No, you prefer mothers-in-law—in someone else's house, of course.

PASTOR. Well, well, we all have our burdens to bear.

CAPTAIN. I daresay, but I have more than my share. There's my old nurse too, who treats me as if I still wore a bib. She's a good old soul, to be sure, but she shouldn't be here.

PASTOR. You should keep your women-folk in order, Adolf. You give them too much rope.

CAPTAIN. My dear fellow, can you tell me how to keep women in order?

PASTOR. To tell the truth, although she's my sister, Laura was always a bit of a handful.

CAPTAIN. Laura has her faults, of course, but they are not very serious ones.

PASTOR. Oh come now, I know her!

CAPTAIN. She was brought up with romantic ideas and has always found it a little difficult to come to terms with life. But she is my wife and . . .

PASTOR. And because she is your wife she must be the best of

women. No, brother-in-law, it's she not you who wears the
trousers.

CAPTAIN. In any case, the whole household has gone mad.
Laura's determined Bertha shan't leave her, and I won't
let her stay in this lunatic asylum.

PASTOR. So Laura's determined, is she? Then there's bound
to be trouble, I'm afraid. As a child she used to lie down
and sham dead until they gave in to her. Then she would
calmly hand back whatever she'd set her mind on, explaining it wasn't the thing she wanted, but simply to get
her own way.

CAPTAIN. So she was like that even then, was she? Hm. As
a matter of fact, she does sometimes get so overwrought
I'm frightened for her and think she must be ill.

PASTOR. What is it you want Bertha to do that's such a bone
of contention? Can't you come to some agreement?

CAPTAIN. Don't think I want to turn her into a prodigy—or
into some image of myself. But I will not play pander and
have my daughter fitted for nothing but the marriage
market. For then, if she didn't marry after all, she'd have
a wretched time of it. On the other hand, I don't want to
start her off in some man's career with a long training that
would be entirely wasted if she did marry.

PASTOR. Well, what do you want then?

CAPTAIN. I want her to be a teacher. Then, if she doesn't
marry she'll be able to support herself, and at least be no
worse off than those unfortunate schoolmasters who have
to support families on their earnings. And if she does
marry, she can educate her own children. Isn't that reasonable?

PASTOR. Reasonable, yes—but what about her artistic talent?
Wouldn't it be against the grain to repress that?

CAPTAIN. No. I showed her attempts to a well-known painter
who told me they were nothing but the usual sort of thing
learnt at school. Then, during the summer, some young
jackanapes came along who knew better and said she was
a genius—whereupon the matter was settled in Laura's
favour.

PASTOR. Was he in love with Bertha?

CAPTAIN. I take that for granted.

PASTOR. Well, God help you, old boy, I don't see any solution. But it's a tiresome business, and I suppose Laura has supporters . . . *indicates other rooms* in there.

CAPTAIN. You may be sure of that. The whole household is in an uproar, and between ourselves the method of attack from that quarter is not exactly chivalrous.

PASTOR, *rising.* Do you think I haven't been through it?

CAPTAIN. You too?

PASTOR. Yes, indeed.

CAPTAIN. But to me the worst thing about it is that Bertha's future should be decided in there from motives of sheer hate. They do nothing but talk about men being made to see that women can do this and do that. It's man versus woman the whole day long . . . Must you go? Won't you stay to supper? I don't know what there is, but do stay. I'm expecting the new doctor, you know. Have you seen him yet?

PASTOR. I caught a glimpse of him on my way here. He looks a decent, reliable sort of man.

CAPTAIN. That's good. Do you think he may be my ally?

PASTOR. Maybe. It depends how well he knows women.

CAPTAIN. But won't you stay?

PASTOR. Thank you, my dear fellow, but I promised to be home this evening, and my wife gets anxious if I'm late.

CAPTAIN. Anxious! Furious, you mean. Well, as you please. Let me help you on with your coat.

PASTOR. It's certainly very cold to-night. Thank you. You must look after yourself, Adolf. You seem a bit on edge.

CAPTAIN. On edge? Do I?

PASTOR. Yes. You aren't very well, are you?

CAPTAIN. Did Laura put this into your head? For the last twenty years she's been treating me as if I had one foot in the grave.

PASTOR. Laura? No, it's just that I'm . . . I'm worried about

you. Take my advice and look after yourself. Goodbye,
old man. By the way, didn't you want to talk about the
confirmation?

CAPTAIN. By no means. But I give you my word this shall
take its own course—and be chalked up to the official
conscience. I am neither a witness to the truth, nor a
martyr. We have got past that sort of thing. Goodbye.
Remember me to your wife.

PASTOR. Goodbye, Adolf. Give my love to Laura.

Exit PASTOR. *The* CAPTAIN *opens the bureau and settles
down to his accounts.*

CAPTAIN. Thirty-four—nine, forty-three—seven, eight, fifty-six.

LAURA, *entering from the next room.* Will you please . . .

CAPTAIN. One moment!—Sixty-six, seventy-one, eighty-four,
eighty-nine, ninety-two, a hundred. What is it?

LAURA. Am I disturbing you?

CAPTAIN. Not in the least. Housekeeping money, I suppose?

LAURA. Yes, housekeeping money.

CAPTAIN. If you put the accounts down there, I will go
through them.

LAURA. Accounts?

CAPTAIN. Yes.

LAURA. Do you expect me to keep accounts now?

CAPTAIN. Of course you must keep accounts. Our position's
most precarious, and if we go bankrupt, we must have
accounts to show. Otherwise we could be accused of negli-
gence.

LAURA. It's not my fault if we're in debt.

CAPTAIN. That's what the accounts will show.

LAURA. It's not my fault the tenant farmer doesn't pay.

CAPTAIN. Who was it recommended him so strongly? You.
Why did you recommend such a—shall we call him a scatterbrain?

LAURA. Why did you take on such a scatterbrain?

CAPTAIN. Because I wasn't allowed to eat in peace, sleep in

peace or work in peace till you got him here. You wanted him because your brother wanted to get rid of him; my mother-in-law wanted him because I didn't; the governess wanted him because he was a Methodist, and old Margaret because she had known his grandmother as a child. That's why, and if I hadn't taken him I should be in a lunatic asylum by now, or else in the family vault. However, here's the housekeeping allowance and your pin money. You can give me the accounts later.

LAURA, *with an ironic bob.* Thank you so much.—By the way, do you keep accounts yourself—of what you spend outside the household?

CAPTAIN. That's none of your business.

LAURA. True. As little my business as the future of my own child. Did you gentlemen come to any decision at this evening's conference?

CAPTAIN. I had already made my decision, so I merely had to communicate it to the only friend I have in the family. Bertha is going to live in town. She will leave in a fortnight's time.

LAURA. Where, if I may ask, is she going to stay?

CAPTAIN. At Sävberg's—the solicitor's.

LAURA. That Freethinker!

CAPTAIN. According to the law as it now stands, children are brought up in their father's faith.

LAURA. And the mother has no say in the matter?

CAPTAIN. None whatever. She sells her birthright by legal contract and surrenders all her rights. In return the husband supports her and her children.

LAURA. So she has no rights over her own child?

CAPTAIN. None at all. When you have sold something, you don't expect to get it back and keep the money too.

LAURA. But supposing the father and mother were to decide things together . . . ?

CAPTAIN. How would that work out? I want her to live in town; you want her to live at home. The mathematical mean would be for her to stop at the railway station,

midway between home and town. You see? It's a dead-
lock.

LAURA. Then the lock must be forced. . . . What was Nöjd
doing here?

CAPTAIN. That's a professional secret.

LAURA. Which the whole kitchen knows.

CAPTAIN. Then doubtless you know it too.

LAURA. I do.

CAPTAIN. And are ready to sit in judgment?

LAURA. The law does that.

CAPTAIN. The law doesn't say who the child's father is.

LAURA. Well, people know that for themselves.

CAPTAIN. Discerning people say that's what one never can
know.

LAURA. How extraordinary! Can't one tell who a child's father
is?

CAPTAIN. Apparently not.

LAURA. How perfectly extraordinary! Then how can the father
have those rights over the mother's child?

CAPTAIN. He only has them when he takes on the responsibility—or has it forced on him. But of course in marriage
there is no doubt about the paternity.

LAURA. No doubt?

CAPTAIN. I should hope not.

LAURA. But supposing the wife has been unfaithful?

CAPTAIN. Well, such a supposition has no bearing on our
problem. Is there anything else you want to ask me about?

LAURA. No, nothing.

CAPTAIN. Then I shall go up to my room. Please let me know
when the doctor comes. *Closes the bureau and rises.*

LAURA. I will.

CAPTAIN, *going out by the wall-papered door.* As soon as he
comes, mind. I don't want to be discourteous, you understand.
Exit.

LAURA. I understand. *She looks at the bank-notes she is holding.*

MOTHER-IN-LAW, *off.* Laura!

LAURA. Yes, Mother?

MOTHER-IN-LAW. Is my tea ready?

LAURA, *at the door to the next room.* It's coming in a moment.
The ORDERLY *opens the hall door.*

ORDERLY. Dr. Östermark.
Enter DOCTOR. *Exit* ORDERLY, *closing the door.*

LAURA, *shaking hands.* How do you do, Dr. Östermark. Let
me welcome you to our home. The Captain is out, but
he will be back directly.

DOCTOR. I must apologize for calling so late, but I have
already had to pay some professional visits.

LAURA. Won't you sit down?

DOCTOR. Thank you.

LAURA. Yes, there is a lot of illness about just now, but I hope
all the same that you will find this place suits you. It is so
important for people in a lonely country district like this
to have a doctor who takes a real interest in his patients.
I have heard you so warmly spoken of, Dr. Östermark,
I hope we shall be on the best of terms.

DOCTOR. You are too kind, dear lady. I hope, however, for
your sake that my visits here will not often be of a professional nature. I take it that the health of your family is, on
the whole, good, and that . . .

LAURA. Yes, we have been fortunate enough not to have any
serious illnesses, but all the same things are not quite as
they should be.

DOCTOR. Indeed?

LAURA. No, I'm afraid not really at all as one would wish.

DOCTOR. Dear, dear, you quite alarm me!

LAURA. In a family there are sometimes things which honour
and duty compel one to keep hidden from the world.

DOCTOR. But not from one's doctor.

LAURA. No. That is why it is my painful duty to tell you the whole truth from the start.

DOCTOR. May we not postpone this conversation until I have had the honour of meeting the Captain?

LAURA. No. You must hear what I have to say before you see him.

DOCTOR. Does it concern him then?

LAURA. Yes, him. My poor, dear husband.

DOCTOR. You are making me most uneasy. Whatever your trouble, Madam, you can confide in me.

LAURA, *taking out her handkerchief*. My husband's mind is affected. Now you know, and later on you will be able to judge for yourself.

DOCTOR. You astound me. The Captain's learned treatise on mineralogy, for which I have the greatest admiration, shows a clear and powerful intellect.

LAURA. Does it? I shall be overjoyed if we—his relatives—are mistaken.

DOCTOR. It is possible, of course, that his mind is disturbed in other ways. Tell me . . .

LAURA. That is exactly what we fear. You see, at times he has the most peculiar ideas, which wouldn't matter much for a scientist, if they weren't such a burden on his family. For instance, he has an absolute mania for buying things.

DOCTOR. That is significant. What kind of things?

LAURA. Books. Whole cases of them, which he never reads.

DOCTOR. Well, that a scholar should buy books isn't so alarming.

LAURA. You don't believe what I am telling you?

DOCTOR. I am convinced, Madam, that you believe what you are telling me.

LAURA. Well, then, is it possible for anyone to see in a microscope what's happening on another planet?

DOCTOR. Does he say he can do that?

LAURA. Yes, that's what he says.

DOCTOR. In a microscope?

LAURA. In a microscope. Yes.

DOCTOR. That is significant, if it is so.

LAURA. If it is so! You don't believe me, Doctor. And here have I let you in to the family secret.

DOCTOR. My dear lady, I am honoured by your confidence, but as a physician I must observe and examine before giving an opinion. Has the Captain shown any symptoms of instability, any lack of will power?

LAURA. Has he, indeed! We have been married twenty years, and he has never yet made a decision without going back on it.

DOCTOR. Is he dogmatic?

LAURA. He certainly lays down the law, but as soon as he gets his own way, he loses interest and leaves everything to me.

DOCTOR. That is significant and requires careful consideration. The will, you see, Madam, is the backbone of the mind. If it is injured, the mind falls to pieces.

LAURA. God knows how I have schooled myself to meet his every wish during these long hard years. Oh, if you knew what I have been through with him, if you only knew!

DOCTOR. I am profoundly distressed to learn of your trouble, Madam, and I promise I will do what I can. You have my deepest sympathy and I beg you to rely on me implicitly. But now you have told me this, I am going to ask one thing of you. Don't allow anything to prey on the patient's mind. In a case of instability, ideas can sometimes take hold and grow into an obsession—or even monomania. Do you follow me?

LAURA. . . . . You mean don't let him get ideas into his head.

DOCTOR. Precisely. For a sick man can be made to believe anything. He is highly susceptible to suggestion.

LAURA. I see . . . I understand. Yes, indeed. *A bell rings within.* Excuse me. That's my mother ringing. I won't be a moment . . . Oh, here's Adolf!

As LAURA *goes out, the* CAPTAIN *enters by the wall-papered door.*

CAPTAIN. Ah, so you have arrived, Doctor! You are very welcome.

DOCTOR. How do you do, Captain. It's a great honour to meet
such a distinguished scientist.

CAPTAIN. Oh please! Unfortunately, my military duties don't
give me much time for research . . . All the same, I do
believe I am now on the brink of a rather exciting discovery.

DOCTOR. Really?

CAPTAIN. You see, I have been subjecting meteoric stones to
spectrum analysis, and I have found carbon—an indication of organic life. What do you say to that?

DOCTOR. Can you see that in a microscope?

CAPTAIN. No, in a spectroscope, for heaven's sake!

DOCTOR. Spectroscope! I beg your pardon. Then you will soon
be telling us what is happening on Jupiter.

CAPTAIN. Not what is happening, what *has* happened. If only
that blasted Paris bookseller would send my books. I
really think the whole book-trade must be in league
against me. Think of it, for two months I've not had one
single answer to my orders, my letters or my abusive tele-
grams! It's driving me mad. I can't make out what's happened.

DOCTOR. Well, what could it be but ordinary carelessness?
You shouldn't let it upset you.

CAPTAIN. Yes, but the devil of it is I shan't be able to get my
article finished in time.—I know they're working on the
same lines in Berlin . . . However, that's not what we
should be talking about now, but about you. If you would
care to live here, we can give you a small suite of rooms
in that wing. Or would you prefer your predecessor's
house?

DOCTOR. Whichever you please.

CAPTAIN. No, whichever *you* please. You have only to say.

DOCTOR. It's for you to decide, Captain.

CAPTAIN. Nothing of the kind. It's for you to say which you
prefer. I don't care one way or the other.

DOCTOR. But I really can't . . .

CAPTAIN. For Christ's sake, man, say what you want! I haven't any opinion, any inclination, any choice, any preference at all. Are you such a milksop that you don't know what you want? Make up your mind, or I shall lose my temper.

DOCTOR. If I am to choose, I should like to live here.

CAPTAIN. Good!—Thank you. *Rings.* Oh dear me!—I apologise, Doctor, but nothing irritates me so much as to hear people say they don't care one way or the other.

The NURSE *enters.*

Ah, it's you, Margaret. Look here, my dear, do you know if the rooms in the wing are ready for the doctor?

NURSE. Yes, Captain, they're ready.

CAPTAIN. Good. Then I won't detain you, Doctor, for you must be tired. Goodnight, and once again—welcome. I look forward to seeing you in the morning.

DOCTOR. Thank you. Goodnight.

CAPTAIN. By the way, I wonder if my wife told you anything about us—if you know at all how the land lies?

DOCTOR. Your good lady did suggest one or two things it might be as well for a newcomer to know. Goodnight, Captain.

The NURSE *shows the* DOCTOR *out and returns.*

CAPTAIN. What is it, old girl? Anything the matter?

NURSE. Now listen, Mr. Adolf, dear.

CAPTAIN. Yes, go on, Margaret, talk. You're the only one whose talk doesn't get on my nerves.

NURSE. Then listen, Mr. Adolf. Couldn't you go halfway to meet the mistress in all this bother over the child? Think of a mother . . .

CAPTAIN. Think of a father, Margaret.

NURSE. Now, now, now! A father has many things besides his child, but a mother has nothing but her child.

CAPTAIN. Quite so, my friend. She has only one burden, while I have three and bear hers too. Do you think I'd have been stuck in the army all my life if I hadn't had her and her child to support?

NURSE. I know, but that wasn't what I wanted to talk about.

CAPTAIN. Quite. What you want is to make out I'm in the wrong.

NURSE. Don't you believe I want what's best for you, Mr. Adolf?

CAPTAIN. I'm sure you do, my dear, but you don't know what is best for me. You see, it's not enough to have given the child life. I want to give her my very soul.

NURSE. Oh, that's beyond me, but I do think you two ought to come to terms.

CAPTAIN. Margaret, you are not my friend.

NURSE. Not your friend! Ah God, what are you saying, Mr. Adolf? Do you think I ever forget you were my baby when you were little?

CAPTAIN. Well, my dear, am I likely to forget it? You have been like a mother to me, and stood by me against all the others. But now that things have come to a head, you're deserting—going over to the enemy.

NURSE. Enemy?

CAPTAIN. Yes, enemy. You know perfectly well how things are here. You've seen it all from beginning to end.

NURSE. Aye, I've seen plenty. But, dear God, why must two people torment the lives out of each other? Two people who are so good and kind to everyone else. The mistress never treats me wrong or . . .

CAPTAIN. Only me. I know. And I tell you, Margaret, if you desert me now, you'll be doing a wicked thing. For a net is closing round me, and that doctor is no friend of mine.

NURSE. Oh, goodness, Mr. Adolf, you believe the worst of everyone! But that's what comes of not having the true faith. That's your trouble.

CAPTAIN. While you and the Baptists have found the one true faith, eh? You're lucky.

NURSE. Aye, luckier than you, Mr. Adolf. Humble your heart

and you will see how happy God will make you in your love for your neighbour.

CAPTAIN. Isn't it strange—as soon as you mention God and love, your voice grows hard and your eyes fill with hate. No, Margaret, I'm sure you haven't found the true faith.

MARGARET. However proud you are and stuffed with book-learning, that won't get you anywhere when the pinch comes.

CAPTAIN. How arrogantly thou speakest, O humble heart! I'm well aware that learning means nothing to creatures like you.

NURSE. Shame on you! Still, old Margaret loves her great big boy best of all. And when the storm breaks, he'll come back to her, sure enough, like the good child he is.

CAPTAIN. Forgive me, Margaret. You see, you really are the only friend I have here. Help me, for something is going to happen. I don't know what, but I know it's evil, this thing that's on its way. *A scream from within.* What's that? Who's screaming?

BERTHA *runs in.*

BERTHA. Father, Father! Help me! Save me!

CAPTAIN. What is it? My darling, tell me.

BERTHA. Please protect me. I know she'll do something terrible to me.

CAPTAIN. Who? What do you mean? Tell me at once.

BERTHA. Grandmother. But it was my fault. I played a trick on her.

CAPTAIN. Go on.

BERTHA. Yes, but you mustn't tell anyone. Promise you won't.

CAPTAIN. Very well, but what happened?

Exit NURSE.

BERTHA. You see, sometimes in the evening she turns the lamp down and makes me sit at the table holding a pen over a piece of paper. And then she says the spirits write.

CAPTAIN. Well, I'll be damned! And you never told me.

BERTHA. I'm sorry, I didn't dare. Grandmother says spirits

revenge themselves on people who talk about them. And then the pen writes, but I don't know if it's me doing it or not. Sometimes it goes well, but sometimes it doesn't work at all. And when I get tired nothing happens, but I have to make something happen all the same. This evening I thought I was doing rather well, but then Grandmother said it was all out of Stagnelius* and I had been playing a trick on her. And she was simply furious.

CAPTAIN. Do you believe there are spirits?

BERTHA. I don't know.

CAPTAIN. But I know there are not.

BERTHA. Grandmother says you don't understand, and that you have worse things that can see into other planets.

CAPTAIN. She says that, does she? And what else does she say?

BERTHA. That you can't work miracles.

CAPTAIN. I never said I could. You know what meteorites are, don't you?—stones that fall from other heavenly bodies. Well, I examine these and see if they contain the same elements as the earth. That's all I do.

BERTHA. Grandmother says there are things she can see and you can't.

CAPTAIN. My dear, she is lying.

BERTHA. Grandmother doesn't lie.

CAPTAIN. How do you know?

BERTHA. Then Mother does too.

CAPTAIN. Hm!

BERTHA. If you say Mother is a liar, I'll never believe a word you say again.

CAPTAIN. I didn't say that, so now you must believe me. Listen. Your happiness, your whole future depends on your leaving home. Will you do this? Will you go and live in town and learn something useful?

BERTHA. Oh yes, I'd love to live in town—anywhere away from here! It's always so miserable in there, as gloomy

*Erik Johan Stagnelius, Swedish poet and dramatist. (1793–1823.)

as a winter night. But when you come home, Father, it's like a spring morning when they take the double windows down.

CAPTAIN. My darling, my beloved child!

BERTHA. But, Father, listen, you must be kind to Mother. She often cries.

CAPTAIN. Hm! . . . So you would like to live in town?

BERTHA. Oh yes!

CAPTAIN. But supposing your mother doesn't agree?

BERTHA. She must.

CAPTAIN. But supposing she doesn't?

BERTHA. Then I don't know what will happen. But she must, she must!

CAPTAIN. Will you ask her?

BERTHA. No, you must ask her—very nicely. She wouldn't pay any attention to me.

CAPTAIN. Hm! . . . Well now, if you want this and I want it and she doesn't want it, what are we to do then?

BERTHA. Oh, then the fuss will begin all over again! Why can't you both . . .

Enter LAURA.

LAURA. Ah, so you're here, Bertha! Well now, Adolf, as the question of her future is still to be decided, let's hear what she has to say herself.

CAPTAIN. The child can hardly have anything constructive to say about the development of young girls, but you and I ought to be able to sum up the pros and cons. We've watched a good number grow up.

LAURA. But as we don't agree, Bertha can give the casting vote.

CAPTAIN. No. I won't allow anyone to interfere with my rights —neither woman nor child. Bertha, you had better leave us.

Exit BERTHA.

LAURA. You were afraid to hear her opinion because you knew she would agree with me.

CAPTAIN. I know she wants to leave home, but I also know you have the power to make her change her mind.

LAURA. Oh, have I much power?

CAPTAIN. Yes, you have a fiendish power of getting your own way, like all people who are unscrupulous about the means they employ. How, for instance, did you get rid of Dr. Norling? And how did you get hold of the new doctor?

LAURA. Yes, how did I?

CAPTAIN. You ran the old doctor down until he had to leave, and then you got your brother to canvass for this one.

LAURA. Well, that was quite simple and perfectly legal. Then is Bertha to leave home?

CAPTAIN. Yes, in a fortnight's time.

LAURA. I warn you I shall do my best to prevent it.

CAPTAIN. You can't.

LAURA. Can't I? Do you expect me to give up my child to be taught by wicked people that all she has learnt from her mother is nonsense? So that I would be despised by my own daughter for the rest of my life.

CAPTAIN. Do you expect me to allow ignorant and bumptious women to teach my daughter that her father is a charlatan?

LAURA. That shouldn't matter so much to you—now.

CAPTAIN. What on earth do you mean?

LAURA. Well, the mother's closer to the child, since the discovery that no one can tell who the father is.

CAPTAIN. What's that got to do with us?

LAURA. You don't know if you are Bertha's father.

CAPTAIN. Don't know?

LAURA. How can you know what nobody knows?

CAPTAIN. Are you joking?

LAURA. No, I'm simply applying your own theory. How do you know I haven't been unfaithful to you?

CAPTAIN. I can believe a good deal of you, but not that. And if it were so, you wouldn't talk about it.

LAURA. Supposing I were prepared for anything, for being turned out and ostracised, anything to keep my child under my own control. Supposing I am telling the truth now when I say: Bertha is my child but not yours. Supposing . . .

CAPTAIN. Stop it!

LAURA. Just supposing . . . then your power would be over.

CAPTAIN. Not till you had proved I wasn't the father.

LAURA. That wouldn't be difficult. Do you want me to?

CAPTAIN. Stop.

LAURA. I should only have to give the name of the real father —with particulars of place and time, of course. For that matter—when was Bertha born? In the third year of our marriage . . .

CAPTAIN. Will you stop it now, or . . .

LAURA. Or what? Very well, let's stop. All the same, I should think twice before you decide anything. And, above all, don't make yourself ridiculous.

CAPTAIN. I find the whole thing tragic.

LAURA. Which makes you still more ridiculous.

CAPTAIN. But not you?

LAURA. No, we're in such a strong position.

CAPTAIN. That's why we can't fight you.

LAURA. Why try to fight a superior enemy?

CAPTAIN. Superior?

LAURA. Yes. It's odd, but I have never been able to look at a man without feeling myself his superior.

CAPTAIN. One day you may meet your master—and you'll never forget it.

LAURA. That will be fascinating.

Enter NURSE.

NURSE. Supper's ready. Come along now, please.

LAURA. Yes, of course. *The* CAPTAIN *lingers and sits down in an armchair near the sofa.* Aren't you coming?

CAPTAIN. No, thank you, I don't want any supper.

LAURA. Why not? Has anything upset you?

CAPTAIN. No, but I'm not hungry.

LAURA. Do come, or they'll start asking questions, and that's not necessary. Do be sensible. You won't? Well, stay where you are then!

Exit.

NURSE. Mr. Adolf, whatever is it now?

CAPTAIN. I don't know yet. Tell me—why do you women treat a grown man as if he were a child?

NURSE. Well, goodness me, you're all some woman's child, aren't you?—All you men, big or small . . .

CAPTAIN. While no woman is born of man, you mean. True. But I must be Bertha's father. You believe that, Margaret, don't you? Don't you?

NURSE. Lord, what a silly boy you are! Of course you're your own child's father. Come along and eat now. Don't sit here sulking. There now, come along, do.

CAPTAIN, *rising.* Get out, woman! To hell with the hags! *At the hall door.* Svärd! Svärd!

ORDERLY, *entering.* Yes, sir?

CAPTAIN. Have the small sleigh got ready at once.

Exit ORDERLY.

NURSE. Now listen, Captain . . .

CAPTAIN. Get out, woman! Get out, I say!

NURSE. God preserve us, whatever's going to happen now?

CAPTAIN, *putting on his cap.* Don't expect me home before midnight.

Exit.

NURSE. Lord Jesus! What *is* going to happen?

ACT TWO

The same as before, late that night. The DOCTOR *and*
LAURA *are sitting talking.*

DOCTOR. My conversation with him has led me to the conclusion that your suspicions are by no means proved. To
begin with, you were mistaken in saying that he had made
these important astronomical discoveries by using a microscope. Now I have learnt that it was a spectroscope. Not
only is there no sign in this of mental derangement—on
the contrary, he has rendered a great service to science.

LAURA. But I never said that.

DOCTOR. I made a memorandum of our conversation, Madam,
and I remember questioning you on this vital point, because I thought I must have misheard. One must be
scrupulously accurate when bringing charges which might
lead to a man being certified.

LAURA. Certified?

DOCTOR. I presume you are aware that if a person is certified
insane, he loses both his civil and his family rights.

LAURA. No, I didn't know that.

DOCTOR. There is one other point I should like to be clear
about. He spoke of not getting any replies from his book-
sellers. May I ask whether—from the best of intentions, of
course—you have been intercepting his correspondence?

LAURA. Yes, I have. It is my duty to protect the family. I
couldn't let him ruin us all and do nothing about it.

DOCTOR. Excuse me, I do not think you understand the
possible consequences of your action. If he realises you
have been interfering with his affairs behind his back, his
suspicions will be aroused and might even develop into a
persecution mania. Particularly, as by thwarting his will,
you have already driven him to the end of his tether.

Surely you know how enraging it is to have your will opposed and your dearest wishes frustrated.

LAURA. Do I not!

DOCTOR. Then think what this means to him.

LAURA, *rising*. It's midnight and he's not back yet. Now we can expect the worst.

DOCTOR. Tell me what happened this evening after I saw him. I must know everything.

LAURA. He talked in the wildest way and said the most fantastic things. Can you believe it—he even suggested he wasn't the father of his own child!

DOCTOR. How extraordinary! What can have put that into his head?

LAURA. Goodness knows, unless it was an interview he had with one of his men about maintenance for a child. When I took the girl's part, he got very excited and said no one could ever tell who a child's father was. God knows I did everything I could to calm him, but I don't believe anything can help him now. *Weeps.*

DOCTOR. This can't go on. Something must be done—without rousing his suspicions. Tell me, has he had any such delusions before?

LAURA. As a matter of fact, he was much the same six years ago, and then he actually admitted—in a letter to his doctor—that he feared for his reason.

DOCTOR. I see, I see. A deep-seated trouble. But . . . er . . . the sanctity of family life . . . and so forth . . . I mustn't probe too far . . . must keep to the surface. Unfortunately what is done cannot be undone, yet the remedy should have been applied to what is done . . . Where do you think he is now?

LAURA. I can't imagine. He has such wild notions these days . . .

DOCTOR. Would you like me to stay until he comes in? I could explain my presence by saying—well, that your mother is ill and I came to see her.

LAURA. That's a very good idea. Please stand by us, Doctor.

If you only knew how worried I am! . . . But wouldn't
it be better to tell him straight out what you think of his
condition?

DOCTOR. We never do that with mental patients, unless they
bring the subject up themselves, and rarely even then.
Everything depends on how the case develops. But we
had better not stay here. May I go into some other room,
to make it more convincing?

LAURA. Yes, that will be best, and Margaret can come in here.
She always waits up for him. *At the door.* Margaret!
Margaret! She is the only one who can manage him.

NURSE, *entering.* Did you call, Madam? Is Master back?

LAURA. No, but you are to wait here for him. And when he
comes, tell him that my mother is unwell and the doctor
is with her.

NURSE. Aye, aye. Leave all that to me.

LAURA, *opening the door.* If you will be so good as to come in
here, Doctor . . .

DOCTOR. Thank you.

They go out. The NURSE *sits at the table, puts on her
glasses and picks up her hymn-book.*

NURSE. Ah me! Ah me! *Reads softly:*

> *A sorrowful and grievous thing*
> *Is life, so swiftly passing by,*
> *Death shadows with his angel's wing*
> *The whole earth, and this his cry:*
> *'Tis Vanity, all Vanity!*

Ah me! Ah me!

> *All that on earth has life and breath,*
> *Falls low before his awful might,*
> *Sorrow alone is spared by Death,*
> *Upon the yawning grave to write:*
> *'Tis Vanity, all Vanity!*

Ah me! Ah me!

During the last lines, BERTHA *enters, carrying a tray with
a coffee-pot and a piece of embroidery.*

BERTHA, *softly.* Margaret, may I sit in here with you? It's so dismal up there.

NURSE. Saints alive! Bertha, are you still up?

BERTHA. Well, you see, I simply must get on with Father's Christmas present. And here's something nice for you.

NURSE. But, sweetheart, this won't do. You have to be up bright and early, and it's past twelve now.

BERTHA. Oh, that doesn't matter! I daren't stay up there all alone. I'm sure there are ghosts.

NURSE. There now! What did I tell you? Mark my words, there's no good fairy in this house. What was it? Did you hear something, Bertha?

BERTHA. Oh Margaret, someone was singing in the attic!

NURSE. In the attic? At this time of night?

BERTHA. Yes. It was such a sad song; the saddest I ever heard. And it seemed to come from the attic—you know, the one on the left where the cradle is.

NURSE. Oh dear, dear, dear! And such a fearful night too. I'm sure the chimneys will blow down. "Alas, what is this earthly life? Sorrow, trouble, grief and strife. Even when it seems most fair, Nought but tribulation there."—Ah, dear child, God grant us a happy Christmas!

BERTHA. Margaret, is it true Father's ill?

NURSE. Aye, that's true enough.

BERTHA. Then I don't expect we shall have a Christmas party. But why isn't he in bed if he's ill?

NURSE. Well, dearie, staying in bed doesn't help his kind of illness. Hush! I hear someone in the porch. Go to bed now —take the tray with you, or the Master will be cross.

BERTHA, *going out with the tray.* Goodnight, Margaret.

NURSE. Goodnight, love. God bless you.

Enter the CAPTAIN.

CAPTAIN, *taking off his overcoat.* Are you still up? Go to bed.

NURSE. Oh, I was only biding till . . .

The CAPTAIN *lights a candle, opens the bureau, sits down at it and takes letters and newspapers from his pocket.*

Mr. Adolf . . .

CAPTAIN. What is it?

NURSE. The old mistress is ill. Doctor's here.

CAPTAIN. Anything serious?

NURSE. No, I don't think so. Just a chill.

CAPTAIN, *rising.* Who was the father of your child, Margaret?

NURSE. I've told you often enough, it was that heedless fellow
    Johansson.

CAPTAIN. Are you sure it was he?

NURSE. Don't talk so silly. Of course I'm sure, seeing he was
    the only one.

CAPTAIN. Yes, but was he sure he was the only one? No, he
    couldn't be sure, only you could be. See? That's the differ-
    ence.

NURSE. I don't see any difference.

CAPTAIN. No, you don't see it, but it's there all the same.
    Turns the pages of the photograph album on the table.

Do you think Bertha's like me?

NURSE. You're as like as two peas in a pod.

CAPTAIN. Did Johansson admit he was the father?

NURSE. Well, he was forced to.

CAPTAIN. How dreadful!—Here's the doctor.

Enter DOCTOR.

Good evening, Doctor. How is my mother-in-law?

DOCTOR. Oh, it's nothing much. Just a slight sprain of the left
    ankle.

CAPTAIN. I thought Margaret said it was a chill. There ap-
    pear to be different diagnoses of the case. Margaret, go
    to bed.

Exit NURSE. *Pause.*

Won't you sit down, Dr. Östermark?

DOCTOR, *sitting.* Thank you.

CAPTAIN. Is it true that if you cross a mare with a zebra you
    get striped foals?

DOCTOR, *astonished*. Perfectly true.

CAPTAIN. And that if breeding is then continued with a stallion, the foals may still be striped?

DOCTOR. That is also true.

CAPTAIN. So, in certain circumstances, a stallion can sire striped foals, and vice versa.

DOCTOR. That would appear to be the case.

CAPTAIN. So the offspring's resemblance to the father proves nothing.

DOCTOR. Oh . . .

CAPTAIN. You're a widower, aren't you? Any children?

DOCTOR. Ye-es.

CAPTAIN. Didn't you sometimes feel rather ridiculous as a father? I myself don't know anything more ludicrous than the sight of a man holding his child's hand in the street, or hearing a father say: "My child." "My wife's child," he ought to say. Didn't you ever see what a false position you were in? Weren't you ever haunted by doubts—I won't say suspicions, as a gentleman I assume your wife was above suspicion?

DOCTOR. No, I certainly wasn't. There it is, Captain, a man— as I think Goethe says—must take his children on trust.

CAPTAIN. Trust, where a woman's concerned? A bit of a risk.

DOCTOR. Ah, but there are many kinds of women!

CAPTAIN. The latest research shows there is only one kind . . . when I was a young fellow and not, if I may say so, a bad specimen, I had two little experiences which afterwards gave me to think. The first was on a steamer. I was in the saloon with some friends, and the young stewardess told us—with tears running down her cheeks—how her sweetheart had been drowned at sea. We condoled with her and I ordered champagne. After the second glass I touched her foot, after the fourth her knee, and before morning I had consoled her.

DOCTOR. One swallow doesn't make a summer.

CAPTAIN. My second experience was a summer swallow. I was staying at Lysekil and got to know a young married

woman who was there with her children—her husband
was in town. She was religious and high-minded, kept
preaching at me and was—or so I thought—the soul of
virtue. I lent her a book or two which, strange to relate,
she returned. Three months later, I found her card in one
of those books with a pretty outspoken declaration of
love. It was innocent—as innocent, that's to say, as such
a declaration from a married woman could be—to a
stranger who had never made her any advances. Moral:
don't believe in anyone too much.

DOCTOR. Don't believe too little either.

CAPTAIN. The happy mean, eh? But you see, Doctor, that
woman was so unaware of her motives she actually told
her husband of her infatuation for me. That's where the
danger lies, in the fact that women are unconscious of
their instinctive wickedness. An extenuating circumstance,
perhaps, but that can only mitigate the judgment, not
revoke it.

DOCTOR. You have a morbid turn of mind, Captain. You
should be on your guard against this.

CAPTAIN. There's nothing morbid about it. Look here. All
steam-boilers explode when the pressure-gauge reaches
the limit, but the limit isn't the same for all boilers. Got
that? After all, you're here to observe me. Now if I were
not a man I could sniff and snivel and explain the case to
you, with all its past history. But as unfortunately I am
a man, like the ancient Roman I must cross my arms upon
my breast and hold my breath until I die. Goodnight.

DOCTOR. If you are ill, Captain, there's no reflection on your
manhood in telling me about it. Indeed, it is essential for
me to hear both sides of the case.

CAPTAIN. I thought you were quite satisfied with one side.

DOCTOR. You're wrong. And I should like you to know, Captain, that when I heard that Mrs. Alving* blackening her
late husband's memory, I thought what a damned shame
it was that the fellow should be dead.

CAPTAIN. Do you think if he'd been alive he'd have said any-

*Reference to Mrs. Alving in Ibsen's GHOSTS.

thing? Do you think if any husband rose from the dead he'd be believed? Goodnight, Doctor. Look how calm I am. It's quite safe for you to go to bed.

DOCTOR. Then I will bid you goodnight. I wash my hands of the whole business.

CAPTAIN. So we're enemies?

DOCTOR. By no means. It's just a pity we can't be friends. Goodnight.

The CAPTAIN *shows the* DOCTOR *out by the hall door, then crosses to the other and slightly opens it.*

CAPTAIN. Come in and let's talk. I knew you were eavesdropping.

Enter LAURA, *embarrassed. The* CAPTAIN *sits at the bureau.*

It's very late, but we'd better have things out now. Sit down. *She sits. Pause.* This evening it was I who went to the post office and fetched the mail, and from my letters it is clear to me that you have been intercepting my correspondence—both in and out. The result of this has been a loss of time which has pretty well shattered the expectations I had for my work.

LAURA. I acted from the best of intentions. You were neglecting your military duties for this other work.

CAPTAIN. Scarcely the best of intentions. You knew very well that one day I should win more distinction in this field than in the Army, but what you wanted was to stop me winning laurels of any kind, because this would stress your own inferiority. Now, for a change, I have intercepted letters addressed to you.

LAURA. How chivalrous!

CAPTAIN. In keeping with the high opinion you have of me. From these letters it appears that for a long time now you've been setting my old friends against me, by spreading rumours about my mental condition. So successful have your efforts been that now scarcely one person from Colonel to kitchen-maid believes I am sane. The actual facts about my condition are these. My reason is, as you know, unaffected, and I am able to discharge my duties both as soldier and father. My emotions are still pretty well under control, but only so long as my will-power remains intact. And you have so gnawed and gnawed at my will that at any moment it may slip its cogs, and then the whole bag of tricks will go to pieces. I won't appeal to your feelings, because you haven't any—that is your strength. I appeal to your own interests.

LAURA. Go on.

CAPTAIN. By behaving in this way you have made me so full of suspicion that my judgment is fogged and my mind is beginning to stray. This means that the insanity you have been waiting for is on its way and may come at any moment. The question you now have to decide is whether it is more to your advantage for me to be well or ill. Consider. If I go to pieces, I shall have to leave the Service, and where will you be then? If I die, you get my life-insurance. But if I take my own life, you get nothing. It is therefore to your advantage that I should live my life out.

LAURA. Is this a trap?

CAPTAIN. Certainly. You can avoid it or stick your head in it.

LAURA. You say you'd kill yourself, but you never would.

CAPTAIN. Are you so sure? Do you think a man can go on living when he has nothing and nobody to live for?

LAURA. Then you give in?

CAPTAIN. No, I offer peace.

LAURA. On what terms?

CAPTAIN. That I may keep my reason. Free me from doubt and I will give up the fight.

LAURA. Doubt about what?   .

CAPTAIN. Bertha's parentage.

LAURA. Are there doubts about that?

CAPTAIN. Yes, for me there are, and it was you who roused them.

LAURA. I?

CAPTAIN. Yes. You dropped them like henbane in my ear, and

circumstances encouraged them to grow. Free me from uncertainty. Tell me straight out it is so, and I will forgive you in advance.

LAURA. I can scarcely admit to guilt that isn't mine.

CAPTAIN. What can it matter to you, when you know I won't reveal it? Do you think any man would proclaim his shame from the housetops?

LAURA. If I say it isn't so, you still won't be certain, but if I say it is, you will believe me. You must want it to be true.

CAPTAIN. Strangely enough I do. Perhaps because the first supposition can't be proved, while the second can.

LAURA. Have you any grounds for suspicion?

CAPTAIN. Yes and no.

LAURA. I believe you want to make out I'm guilty, so you can get rid of me and have absolute control of the child. But you won't catch me in any such trap.

CAPTAIN. Do you think, if I were convinced of your guilt, I should want to take on another man's child?

LAURA. No, I'm sure you wouldn't. So evidently you were lying when you said you'd forgive me in advance.

CAPTAIN, *rising*. Laura, save me and my reason! You can't have understood what I was saying. If the child's not mine, I have no rights over her, nor do I want any. And that's how you'd like it, isn't it? But that's not all. You want complete power over the child, don't you, with me still there to support you both?

LAURA. Power, that's it. What's this whole life and death struggle for if not power?

CAPTAIN. For me, as I don't believe in a life to come, this child was my life after death, my conception of immortality—the only one, perhaps, that's valid. If you take her away, you cut my life short.

LAURA. Why didn't we separate sooner?

CAPTAIN. Because the child bound us together, but the bond became a chain. How was that? I never thought of this before, but now memories return, accusing, perhaps condemning. After two years of marriage we were still child-

less—you know best why. Then I was ill and almost died.
One day, between bouts of fever, I heard voices in the
next room. You and the lawyer were discussing the property I still owned then. He was explaining that as there
were no children, you could not inherit, and he asked if
by any chance you were pregnant. I did not hear your
reply. I recovered and we had a child. Who is the father?

LAURA. You are.

CAPTAIN. No, I am not. There's a crime buried here that's
beginning to stink. And what a fiendish crime! You
women, who were so tender-hearted about freeing black
slaves, kept the white ones. I have slaved for you, your
child, your mother, your servants. I have sacrificed career
and promotion. Tortured, beaten, sleepless—my hair has
gone grey through the agony of mind you have inflicted
on me. All this I have suffered in order that you might
enjoy a care-free life and, when you were old, relive it in
your child. This is the lowest form of theft, the cruellest
slavery. I have had seventeen years of penal servitude—
and I was innocent. How can you make up to me for
this?

LAURA. Now you really are mad.

CAPTAIN, *sitting*. So you hope. I have watched you trying to
conceal your crime, but because I didn't understand I
pitied you. I've soothed your conscience, thinking I was
chasing away some nightmare. I've heard you crying out
in your sleep without giving your words a second thought.
But now . . . now! The other night—Bertha's birthday—
comes back to me. I was still up in the early hours, reading, and you suddenly screamed as if someone were trying
to strangle you. "Don't! Don't!" you cried. I knocked on
the wall—I didn't want to hear any more. For a long time
I have had vague suspicions. I did not want them confirmed. This is what I have suffered for you. What will
you do for me?

LAURA. What can I do? Swear before God and all that I hold
sacred that you are Bertha's father?

CAPTAIN. What good would that do? You have already said

that a mother can and ought to commit any crime for her child. I implore you by the memory of the past, I implore you as a wounded man begs to be put out of his misery, tell me the truth. Can't you see I'm helpless as a child? Can't you hear me crying to my mother that I'm hurt? Forget I'm a man, a soldier whose word men—and even beasts—obey. I am nothing but a sick creature in need of pity. I renounce every vestige of power and only beg for mercy on my life.

LAURA, *laying her hand on his forehead.* What? You, a man, in tears?

CAPTAIN. Yes, a man in tears. Has not a man eyes? Has not a man hands, limbs, senses, opinions, passions? Is he not nourished by the same food as a woman, wounded by the same weapons, warmed and chilled by the same winter and summer? If you prick us, do we not bleed? If you tickle us, do we not laugh? If you poison us, do we not die? Why should a man suffer in silence or a soldier hide his tears? Because it's not manly? Why isn't it manly?

LAURA. Weep, then, my child, and you shall have your mother again. Remember, it was as your second mother that I came into your life. You were big and strong, yet not fully a man. You were a giant child who had come into the world too soon, or perhaps an unwanted child.

CAPTAIN. That's true. My father and mother had me against their will, and therefore I was born without a will. That is why, when you and I became one, I felt I was completing myself—and that is why you dominated. I—in the army the one to command—became at home the one to obey. I grew up at your side, looked up to you as a superior being and listened to you as if I were your foolish little boy.

LAURA. Yes, that's how it was, and I loved you as if you were my little boy. But didn't you see how, when your feelings changed and you came to me as a lover, I was ashamed? The joy I felt in your embraces was followed by such a sense of guilt my very blood seemed tainted. The mother became the mistress—horrible!

CAPTAIN. I saw, but I didn't understand. I thought you despised my lack of virility, so I tried to win you as a woman by proving myself as a man.

LAURA. That was your mistake. The mother was your friend, you see, but the woman was your enemy. Sexual love is conflict. And don't imagine I gave myself. I didn't give. I only took what I meant to take. Yet you did dominate me . . . I felt it and wanted you to feel it.

CAPTAIN. You always dominated me. You could hypnotise me when I was wide awake, so that I neither saw nor heard, but simply obeyed. You could give me a raw potato and make me think it was a peach; you could make me take your ridiculous ideas for flashes of genius. You could corrupt me—yes, make me do the shabbiest things. You never had any real intelligence, yet, instead of being guided by me, you would take the reins into your own hands. And when at last I woke to the realisation that I had lost my integrity, I wanted to blot out my humiliation by some heroic action—some feat, some discovery—even by committing *hara-kiri*. I wanted to go to war, but I couldn't. It was then that I gave all my energies to science. And now—now when I should be stretching out my hand to gather the fruit, you chop off my arm. I'm robbed of my laurels; I'm finished. A man cannot live without repute.

LAURA. Can a woman?

CAPTAIN. Yes—she has her children, but he has not . . . Yet you and I and everyone else went on living, unconscious as children, full of fancies and ideals and illusions, until we woke up. Right—but we woke topsy-turvy, and what's more, we'd been woken by someone who was talking in his own sleep. When women are old and stop being women, they grow beards on their chins. What do men grow, I wonder, when they are old and stop being men? In this false dawn, the birds that crowed weren't cocks, they were capons, and the hens that answered their call were sexless, too. So when the sun should have risen for us, we found ourselves back among the ruins in the full moonlight, just as in the good old times. Our light morning sleep had only been troubled by fantastic dreams— there had been no awakening.

LAURA. You should have been a writer, you know.

CAPTAIN. Perhaps.

LAURA. But I'm sleepy now, so if you have any more fantasies, keep them till to-morrow.

CAPTAIN. Just one thing more—a fact. Do you hate me?

LAURA. Sometimes—as a man.

CAPTAIN. It's like race-hatred. If it's true we are descended from the ape, it must have been from two different species. There's no likeness between us, is there?

LAURA. What are you getting at?

CAPTAIN. In this fight, one of us must go under.

LAURA. Which?

CAPTAIN. The weaker naturally.

LAURA. Then is the stronger in the right?

CAPTAIN. Bound to be as he has the power.

LAURA. Then I am in the right.

CAPTAIN. Why, what power have you?

LAURA. All I need. And it will be legal power to-morrow when I've put you under restraint.

CAPTAIN. Under restraint?

LAURA. Yes. Then I shall decide my child's future myself out of reach of your fantasies.

CAPTAIN. Who will pay for her if I'm not there?

LAURA. Your pension.

CAPTAIN, *moving towards her menacingly.* How can you have me put under restraint?

LAURA, *producing a letter.* By means of this letter, an attested copy of which is already in the hands of the authorities.

CAPTAIN. What letter?

LAURA, *retreating.* Your own. The one in which you told the doctor you were mad. *He stares at her in silence.* Now you have fulfilled the unfortunately necessary functions of father and bread-winner. You are no longer needed, and you must go. You must go, now that you realise my wits are as strong as my will—you won't want to stay and acknowledge my superiority.

The CAPTAIN *goes to the table, picks up the lighted lamp and throws it at* LAURA, *who escapes backward through the door.*

ACT THREE

The same. The following evening. A new lamp, lighted, is on the table. The wall-papered door is barricaded with a chair. From the room above comes the sound of pacing footsteps. The NURSE *stands listening, troubled. Enter* LAURA *from within.*

LAURA. Did he give you the keys?

NURSE. Give? No, God help us, I took them from the coat Nöjd had out to brush.

LAURA. Then it's Nöjd who's on duty?

NURSE. Aye, it's Nöjd.

LAURA. Give me the keys.

NURSE. Here you are, but it's no better than stealing. Hark at him up there! To and fro, to and fro.

LAURA. Are you sure the door's safely bolted?

NURSE. It's bolted safe enough. *Weeps.*

LAURA, *opening the bureau and sitting down at it.* Pull yourself together, Margaret. The only way we can protect ourselves is by keeping calm. *A knock at the hall door.* See who that is.

NURSE, *opening door.* It's Nöjd.

LAURA. Tell him to come in.

NÖJD, *entering.* Despatch from the Colonel.

LAURA. Give it to me. *Reads.* I see . . . Nöjd, have you removed the cartridges from all the guns and pouches?

NÖJD. Yes, Ma'am, just as you said.

LAURA. Wait outside while I write to the Colonel.

Exit NÖJD. LAURA *writes. Sound of sawing above.*

NURSE. Listen, Madam. Whatever is he doing now?

LAURA. Do be quiet. I'm writing.

NURSE, *muttering.* Lord have mercy on us! What will be the end of all this?

LAURA, *holding out the note.* Here you are. Give it to Nöjd. And, remember, my mother's to know nothing of all this.

Exit NURSE *with note.* LAURA *opens the bureau drawers and takes out papers. Enter* PASTOR.

PASTOR. My dear Laura! As you probably gathered, I have been out all day and only just got back. I hear you've been having a terrible time.

LAURA. Yes, brother, I've never been through such a night and day in all my life!

PASTOR. Well, I see you're looking none the worse for it.

LAURA. No, thank heaven, I wasn't hurt. But just think what might have happened!

PASTOR. Tell me all about it. I've only heard rumours. How did it begin?

LAURA. It began by him raving about not being Bertha's father, and ended by him throwing the lighted lamp in my face.

PASTOR. But this is appalling. He must be quite out of his mind. What in heaven's name are we to do?

LAURA. We must try to prevent further violence. The doctor has sent to the hospital for a strait-jacket. I have just written a note to the Colonel, and now I'm trying to get some idea of the state of our affairs, which Adolf has so shockingly mismanaged. *Opens another drawer.*

PASTOR. It's a miserable business altogether, but I always feared something of the kind might happen. When fire and water meet, there's bound to be an explosion. *Looks in drawer.* Whatever's all this?

LAURA. Look! This is where he's kept everything hidden.

PASTOR. Good heavens! Here's your old doll! And there's your christening cap . . . and Bertha's rattle . . . and your letters . . . and that locket . . . *Wipes his eyes.* He must have loved you very dearly, Laura. I never kept this kind of thing.

LAURA. I believe he did love me once, but time changes everything.

PASTOR. What's this imposing document? *Examines it.* The purchase of a grave! Well, better a grave than the asylum! Laura, be frank with me. Aren't you at all to blame?

LAURA. How can I be to blame because someone goes out of his mind?

PASTOR. We—ell! I will say no more. After all, blood's thicker than water.

LAURA. Meaning what, if I may ask?

PASTOR, *gazing at her.* Oh come now!

LAURA. What?

PASTOR. Come, come! You can scarcely deny that it would suit you down to the ground to have complete control of your daughter.

LAURA. I don't understand.

PASTOR. I can't help admiring you.

LAURA. Really?

PASTOR. And as for me—I shall be appointed guardian to that Freethinker whom, as you know, I always regarded as a tare among our wheat.

LAURA *gives a quick laugh which she suppresses.*

LAURA. You dare say that to me, his wife?

PASTOR. How strong-willed you are, Laura, how amazingly strong-willed! Like a fox in a trap that would gnaw off its own leg rather than be caught. Like a master-thief working alone, without even a conscience for accomplice. Look in the mirror! You daren't.

LAURA. I never use a mirror.

PASTOR. No. You daren't look at yourself. Let me see your hand. Not one tell-tale spot of blood, not a trace of that subtle poison. A little innocent murder that the law cannot touch. An unconscious crime. Unconscious? A stroke of genius that. Listen to him up there! Take care, Laura! If that man gets loose, he will saw you in pieces too.

LAURA. You must have a bad conscience to talk like that. Pin the guilt on me if you can.

PASTOR. I can't.

LAURA. You see? You can't, and so—I am innocent. And now, you look after your charge and I'll take care of mine. *Enter* DOCTOR.

Ah, here is the Doctor! *Rises.* I'm so glad to see you, Doctor. I know I can count on you to help me, although I'm afraid not much can be done now. You hear him up there. Are you convinced at last?

DOCTOR. I am convinced there has been an act of violence. But the question is—should that act of violence be regarded as an outbreak of temper or insanity?

PASTOR. But apart from this actual outbreak, you must admit that he suffers from fixed ideas.

DOCTOR. I have a notion, Pastor, that *your* ideas are even more fixed.

PASTOR. My firmly rooted convictions of spiritual . . .

DOCTOR. Convictions apart, it rests with you, Madam, to decide if your husband is to be fined or imprisoned or sent to the asylum. How do you regard his conduct?

LAURA. I can't answer that now.

DOCTOR. Oh? Have you no—er—firmly rooted convictions of what would be best for the family? And you, Pastor?

PASTOR. There's bound to be a scandal either way. It's not easy to give an opinion.

LAURA. But if he were only fined for violence he could be violent again.

DOCTOR. And if he were sent to prison he would soon be out again. So it seems best for all parties that he should be treated as insane. Where is the nurse?

LAURA. Why?

DOCTOR. She must put the strait-jacket on the patient. Not at once, but after I have had a talk with him—and not then until I give the order. I have the—er—garment outside. *Goes out to hall and returns with a large parcel.* Kindly call the nurse.

LAURA *rings. The* DOCTOR *begins to unpack the strait-jacket.*

PASTOR. Dreadful! Dreadful!

Enter NURSE.

DOCTOR. Ah, Nurse! Now please pay attention. You see this jacket. When I give you the word I want you to slip it on the Captain from behind. So as to prevent any further violence, you understand. Now it has, you see, unusually long sleeves. That is to restrict his movements. These sleeves must be tied together behind his back. And now here are two straps with buckles, which afterwards you must fasten to the arm of a chair—or to whatever's easiest. Can you do this, do you think?

NURSE. No, Doctor, I can't. No, not that.

LAURA. Why not do it yourself, Doctor?

DOCTOR. Because the patient distrusts me. You, Madam, are the proper person, but I'm afraid he doesn't trust you either. LAURA *grimaces.* Perhaps you, Pastor . . .

PASTOR. I must beg to decline.

Enter NÖJD.

LAURA. Did you deliver my note?

NÖJD. Yes, Madam.

DOCTOR. Oh, it's you, Nöjd! You know the state of things here, don't you? You know the Captain has had a mental break-down. You must help us look after the patient.

NÖJD. If there's aught I can do for Captain, he knows I'll do it.

DOCTOR. You are to put this jacket on him.

NURSE. He's not to touch him. Nöjd shan't hurt him. I'd rather do it myself, gently, gently. But Nöjd can wait outside and help me if need be—yes, that's what he'd best do. *A pounding on the paper-covered door.*

DOCTOR. Here he is! *To* NURSE. Put the jacket on that chair under your shawl. And now go away, all of you, while the Pastor and I talk to him. That door won't hold long. Hurry!

NURSE, *going out.* Lord Jesus, help us!

LAURA *shuts the bureau and follows the* NURSE. NÖJD *goes out to the hall. The paper-covered door bursts open, the lock broken and the chair hurled to the floor. The* CAPTAIN *comes out, carrying a pile of books.*

CAPTAIN, *putting the books on the table.* Here it all is. You can read it in every one of these volumes. So I wasn't mad after all. *Picks one up.* Here it is in the Odyssey, Book I, page 6, line 215 in the Uppsala translation. Telemachus speaking to Athene: "My mother says I am Odysseus' son; but for myself I cannot tell. It's a wise child that knows its own father."* And that's the suspicion Telemachus has about Penelope, the most virtuous of women. Fine state of affairs, eh? *Takes up another book.* And here we have the Prophet Ezekiel: "The fool saith, Lo, here is my father; but who can tell whose loins have engendered him?" That's clear enough. *Picks up another.* And what's this? A history of Russian literature by Merzlyakov. Alexander Pushkin, Russia's greatest poet, was mortally wounded—but more by the rumours of his wife's unfaithfulness than by the bullet he received in his breast at the duel. On his deathbed he swore she was innocent. Jackass! How could he swear any such thing? I *do* read my books, you see! Hullo, Jonas, are you here? And the Doctor, of course. Did I ever tell you what I said to the English lady who was deploring the habit Irishmen have of throwing lighted lamps in their wives' faces? "God, what women!" I said. "Women?" she stammered. "Of course," I replied. "When things get to such a pass that a man who has loved, has worshipped a woman, picks up a lighted lamp and flings it in her face, then you may be sure . . ."

PASTOR. Sure of what?

*English translation E. V. Rieu. Penguin Classics.

CAPTAIN. Nothing. You can never be sure of anything—you can only believe. That's right, isn't it, Jonas? One believes and so one is saved. Saved, indeed! No. One can be damned through believing. That's what I've learnt.

DOCTOR. But, Captain . . .

CAPTAIN. Hold your tongue! I don't want any chat from you. I don't want to hear you relaying all the gossip from in there like a telephone. In there—you know what I mean. Listen to me, Jonas. Do you imagine you're the father of your children? I seem to remember you had a tutor in the house, a pretty boy about whom there was quite a bit of gossip.

PASTOR. Take care, Adolf!

CAPTAIN. Feel under your wig and see if you don't find two little nobs. Upon my soul, he's turning pale! Well, well! It was only talk, of course, but my God, how they talked! But we married men are all figures of fun, every man Jack of us. Isn't that right, Doctor? What about your own marriage bed? Didn't you have a certain lieutenant in your house, eh? Wait now, let me guess. He was called . . . *Whispers in the* DOCTOR's *ear*. By Jove, he's turned pale too! But don't worry. She's dead and buried, so what was done can't be done again. As a matter of fact, I knew him, and he's now—look at me, Doctor—no, straight in the eyes! He is now a major of Dragoons. Good Lord, I believe *he* has horns too!

DOCTOR, *angrily*. Be so good as to change the subject, Captain.

CAPTAIN. See! As soon as I mention horns he wants to change the subject.

PASTOR. I suppose you know, brother-in-law, that you're not in your right mind?

CAPTAIN. Yes, I do know. But if I had the handling of your decorated heads, I should soon have you shut up too. I am mad. But how did I become mad? Doesn't that interest you? No, it doesn't interest anyone. *Takes the photograph album from the table*. Christ Jesus, there is my daughter! Mine? That's what we can never know.

Shall I tell you what we should have to do so as to know? First marry, in order to be accepted by society, then immediately divorce; after that become lovers and finally adopt the children. That way one could at least be sure they were one's own adopted children. Eh? But what good's that to me? What good's anything now you have robbed me of my immortality? What can science or philosophy do for me when I have nothing left to live for? How can I live without honour? I grafted my right arm and half my brain and spinal cord on to another stem. I believed they would unite and grow into a single, more perfect tree. Then someone brought a knife and cut below the graft, so now I'm only half a tree. The other part, with my arm and half my brain, goes on growing. But I wither—I am dying, for it was the best part of myself I gave away. Let me die. Do what you like with me. I'm finished.

The DOCTOR *and* PASTOR *whisper, then go out. The* CAPTAIN *sinks into a chair by the table.* BERTHA *enters.*

BERTHA, *going to him.* Are you ill, Father?

CAPTAIN, *looking up stupidly at word "Father."* Me?

BERTHA. Do you know what you did? You threw a lamp at Mother.

CAPTAIN. Did I?

BERTHA. Yes. Supposing she'd been hurt!

CAPTAIN. Would that have mattered?

BERTHA. You're not my father if you talk like that.

CAPTAIN. What d'you say? Not your father? How d'you know? Who told you? Who is your father, then? Who?

BERTHA. Not you, anyway.

CAPTAIN. Anyone but me! Who then? Who? You seem well informed. Who told you? That I should live to hear my own child tell me to my face I am not her father! Do you realise you're insulting your mother by saying this? Don't you understand that, if it's true, *she* is disgraced?

BERTHA. You're not to say anything against Mother, I tell you!

CAPTAIN. Yes, all in league against me, just as you've always been.

BERTHA. Father!

CAPTAIN. Don't call me that again!

BERTHA. Father, Father!

CAPTAIN, *drawing her to him*. Bertha, my beloved child, yes, you *are* my child. Yes, yes, it must be so—it *is* so. All that was only a sick fancy—it came on the wind like an infection or a fever. Look at me! Let me see my soul in your eyes . . . But I see *her* soul as well. You have two souls. You love me with one and hate me with the other. You must love me and only me. You must have only one soul or you'll have no peace—neither shall I. You must have only one mind, fruit of my mind. You must have only one will—mine!

BERTHA. No, no! I want to be myself.

CAPTAIN. Never! I am a cannibal, you see, and I'm going to eat you. Your mother wanted to eat me, but she didn't succeed. I am Saturn who devoured his children because it was foretold that otherwise they would devour him. To eat or to be eaten—that is the question. If I don't eat you, you will eat me—you've shown your teeth already. *Goes to the rack.* Don't be afraid, my darling child. I shan't hurt you. *Takes down a revolver.*

BERTHA, *dodging away from him*. Help! Mother, help! He wants to kill me!

NURSE, *hurrying in*. What in heaven's name are you doing, Mr. Adolf?

CAPTAIN, *examining the revolver*. Did you remove the cartridges?

NURSE. Well, I did just tidy them away, but sit down here and take it easy and I'll soon fetch them back.

She takes the CAPTAIN *by the arm and leads him to a chair. He slumps down. She picks up the strait-jacket and goes behind the chair.* BERTHA *creeps out.*

Mr. Adolf, do you remember when you were my dear little boy, and I used to tuck you up at night and say your prayers with you? And do you remember how I used to get up in the night to get you a drink when you were thirsty? And how, when you had bad dreams and couldn't go to sleep again, I'd light the candle and tell you pretty stories. Do you remember?

CAPTAIN. Go on talking, Margaret. It soothes my mind. Go on talking.

NURSE. Aye, that I will, but you listen carefully. D'you remember how once you took a great big kitchen knife to carve a boat with, and I came in and had to trick the knife away from you? You were such a silly little lad, one had to trick you, you never would believe what anyone did was for your own good . . . "Give me that snake," I said, "or else he'll bite you." And then, see, you let go of the knife. *Takes the revolver from his hand.* And then, too, when it was time for you to dress yourself, and you wouldn't. I had to coax you, and say· you should have a golden coat and be dressed just like a prince. Then I took your little tunic, that was just made of green wool, and held it up in front of you and said: "In with your arms, now, both together." *Gets the jacket on.* And then I said: "Sit nice and still now, while I button it up behind." *Ties the sleeves behind him.* And then I said: "Up with you, and walk across the floor like a good boy, so Nurse can see how it fits." *Leads him to the sofa.* And then I said: "Now you must go to bed."

CAPTAIN. What's that? Go to bed, when I'd just been dressed? My God! What have you done to me? *Tries to get free.* Oh you fiendish woman, what devilish cunning! Who would have thought you had the brains for it? *Lies down on the sofa.* Bound, fleeced, outwitted and unable to die!

NURSE. Forgive me, Mr. Adolf, forgive me! I had to stop you killing the child.

CAPTAIN. Why didn't you let me kill her? If life's hell and death's heaven, and children belong to heaven?

NURSE. What do you know of the hereafter?

CAPTAIN. It's the only thing one does know. Of life one knows nothing. Oh, if one had known from the beginning!

NURSE. Humble your stubborn heart, Mr. Adolf, and cry to God for mercy! Even now it's not too late. It wasn't too late for the thief on the Cross, for Our Saviour said: "To-day shalt thou be with me in paradise."

CAPTAIN. Croaking for a corpse already, old crow? *She takes her hymn-book from her pocket. He calls.* Nöjd! Are you there, Nöjd?

Enter NÖJD.

Throw this woman out of the house or she'll choke me to death with her hymn-book. Throw her out of the window, stuff her up the chimney, do what you like only get rid of her!

NÖJD, *staring at the* NURSE. God save you, Captain—and that's from the bottom of my heart—but I can't do that, I just can't. If it were six men now, but a woman!

CAPTAIN. What? You can't manage one woman?

NÖJD. I could manage her all right, but there's something stops a man laying hands on a woman.

CAPTAIN. What is this something? Haven't they laid hands on me?

NÖJD. Yes, but I just can't do it, Sir. Same as if you was to tell me to hit Pastor. It's like religion, it's in your bones. I can't do it.

Enter LAURA. *She signs to* NÖJD, *who goes out.*

CAPTAIN. Omphale! Omphale! Playing with the club while Hercules spins your wool.

LAURA, *approaching the sofa.* Adolf, look at me! Do you believe I'm your enemy?

CAPTAIN. Yes, I do. I believe all you women are my enemies. My mother did not want me to come into the world because my birth would give her pain. She was my enemy. She robbed my embryo of nourishment, so I was born incomplete. My sister was my enemy when she made me knuckle under to her. The first woman I took in my arms was my enemy. She gave me ten years of sickness in return for the love I gave her. When my daughter had to choose between you and me, she became my enemy. And you, you, my wife, have been my mortal enemy, for you have not let go your hold until there is no life left in me.

LAURA. But I didn't mean this to happen. I never really thought it out. I may have had some vague desire to get rid of you—you were in my way—and perhaps, if you see some plan in my actions, there was one, but I was unconscious of it. I have never given a thought to my actions—they simply ran along the rails you laid down. My conscience is clear, and before God I feel innocent, even if I'm not. You weighed me down like a stone, pressing and pressing till my heart tried to shake off its intolerable burden. That's how it's been, and if without meaning to I have brought you to this, I ask your forgiveness.

CAPTAIN. Very plausible, but how does that help me? And whose fault is it? Perhaps our cerebral marriage is to blame. In the old days one married a wife. Now one goes into partnership with a business woman or sets up house with a friend. Then one rapes the partner or violates the friend. What becomes of love, the healthy love of the senses? It dies of neglect. And what happens to the dividends from those love shares, payable to holder, when there's no joint account? Who is the holder when the crash comes? Who is the bodily father of the cerebral child?

LAURA. Your suspicions about our daughter are entirely unfounded.

CAPTAIN. That's the horror of it. If they had some foundation, there would at least be something to catch hold of, to cling to. Now there are only shadows, lurking in the undergrowth, peering out with grinning faces. It's like fighting with air, a mock battle with blank cartridges. Reality, however deadly, puts one on one's mettle, nerves body and soul for action, but as it is . . . my thoughts dissolve in fog, my brain grinds a void till it catches fire . . . Put a pillow under my head. Lay something over me. I'm cold. I'm terribly cold.

LAURA *takes off her shawl and spreads it over him. Exit* NURSE.

LAURA. Give me your hand, my dear.

CAPTAIN. My hand! Which you have bound behind my back. Omphale, Omphale! But I can feel your shawl soft against my mouth. It's warm and gentle like your arms and smells of vanilla like your hair when you were young. When you were young, Laura, and we used to walk in the birch woods. There were primroses and thrushes—lovely, lovely! Think how beautiful life was then—and what it has become! You did not want it to become like this, neither did I. Yet it has. Who then rules our lives?

LAURA. God.

CAPTAIN. The God of strife then—or nowadays the Goddess! *Enter* NURSE *with a pillow.*

Take away this cat that's lying on me. Take it away! NURSE *removes the shawl and puts the pillow under his head.* Bring my uniform. Put my tunic over me. *The* NURSE *takes the tunic from a peg and spreads it over him. To* LAURA. Ah, my tough lion's-skin that you would take from me! Omphale! Omphale! You cunning woman, lover of peace and contriver of disarmament. Wake, Hercules, before they take away your club! You would trick us out of our armour, calling it tinsel. It was iron, I tell you, before it became tinsel. In the old days the smith forged the soldier's coat, now it is made by the needlewoman. Omphale! Omphale! Rude strength has fallen before treacherous weakness. Shame on you, woman of Satan, and a curse on all your sex! *He raises himself to spit at her, but sinks back again.* What sort of a pillow have you given me, Margaret? How hard and cold it is! So cold! Come and sit beside me on this chair. *She does so.* Yes, like that. Let me put my head on your lap. Ah, that's warmer! Lean over me so I can feel your breast. Oh how sweet it is to sleep upon a woman's breast, be she mother or mistress! But sweetest of all a mother's.

LAURA. Adolf, tell me, do you want to see your child?

CAPTAIN. My child? A man has no children. Only women have children. So the future is theirs, while we die childless. O God, who holds all children dear!

NURSE. Listen! He's praying to God.

CAPTAIN. No, to you, to put me to sleep. I'm tired, so tired. Goodnight, Margaret. "Blessed art thou among women." *He raises himself, then with a cry falls back on the* NURSES'S *knees.*

LAURA, *at the door, calling.* Doctor!

Enter DOCTOR *and* PASTOR.

Help him, Doctor—if it's not too late! Look, he has stopped breathing!

DOCTOR, *feeling his pulse.* It is a stroke.

PASTOR. Is he dead?

DOCTOR. No, he might still wake—but to what, who can say?

PASTOR. ". . . once to die, but after this the judgment."*

DOCTOR. No judgment—and no recriminations. You who believe that a God rules over human destiny must lay this to his charge.

NURSE. Ah Pastor, with his last breath he prayed to God!

PASTOR, *to* LAURA. Is this true?

LAURA. It is true.

DOCTOR. If this be so, of which I am as poor a judge as of the cause of his illness, in any case my skill is at an end. Try yours now, Pastor.

LAURA. Is that all you have to say at this deathbed, Doctor?

DOCTOR. That is all. I know no more. Let him who knows more, speak.

BERTHA *comes in and runs to* LAURA.

BERTHA. Mother! Mother!

LAURA. My child! My own child!

PASTOR. Amen.

*HEBREWS: ix, 27.

END

MISS JULIE

A Tragedy in One Act
by

AUGUST STRINDBERG

AUTHOR'S FOREWORD

Theatre has long seemed to me—in common with much other art—a *Biblia Pauperum*, a Bible in pictures for those who cannot read what is written or printed; and I see the playwright as a lay preacher peddling the ideas of his time in popular form, popular enough for the middle-classes, mainstay of theatre audiences, to grasp the gist of the matter without troubling their brains too much. For this reason theatre has always been an elementary school for the young, the semi-educated and for women who still have a primitive capacity for deceiving themselves and letting themselves be deceived—who, that is to say, are susceptible to illusion and to suggestion from the author. I have therefore thought it not unlikely that in these days, when that rudimentary and immature thought-process operating through fantasy appears to be developing into reflection, research and analysis, that theatre, like religion, might be discarded as an outworn form for whose appreciation we lack the necessary conditions. This opinion is confirmed by the major crisis still prevailing in the theatres of Europe, and still more by the fact that in those countries of culture, producing the greatest thinkers of the age, namely England and Germany, drama—like other fine arts—is dead.

Some countries, it is true, have attempted to create a new drama by using the old forms with up-to-date contents, but not only has there been insufficient time for these new ideas to be popularized, so that the audience can grasp them, but also people have been so wrought up by the taking of sides that pure, disinterested appreciation has become impossible. One's deepest impressions are upset when an applauding or a hissing majority dominates as forcefully and openly as it can in the theatre. Moreover, as no new form has been devised for these new contents, the new wine has burst the old bottles.

In this play I have not tried to do anything new, for this cannot be done, but only to modernize the form to meet the demands which may, I think, be made on this art today. To this end I chose—or surrendered myself to—a theme which claims to be outside the controversial issues of today, since questions of social climbing or falling, of higher or lower, better or worse, of man and woman, are, have been and will be of lasting interest. When I took this theme from a true story told me some years ago, which made a deep impression, I saw it as a subject for tragedy, for as yet it is tragic to see one favoured by fortune go under, and still more to see a family heritage die out, although a time may come when we have grown so developed and enlightened that we shall view with indifference life's spectacle, now seeming so brutal, cynical and heartless. Then we shall have dispensed with those inferior, unreliable instruments of thought called feelings, which become harmful and superfluous as reasoning develops.

The fact that my heroine rouses pity is solely due to weakness; we cannot resist fear of the same fate overtaking us. The hyper-sensitive spectator may, it is true, go beyond this kind of pity, while the man with belief in the future may actually demand some suggestion for remedying the evil—in other words some kind of policy. But, to begin with, there is no such thing as absolute evil; the downfall of one family is the good fortune of another, which thereby gets a chance to rise, and, fortune being only comparative, the alternation of rising and falling is one of life's principal charms. Also, to the man of policy, who wants to remedy the painful fact that the bird of prey devours the dove, and lice the bird of prey, I should like to put the question: why should it be remedied? Life is not so mathematically idiotic as only to permit the big to eat the small; it happens just as often that the bee kills the lion or at least drives it mad.

That my tragedy depresses many people is their own fault. When we have grown strong as the pioneers of the French revolution, we shall be happy and relieved to see the national parks cleared of ancient rotting trees which have stood too long in the way of others equally entitled to a period of growth—as relieved as we are when an incurable invalid dies.

My tragedy "The Father" was recently criticised for being too sad—as if one wants cheerful tragedies! Everybody is clamouring for this supposed "joy of life," and theatre managers demand farces, as if the joy of life consisted in being ridiculous and portraying all human beings as suffering from St. Vitus's dance or total idiocy. I myself find the joy of life in its strong and cruel struggles, and my pleasure in learning, in adding to my knowledge. For this reason I have chosen for this play an unusual situation, but an instructive one—an exception, that is to say, but a great exception, one proving the rule, which will no doubt annoy all lovers of the commonplace. What will offend simple minds is that my plot is not simple, nor its point of view single. In real life an action—this, by the way, is a somewhat new discovery—is generally caused by a whole series of motives, more or less fundamental, but as a rule the spectator chooses just one of these—the one which his mind can most easily grasp or that does most credit to his intelligence. A suicide is committed. Business troubles, says the man of affairs. Unrequited love, say the women. Sickness, says the invalid. Despair, says the down-and-out. But it is possible that the motive lay in all or none of these directions, or that the dead man concealed his actual motive by revealing quite another, likely to reflect more to his glory.

I see Miss Julie's tragic fate to be the result of many circumstances: the mother's character, the father's mistaken upbringing of the girl, her own nature, and the influence of her fiancé on a weak, degenerate mind. Also, more directly, the festive mood of Midsummer Eve, her father's absence, her monthly indisposition, her pre-occupation with animals, the excitement of dancing, the magic of dusk, the strongly aphrodisiac influence of flowers, and finally the chance that drives the couple into a room alone —to which must be added the urgency of the excited man.

My treatment of the theme, moreover, is neither exclusively physiological nor psychological. I have not put the blame wholly on the inheritance from her mother, nor on her physical condition at the time, nor on immorality. I have not even preached a moral sermon; in the absence of a priest I leave this to the cook.

I congratulate myself on this multiplicity of motives as being up-to-date, and if others have done the same thing before me, then I congratulate myself on not being alone in my "paradoxes," as all innovations are called.

In regard to the drawing of the characters, I have made my people somewhat "characterless" for the following reasons. In the course of time the word character has assumed manifold meanings. It must have originally signified the dominating trait of the soul-complex, and this was confused with temperament. Later it became the middle-class term for the automaton, one whose nature had become fixed or who had adapted himself to a particular rôle in life. In fact a person who had ceased to grow was called a character, while one continuing to develop—the skilful navigator of life's river, sailing not with sheets set fast, but veering before the wind to luff again—was called characterless, in a derogatory sense, of course, because he was so hard to catch, classify and keep track of. This middle-class conception of the immobility of the soul was transferred to the stage where the middle-class has always ruled. A character came to signify a man fixed and finished: one who invariably appeared either drunk or jocular or melancholy, and characterization required nothing more than a physical defect such as a club-foot, a wooden leg, a red nose; or the fellow might be made to repeat some such phrase as: "That's capital!" or: "Barkis is willin'!" This simple way of regarding human beings still survives in the great Molière. Harpagon is nothing but a miser, although Harpagon might have been not only a miser, but also a first-rate financier, an excellent father and a good citizen. Worse still, his "failing" is a distinct advantage to his son-in-law and his daughter, who are his heirs, and who therefore cannot criticise him, even if they have to wait a while to get to bed. I do not believe, therefore, in simple stage characters; and the summary judgments of authors—this man is stupid, that one brutal, this jealous, that stingy, and so forth—should be challenged by the Naturalists who know the richness of the soul-complex and realise that vice has a reverse side very much like virtue.

Because they are modern characters, living in a period of transition more feverishly hysterical than its predecessor at least, I have drawn my figures vacillating, disintegrated, a blend of old and new. Nor does it seem to me unlikely that, through newspapers and conversations, modern ideas may have filtered down to the level of the domestic servant.

My souls (characters) are conglomerations of past and present stages of civilization, bits from books and newspapers, scraps of humanity, rags and tatters of fine clothing, patched together as is the human soul. And I have added a little evolutionary history by making the weaker steal and repeat the words of the stronger, and by making the characters borrow ideas or "suggestions" from one another.

Miss Julie is a modern character, not that the half-woman, the man-hater, has not existed always, but because now that she has been discovered she has stepped to the front and begun to make a noise. The half-woman is a type who thrusts herself forward, selling herself nowadays for power, decorations, distinctions, diplomas, as formerly for money. The type implies degeneration; it is not a good type and it does not endure; but it can unfortunately transmit its misery, and degenerate men seem instinctively to choose their mates from among such women, and so they breed, producing offspring of indeterminate sex to whom life is torture. But fortunately they perish, either because they cannot come to terms with reality, or because their repressed instincts break out uncontrollably, or again because their hopes of catching up with men are shattered. The type is tragic, revealing a desperate fight against nature, tragic too in its Romantic inheritance now dissipated by Naturalism, which wants nothing but happiness—and for happiness strong and sound species are required.

But Miss Julie is also a relic of the old warrior nobility now giving way to the new nobility of nerve and brain. She is a victim of the discord which a mother's "crime" has produced in a family, a victim too of the day's complaisance, of circumstances, of her own defective constitution, all of which are equivalent to the Fate or Universal Law of former days. The Naturalist has abolished guilt with God, but the consequences of the action—punishment, imprisonment or the fear of it—he cannot abolish, for the simple reason that they remain whether he is acquitted or not. An injured fellow-being is not so complacent as outsiders, who have not been injured, can afford to be. Even if the father had felt impelled to take no vengeance, the daughter would have taken vengeance on herself, as she does here, from that innate or acquired sense of honour which the upper-classes inherit—whether from Barbarism or Aryan forebears, or from the chivalry of the Middle Ages, who knows? It is a very beautiful thing, but it has become a danger nowadays to the preservation of the race. It is the nobleman's *hara-kiri*, the Japanese law of inner conscience which compels him to cut his own stomach open at the insult of another, and which survives in modified form in the duel, a privilege of the nobility. And so the valet Jean lives on, but Miss Julie cannot live without honour. This is the thrall's advantage over the nobleman, that he lacks this fatal preoccupation with honour. And in all of us Aryans there is something of the nobleman, or the Don Quixote, which makes us sympathize with the man who commits suicide because he has done something ignoble and lost his honour. And we are noblemen enough to suffer at the sight of fallen greatness littering the earth like a corpse— yes, even if the fallen rise again and make restitution by honourable deeds. Jean, the valet, is a race-builder, a man of marked characteristics. He was a labourer's son who has educated himself towards becoming a gentleman.

He has learnt easily, through his well-developed senses (smell, taste, vision)—and he also has a sense of beauty. He has already bettered himself, and is thick-skinned enough to have no scruples about using other people's services. He is already foreign to his associates, despising them as part of the life he has turned his back on, yet also fearing and fleeing from them because they know his secrets, pry into his plans, watch his rise with envy, and look forward with pleasure to his fall. Hence his dual, indeterminate character, vacillating between love of the heights and hatred of those who have already achieved them. He is, he says himself, an aristocrat; he has learned the secrets of good society. He is polished, but vulgar within; he already wears his tails with taste, but there is no guarantee of his personal cleanliness.

He has some respect for his young lady, but he is frightened of Kristin, who knows his dangerous secrets, and he is sufficiently callous not to allow the night's events to wreck his plans for the future. Having both the slave's brutality and the master's lack of squeamishness, he can see blood without fainting and take disaster by the horns. Consequently he emerges from the battle unscathed, and probably ends his days as a hotel-keeper. And even if *he* does not become a Roumanian Count, his son will doubtless go to the university and perhaps become a county attorney.

The light which Jean sheds on a lower-class conception of life, life seen from below, is on the whole illuminating —when he speaks the truth, which is not often, for he says what is favourable to himself rather than what is true. When Miss Julie suggests that the lower-classes must be oppressed by the attitude of their superiors, Jean naturally agrees, as his object is to gain her sympathy; but when he perceives the advantage of separating himself from the common herd, he at once takes back his words.

It is not because Jean is now rising that he has the upper hand of Miss Julie, but because he is a man. Sexually he is the aristocrat because of his virility, his keener senses and his capacity for taking the initiative. His inferiority is mainly due to the social environment in which he lives, and he can probably shed it with his valet's livery.

The slave mentality expresses itself in his worship of the Count (the boots), and his religious superstition; but he worships the Count chiefly because he holds that higher position for which Jean himself is striving. And this worship remains even when he has won the daughter of the house and seen how empty is that lovely shell.

I do not believe that a love relationship in the "higher" sense could exist between two individuals of such different quality, but I have made Miss Julie imagine that she is in love, so as to lessen her sense of guilt, and I let Jean suppose that if his social position were altered he would truly love her. I think love is like the hyacinth which has to strike roots in darkness *before* it can produce a vigorous flower. In this case it shoots up quickly, blossoms and goes to seed all at the same time, which is why the plant dies so soon.

As for Kristin, she is a female slave, full of servility and sluggishness acquired in front of the kitchen fire, and stuffed full of morality and religion, which are her cloak and scape-goat. She goes to church as a quick and easy way of unloading her household thefts on to Jesus and taking on a fresh cargo of guiltlessness. For the rest she is a minor character, and I have therefore sketched her in the same manner as the Pastor and the Doctor in "The Father," where I wanted ordinary human beings, as are most country pastors and provincial doctors. If these minor characters seem abstract to some people this is due to the fact that ordinary people are to a certain extent abstract in pursuit of their work; that is to say, they are without individuality, showing, while working, only one side of themselves. And as long as the spectator does not feel a need to see them from other sides, there is nothing wrong with my abstract presentation.

In regard to the dialogue, I have departed somewhat from tradition by not making my characters catechists who ask stupid questions in order to elicit a smart reply.

I have avoided the symmetrical, mathematical construction of French dialogue, and let people's minds work irregularly, as they do in real life where, during a conversation, no topic is drained to the dregs, and one mind finds in another a chance cog to engage in. So too the dialogue wanders, gathering in the opening scenes material which is later picked up, worked over, repeated, expounded and developed like the theme in a musical composition.

The plot speaks for itself, and as it really only concerns two people, I have concentrated on these, introducing only one minor character, the cook, and keeping the unhappy spirit of the father above and behind the action. I have done this because it seems to me that the psychological process is what interests people most today. Our inquisitive souls are no longer satisfied with seeing a thing happen; we must also know how it happens. We want to see the wires themselves, to watch the machinery, to examine the box with the false bottom, to take hold of the magic ring in order to find the join, and look at the cards to see how they are marked.

In this connection I have had in view the documentary novels of the brothers de Goncourt, which appeal to me more than any other modern literature.

As far as the technical side of the work is concerned I have made the experiment of abolishing the division into acts. This is because I have come to the conclusion that our capacity for illusion is disturbed by the intervals, during which the audience has time to reflect and escape from the suggestive influence of the author-hypnotist. My play will probably take an hour and a half, and as one can listen to a lecture, a sermon or a parliamentary debate for as long as that or longer, I do not think a theatrical performance will be fatiguing in the same length of time. As early as 1872, in one of my first dramatic attempts, "The Outlaw," I tried this concentrated form, although with scant success. The play was written in five acts, and only when finished did I become aware of the restless, disjointed effect that it produced. The script

was burnt and from the ashes rose a single well-knit act—
fifty pages of print, playable in one hour. The form of
the present play is, therefore, not new, but it appears to
be my own, and changing tastes may make it timely. My
hope is one day to have an audience educated enough to
sit through a whole evening's entertainment in one act,
but one would have to try this out to see. Meanwhile, in
order to provide respite for the audience and the players,
without allowing the audience to escape from the illusion,
I have introduced three art forms: monologue, mime and
ballet. These are all part of drama, having their origins
in classic tragedy, monody having become monologue
and the chorus, ballet.

Monologue is now condemned by our realists as unnatural, but if one provides motives for it one makes it
natural, and then can use it to advantage. It is, surely,
natural for a public speaker to walk up and down the
room practicing his speech, natural for an actor to read
his part aloud, for a servant girl to talk to her cat, a
mother to prattle to her child, an old maid to chatter to
her parrot, and a sleeper to talk in his sleep. And in order
that the actor may have a chance, for once, of working
independently, free from the author's direction, it is better
that the monologue should not be written, but only indi-
cated. For since it is of small importance what is said in
one's sleep or to the parrot or to the cat—none of it influ-
ences the action—a talented actor, identifying himself
with the atmosphere and the situation, may improvise
better than the author, who cannot calculate ahead how
much may be said or how long taken without waking the
audience from the illusion.

Some Italian theatres have, as we know, returned to
improvisation, thereby producing actors who are creative,
although within the bounds set by the author. This may
well be a step forward, or even the beginning of a new
art-form worthy to be called *productive*.

In places where monologue would be unnatural I have
used mime, leaving here an even wider scope for the
actor's imagination, and more chance for him to win

independent laurels. But so as not to try the audience beyond endurance, I have introduced music—fully justified by the Midsummer Eve dance—to exercise its powers of persuasion during the dumb show. But I beg the musical director to consider carefully his choice of compositions, so that conflicting moods are not induced by selections from the current operetta or dance show, or by folk-tunes of too local a character.

The ballet I have introduced cannot be replaced by the usual kind of "crowd-scene," for such scenes are too badly played—a lot of grinning idiots seizing the opportunity to show off and thus destroying the illusion. And as peasants cannot improvise their taunts, but use ready-made phrases with a double meaning, I have not composed their lampoon, but taken a little-known song and dance which I myself noted down in the Stockholm district. The words are not quite to the point, but this too is intentional, for the cunning, i.e. weakness, of the slave prevents him from direct attack. Nor can there be clowning in a serious action, or coarse joking in a situation which nails the lid on a family coffin.

As regards the scenery, I have borrowed from impressionist painting its asymmetry and its economy; thus, I think, strengthening the illusion. For the fact that one does not see the whole room and all the furniture leaves scope for conjecture—that is to say imagination is roused and complements what is seen. I have succeeded too in getting rid of those tiresome exits through doors, since scenery doors are made of canvas, and rock at the slightest touch. They cannot even express the wrath of an irate head of the family who, after a bad dinner, goes out slamming the door behind him, "so that the whole house shakes." On the stage it rocks. I have also kept to a single set, both in order to let the characters develop in their métier and to break away from over-decoration. When one has only one set, one may expect it to be realistic; but as a matter of fact nothing is harder than to get a stage room that looks something like a room, however easily the scene painter can produce flaming volcanoes and water-falls. Presumably the walls must be of canvas; but it seems about time to dispense with painted shelves and cooking utensils. We are asked to accept so many stage conventions that we might as least be spared the pain of painted pots and pans.

I have set the back wall and the table diagonally so that the actors may play full-face and in half-profile when they are sitting opposite one another at the table. In the opera AIDA I saw a diagonal background, which led the eye to unfamiliar perspectives and did not look like mere reaction against boring straight lines.

Another much needed innovation is the abolition of foot-lights. This lighting from below is said to have the purpose of making the actors' faces fatter. But why, I ask, should all actors have fat faces? Does not this under-lighting flatten out all the subtlety of the lower part of the face, specially the jaw, falsify the shape of the nose and throw shadows up over the eyes? Even if this were not so, one thing is certain: that the lights hurt the per-formers' eyes, so that the full play of their expression is lost. The foot-lights strike part of the retina usually protected—except in sailors who have to watch sunlight on water—and therefore one seldom sees anything other than a crude rolling of the eyes, either sideways or up towards the gallery, showing their whites. Perhaps this too causes that tiresome blinking of the eyelashes, especially by actresses. And when anyone on the stage wants to speak with his eyes, the only thing he can do is to look straight at the audience, with whom he or she then gets into direct communication, outside the framework of the set—a habit called, rightly or wrongly, "greeting one's friends."

Would not sufficiently strong side-lighting, with some kind of reflectors, add to the actor's powers of expression by allowing him to use the face's greatest asset:—the play of the eyes?

I have few illusions about getting the actors to play *to* the audience instead of *with* it, although this is what I want. That I shall see an actor's back throughout a critical scene is beyond my dreams, but I do wish crucial scenes could be played, not in front of the prompter's box, like duets expecting applause, but in the place required by the action. So, no revolutions, but just some small modifications, for to make the stage into a real room with the fourth wall missing would be too upsetting altogether.

I dare not hope that the actresses will listen to what I have to say about make-up, for they would rather be beautiful than life-like, but the actor might consider whether it is to his advantage to create an abstract character with grease-paints, and cover his face with it like a mask. Take the case of a man who draws a choleric charcoal line between his eyes and then, in this fixed state of wrath, has to smile at some repartee. What a frightful grimace the result is! And equally, how is that false forehead, smooth as a billiard ball, to wrinkle when the old man loses his temper?

In a modern psychological drama, where the subtlest reactions of a character need to be mirrored in the face rather than expressed by sound and gesture, it would be worth while experimenting with powerful side-lighting on a small stage and a cast without make-up, or at least with the minimum.

If, in addition, we could abolish the visible orchestra, with its distracting lamps and its faces turned toward the audience; if we could have the stalls raised so that the spectators' eyes were higher than the players' knees; if we could get rid of the boxes (the centre of my target), with their tittering diners and supper-parties, and have total darkness in the auditorium during the performance; and if, first and foremost, we could have a *small* stage and a *small* house, then perhaps a new dramatic art might arise, and theatre once more become a place of entertainment for educated people. While waiting for such a theatre it is as well for us to go on writing so as to stock that repertory of the future.

I have made an attempt. If it has failed, there is time enough to try again.

Characters

MISS JULIE, *aged 25*
JEAN, *the valet, aged 30*
KRISTIN, *the cook, aged 35*

Scene: The large kitchen of a Swedish manor house in a
country district in the eighties.
Midsummer eve.
The kitchen has three doors, two small ones into Jean's
and Kristin's bedrooms, and a large, glass-fronted double
one, opening on to a courtyard. This is the only way to
the rest of the house.
Through these glass doors can be seen part of a foun-
tain with a cupid, lilac bushes in flower and the tops of
some Lombardy poplars. On one wall are shelves edged
with scalloped paper on which are kitchen utensils of
copper, iron and tin.
To the left is the corner of a large tiled range and part
of its chimney-hood, to the right the end of the servants'
dinner table with chairs beside it.
The stove is decorated with birch boughs, the floor
strewn with twigs of juniper. On the end of the table is a
large Japanese spice jar full of lilac.
There are also an ice-box, a scullery table and a sink.
Above the double door hangs a big old-fashioned bell;
near it is a speaking-tube.
A fiddle can be heard from the dance in the barn near-by.
Kristin is standing at the stove, frying something in a
pan. She wears a light-coloured cotton dress and a big
apron.
Jean enters, wearing livery and carrying a pair of large
riding-boots with spurs, which he puts in a conspicuous
place.

JEAN. Miss Julie's crazy again to-night, absolutely crazy.

KRISTIN. Oh, so you're back, are you?

JEAN. When I'd taken the Count to the station, I came back
    and dropped in at the Barn for a dance. And who did I
    see there but our young lady leading off with the game-
    keeper. But the moment she sets eyes on me, up she

rushes and invites me to waltz with her. And how she waltzed—I've never seen anything like it! She's crazy.

KRISTIN. Always has been, but never so bad as this last fortnight since the engagement was broken off.

JEAN. Yes, that was a pretty business, to be sure. He's a decent enough chap, too, even if he isn't rich. Oh, but they're choosy! *Sits down at the end of the table.* In any case, it's a bit odd that our young—er—lady would rather stay at home with the yokels than go with her father to visit her relations.

KRISTIN. Perhaps she feels a bit awkward, after that bust-up with her fiancé.

JEAN. Maybe. That chap had some guts, though. Do you know the sort of thing that was going on, Kristin? I saw it with my own eyes, though I didn't let on I had.

KRISTIN. You saw them . . . ?

JEAN. Didn't I just! Came across the pair of them one evening in the stable-yard. Miss Julie was doing what she called "training" him. Know what that was? Making him jump over her riding-whip—the way you teach a dog. He did it twice and got a cut each time for his pains, but when it came to the third go, he snatched the whip out of her hand and broke it into smithereens. And then he cleared off.

KRISTIN. What goings on! I never did!

JEAN. Well, that's how it was with that little affair . . . Now, what have you got for me, Kristin? Something tasty?

KRISTIN, *serving from the pan to his plate.* Well, it's just a little bit of kidney I cut off their joint.

JEAN, *smelling it.* Fine! That's my special delice. *Feels the plate.* But you might have warmed the plate.

KRISTIN. When you choose to be finicky you're worse than the Count himself. *Pulls his hair affectionately.*

JEAN, *crossly.* Stop pulling my hair. You know how sensitive I am.

KRISTIN. There, there! It's only love, you know.

JEAN *eats.* KRISTIN *brings a bottle of beer.*

JEAN. Beer on Midsummer Eve? No thanks! I've got something better than that. *From a drawer in the table brings out a bottle of red wine with a yellow seal.* Yellow seal, see! Now get me a glass. You use a glass with a stem of course when you're drinking it straight.

KRISTIN, *giving him a wine-glass.* Lord help the woman who gets you for a husband, you old fusser! *She puts the beer in the ice-box and sets a small saucepan on the stove.*

JEAN. Nonsense! You'll be glad enough to get a fellow as smart as me. And I don't think it's done you any harm people calling me your fiancé. *Tastes the wine.* Good. Very good indeed. But not quite warmed enough. *Warms the glass in his hand.* We bought this in Dijon. Four francs the litre without the bottle, and duty on top of that. What are you cooking now? It stinks.

KRISTIN. Some bloody muck Miss Julie wants for Diana.

JEAN. You should be more refined in your speech, Kristin. But why should you spend a holiday cooking for that bitch? Is she sick or what?

KRISTIN. Yes, she's sick. She sneaked out with the pug at the lodge and got in the usual mess. And that, you know, Miss Julie won't have.

JEAN. Miss Julie's too high-and-mighty in some respects, and not enough in others, just like her mother before her. The Countess was more at home in the kitchen and cowsheds than anywhere else, but would she ever go driving with only one horse? She went round with her cuffs filthy, but she had to have the coronet on the cuff-links. Our young lady—to come back to her—hasn't any proper respect for herself or her position. I mean she isn't refined. In the Barn just now she dragged the gamekeeper away from Anna and made him dance with her—no waiting to be asked. We wouldn't do a thing like that. But that's what happens when the gentry try to behave like the common people—they become common . . . Still she's a fine girl. Smashing! What shoulders! And what—er—etcetera!

KRISTIN. Oh come off it! I know what Clara says, and she dresses her.

JEAN. Clara? Pooh, you're all jealous! But I've been out riding with her . . . and as for her dancing!

KRISTIN. Listen, Jean. You will dance with me, won't you, as soon as I'm through.

JEAN. Of course I will.

KRISTIN. Promise?

JEAN. Promise? When I say I'll do a thing I do it. Well, thanks for the supper. It was a real treat. *Corks the bottle.*

JULIE *appears in the doorway, speaking to someone outside.*

JULIE. I'll be back in a moment. Don't wait.

JEAN *slips the bottle into the drawer and rises respectfully.* JULIE *enters and joins* KRISTIN *at the stove.*

Well, have you made it? KRISTIN *signs that* JEAN *is near them.*

JEAN, *gallantly.* Have you ladies got some secret?

JULIE, *flipping his face with her handkerchief.* You're very inquisitive.

JEAN. What a delicious smell! Violets.

JULIE, *coquettishly.* Impertinence! Are you an expert of scent too? I must say you know how to dance. Now don't look. Go away. *The music of a schottische begins.*

JEAN, *with impudent politeness.* Is it some witches' brew you're cooking on Midsummer Eve? Something to tell your stars by, so you can see your future?

JULIE, *sharply.* If you could see that you'd have good eyes. *To* KRISTIN. Put it in a bottle and cork it tight. Come and dance this schottische with me, Jean.

JEAN, *hesitating.* I don't want to be rude, but I've promised to dance this one with Kristin.

JULIE. Well, she can have another, can't you, Kristin? You'll lend me Jean, won't you?

KRISTIN, *bottling.* It's nothing to do with me. When you're so condescending, Miss, it's not his place to say no. Go on, Jean, and thank Miss Julie for the honour.

JEAN. Frankly speaking, Miss, and no offence meant, I wonder if it's wise for you to dance twice running with the same partner, specially as those people are so ready to jump to conclusions.

JULIE, *flaring up.* What did you say? What sort of conclusions? What do you mean?

JEAN, *meekly.* As you choose not to understand, Miss Julie, I'll have to speak more plainly. It looks bad to show a preference for one of your retainers when they're all hoping for the same unusual favour.

JULIE. Show a preference! The very idea! I'm surprised at you. I'm doing the people an honour by attending their ball when I'm mistress of the house, but if I'm really going to dance, I mean to have a partner who can lead and doesn't make me look ridiculous.

JEAN. If those are your orders, Miss, I'm at your service.

JULIE, *gently.* Don't take it as an order. To-night we're all just people enjoying a party. There's no question of class. So now give me your arm. Don't worry, Kristin. I shan't steal your sweetheart.

JEAN gives JULIE his arm and leads her out.

Left alone, KRISTIN plays her scene in an unhurried, natural way, humming to the tune of the schottische, played on a distant violin. She clears JEAN's place, washes up and puts things away, then takes off her apron, brings out a small mirror from a drawer, props it against the jar of lilac, lights a candle, warms a small pair of tongs and curls her fringe. She goes to the door and listens, then turning back to the table finds MISS JULIE's forgotten handkerchief. She smells it, then meditatively smooths it out and folds it.

Enter JEAN.

JEAN. She really *is* crazy. What a way to dance! With people standing grinning at her too from behind the doors. What's got into her, Kristin?

KRISTIN. Oh, it's just her time coming on. She's always queer then. Are you going to dance with me now?

JEAN. Then you're not wild with me for cutting that one.

KRISTIN. You know I'm not—for a little thing like that. Besides, I know my place.

JEAN, *putting his arm round her waist.* You're a sensible girl, Kristin, and you'll make a very good wife . . .

Enter JULIE, *unpleasantly surprised.*

JULIE, *with forced gaiety.* You're a fine beau—running away from your partner.

JEAN. Not away, Miss Julie, but as you see back to the one I deserted.

JULIE, *changing her tone.* You really can dance, you know. But why are you wearing your livery on a holiday. Take it off at once.

JEAN. Then I must ask you to go away for a moment, Miss. My black coat's here. *Indicates it hanging on the door to his room.*

JULIE. Are you so shy of me—just over changing a coat? Go into your room then—or stay here and I'll turn my back.

JEAN. Excuse me then, Miss. *He goes to his room and is partly visible as he changes his coat.*

JULIE. Tell me, Kristin, is Jean your fiancé? You seem very intimate.

KRISTIN. My fiancé? Yes, if you like. We call it that.

JULIE. Call it?

KRISTIN. Well, you've had a fiancé yourself, Miss, and . . .

JULIE. But we really were engaged.

KRISTIN. All the same it didn't come to anything.

JEAN returns in his black coat.

JULIE. Très gentil, Monsieur Jean. Très gentil.

JEAN. Vous voulez plaisanter, Madame.

JULIE. Et vous voulez parler français. Where did you learn it?

JEAN. In Switzerland, when I was sommelier at one of the biggest hotels in Lucerne.

JULIE. You look quite the gentleman in that get-up. Charming. *Sits at the table.*

JEAN. Oh, you're just flattering me!

JULIE, *annoyed.* Flattering you?

JEAN. I'm too modest to believe you would pay real compliments to a man like me, so I must take it you are exaggerating—that this is what's known as flattery.

JULIE. Where on earth did you learn to make speeches like that? Perhaps you've been to the theatre a lot.

JEAN. That's right. And travelled a lot too.

JULIE. But you come from this neighbourhood, don't you?

JEAN. Yes, my father was a labourer on the next estate—the District Attorney's place. I often used to see you, Miss Julie, when you were little, though you never noticed me.

JULIE. Did you really?

JEAN. Yes. One time specially I remember . . . but I can't tell you about that.

JULIE. Oh do! Why not? This is just the time.

JEAN. No, I really can't now. Another time perhaps.

JULIE. Another time means never. What harm in now?

JEAN. No harm, but I'd rather not. *Points to* KRISTIN, *now fast asleep.* Look at her.

JULIE. She'll make a charming wife, won't she? I wonder if she snores.

JEAN. No, she doesn't, but she talks in her sleep.

JULIE, *cynically.* How do you know she talks in her sleep?

JEAN, *brazenly.* I've heard her. *Pause. They look at one another.*

JULIE. Why don't you sit down?

JEAN. I can't take such a liberty in your presence.

JULIE. Supposing I order you to.

JEAN. I'll obey.

JULIE. Then sit down. No, wait a minute. Will you get me a drink first?

JEAN. I don't know what's in the ice-box. Only beer, I expect.

JULIE. There's no only about it. My taste is so simple I prefer it to wine.

JEAN *takes a bottle from the ice-box, fetches a glass and plate and serves the beer.*

JEAN. At your service.

JULIE. Thank you. Won't you have some yourself?

JEAN. I'm not really a beer-drinker, but if it's an order . . .

JULIE. Order? I should have thought it was ordinary manners to keep your partner company.

JEAN. That's a good way of putting it. *He opens another bottle and fetches a glass.*

JULIE. Now drink my health. *He hesitates.* I believe the man really is shy.

JEAN *kneels and raises his glass with mock ceremony.*

JEAN. To the health of my lady!

JULIE. Bravo! Now kiss my shoe and everything will be perfect. *He hesitates, then boldly takes hold of her foot and lightly kisses it.* Splendid. You ought to have been an actor.

JEAN, *rising.* We can't go on like this, Miss Julie. Someone might come in and see us.

JULIE. Why would that matter?

JEAN. For the simple reason that they'd talk. And if you knew the way their tongues were wagging out there just now, you . . .

JULIE. What were they saying? Tell me. Sit down.

JEAN, *sitting.* No offence meant, Miss, but . . . well, their language wasn't nice, and they were hinting . . . oh, you know quite well what. You're not a child, and if a lady's seen drinking alone at night with a man—and a servant at that—then . . .

JULIE. Then what? Besides, we're not alone. Kristin's here.

JEAN. Yes, asleep.

JULIE. I'll wake her up. *Rises.* Kristin, are you asleep? KRISTIN *mumbles in her sleep.* Kristin! Goodness, how she sleeps!

KRISTIN, *in her sleep.* The Count's boots are cleaned—put the coffee on—yes, yes, at once . . . *Mumbles incoherently.*

JULIE, *tweaking her nose.* Wake up, can't you!

JEAN, *sharply.* Let her sleep.

JULIE. What?

JEAN. When you've been standing at the stove all day you're likely to be tired at night. And sleep should be respected.

JULIE, *changing her tone.* What a nice idea. It does you credit. Thank you for it. *Holds out her hand to him.* Now come out and pick some lilac for me.

During the following KRISTIN *goes sleepily in to her bedroom.*

JEAN. Out with you, Miss Julie?

JULIE. Yes.

JEAN. It wouldn't do. It really wouldn't.

JULIE. I don't know what you mean. You can't possibly imagine that . . .

JEAN. I don't, but others do.

JULIE. What? That I'm in love with the valet?

JEAN. I'm not a conceited man, but such a thing's been known to happen, and to these rustics nothing's sacred.

JULIE. You, I take it, are an aristocrat.

JEAN. Yes, I am.

JULIE. And I am coming down in the world.

JEAN. Don't come down, Miss Julie. Take my advice. No one will believe you came down of your own accord. They'll all say you fell.

JULIE. I have a higher opinion of our people than you. Come and put it to the test. Come on. *Gazes into his eyes.*

JEAN. You're very strange, you know.

JULIE. Perhaps I am, but so are you. For that matter everything is strange. Life, human beings, everything, just scum drifting about on the water until it sinks—down and down. That reminds me of a dream I sometimes have, in which I'm on top of a pillar and can't see any way of getting down. When I look down I'm dizzy; I have to get down but I haven't the courage to jump. I can't stay there and I long to fall, but I don't fall. There's no respite. There can't be any peace at all for me until I'm down, right down on the ground. And if I did get to the ground I'd want to be under the ground . . . Have you ever felt like that?

JEAN. No. In my dream I'm lying under a great tree in a dark wood. I want to get up, up to the top of it, and look out over the bright landscape where the sun is shining and rob that high nest of its golden eggs. And I climb and climb, but the trunk is so thick and smooth and it's so far to the first branch. But I know if I can once reach that first branch I'll go to the top just as if I'm on a ladder. I haven't reached it yet, but I shall get there, even if only in my dreams.

JULIE. Here I am chattering about dreams with you. Come on. Only into the park. *She takes his arm and they go towards the door.*

JEAN. We must sleep on nine midsummer flowers tonight; then our dreams will come true, Miss Julie. *They turn at the door. He has a hand to his eye.*

JULIE. Have you got something in your eye? Let me see.

JEAN. Oh, it's nothing. Just a speck of dust. It'll be gone in a minute.

JULIE. My sleeve must have rubbed against you. Sit down and let me see to it. *Takes him by the arm and makes him sit down, bends his head back and tries to get the speck out with the corner of her handkerchief.* Keep still now, quite still. *Slaps his hand.* Do as I tell you. Why, I believe you're trembling, big, strong man though you are! *Feels his biceps.* What muscles!

JEAN, *warning.* Miss Julie!

JULIE. Yes, Monsieur Jean?

JEAN. Attention. Je ne suis qu'un homme.

JULIE. Will you stay still! There now. It's out. Kiss my hand and say thank you.

JEAN, *rising*. Miss Julie, listen. Kristin's gone to bed now. Will you listen?

JULIE. Kiss my hand first.

JEAN. Very well, but you'll have only yourself to blame.

JULIE. For what?

JEAN. For what! Are you still a child at twenty-five? Don't you know it's dangerous to play with fire?

JULIE. Not for me. I'm insured.

JEAN, *bluntly*. No, you're not. And even if you are, there's still stuff here to kindle a flame.

JULIE. Meaning yourself?

JEAN. Yes. Not because I'm me, but because I'm a man and young and . . .

JULIE. And good-looking? What incredible conceit! A Don Juan perhaps? Or a Joseph? Good Lord, I do believe you are a Joseph!

JEAN. Do you?

JULIE. I'm rather afraid so.

JEAN *goes boldly up and tries to put his arms round her and kiss her. She boxes his ears.*

How dare you!

JEAN. Was that in earnest or a joke?

JULIE. In earnest.

JEAN. Then what went before was in earnest too. You take your games too seriously and that's dangerous. Anyhow I'm tired of playing now and beg leave to return to my work. The Count will want his boots first thing and it's past midnight now.

JULIE. Put those boots down.

JEAN. No. This is my work, which it's my duty to do. But I never undertook to be your playfellow and I never will be. I consider myself too good for that.

JULIE. You're proud.

JEAN. In some ways—not all.

JULIE. Have you even been in love?

JEAN. We don't put it that way, but I've been gone on quite
   a few girls. And once I went sick because I couldn't have
   the one I wanted. Sick, I mean, like those princes in the
   Arabian Nights who couldn't eat or drink for love.

JULIE. Who was she? *No answer.* Who was she?

JEAN. You can't force me to tell you that.

JULIE. If I ask as an equal, ask as a—friend? Who was she?

JEAN. You.

JULIE, *sitting.* How absurd!

JEAN. Yes, ludicrous if you like. That's the story I wouldn't
   tell you before, see, but now I will . . . Do you know
   what the world looks like from below? No, you don't. No
   more than the hawks and falcons do whose backs one
   hardly ever sees because they're always soaring up aloft. I
   lived in a labourer's hovel with seven other children and a
   pig, out in the grey fields where there isn't a single tree.
   But from the window I could see the wall round the
   Count's park with apple-trees above it. That was the Garden of Eden, guarded by many terrible angels with flaming
   swords. All the same I and the other boys managed to get
   to the tree of life. Does all this make you despise me?

JULIE. Goodness, all boys steal apples!

JEAN. You say that now, but all the same you do despise me.
   However, one time I went into the Garden of Eden with
   my mother to weed the onion beds. Close to the kitchen
   garden there was a Turkish pavilion hung all over with
   jasmine and honeysuckle. I hadn't any idea what it was
   used for, but I'd never seen such a beautiful building.
   People used to go in and then come out again, and one
   day the door was left open. I crept up and saw the walls
   covered with pictures of kings and emperors, and the windows had red curtains with fringes—you know now what
   the place was, don't you? I . . . *Breaks off a piece of lilac
   and holds it for* JULIE *to smell. As he talks, she takes it
   from him.* I had never been inside the manor, never seen
   anything but the church, and this was more beautiful. No
   matter where my thoughts went, they always came back—
   to that place. The longing went on growing in me to

enjoy it fully, just once. Enfin, I sneaked in, gazed and admired. Then I heard someone coming. There was only one way out for the gentry, but for me there was another and I had no choice but to take it. JULIE *drops the lilac on the table.* Then I took to my heels, plunged through the raspberry canes, dashed across the strawberry beds and found myself on the rose terrace. There I saw a pink dress and a pair of white stockings—it was you. I crawled into a weed pile and lay there right under it among prickly thistles and damp rank earth. I watched you walking among the roses and said to myself: "If it's true that a thief can get to heaven and be with the angels, it's pretty strange that a labourer's child here on God's earth mayn't come in the park and play with the Count's daughter."

JULIE, *sentimentally.* Do you think all poor children feel the way you did?

JEAN, *taken aback, then rallying.* All poor children? . . . Yes, of course they do. Of course.

JULIE. It must be terrible to be poor.

JEAN, *with exaggerated distress.* Oh yes, Miss Julie, yes. A dog may lie on the Countess's sofa, a horse may have his nose stroked by a young lady, but a servant . . . *change of tone* well, yes, now and then you meet one with guts enough to rise in the world, but how often? Anyhow, do you know what I did? Jumped in the millstream with my clothes on, was pulled out and got a hiding. But the next Sunday, when Father and all the rest went to Granny's, I managed to get left behind. Then I washed with soap and hot water, put my best clothes on and went to church so as to see you. I did see you and went home determined to die. But I wanted to die beautifully and peacefully, without any pain. Then I remembered it was dangerous to sleep under an elder bush. We had a big one in full bloom, so I stripped it and climbed into the oats-bin with the flowers. Have you ever noticed how smooth oats are? Soft to touch as human skin . . . Well, I closed the lid and shut my eyes, fell asleep, and when they woke me I was very ill. But I didn't die, as you see. What I meant by all that I don't know. There was no hope of winning you —you were simply a symbol of the hopelessness of ever getting out of the class I was born in.

JULIE. You put things very well, you know. Did you go to school?

JEAN. For a while. But I've read a lot of novels and been to the theatre. Besides, I've heard educated folk talking— that's what's taught me most.

JULIE. Do you stand round listening to what we're saying?

JEAN. Yes, of course. And I've heard quite a bit too! On the carriage box or rowing the boat. Once I heard you, Miss Julie, and one of your young lady friends . . .

JULIE. Oh! Whatever did you hear?

JEAN. Well, it wouldn't be nice to repeat it. And I must say I was pretty startled. I couldn't think where you had learnt such words. Perhaps, at bottom, there isn't as much difference between people as one's led to believe.

JULIE. How dare you! We don't behave as you do when we're engaged.

JEAN, *looking hard at her*. Are you sure? It's no use making out so innocent to me.

JULIE. The man I gave my love to was a rotter.

JEAN. That's what you always say—afterwards.

JULIE. Always?

JEAN. I think it must be always. I've heard the expression several times in similar circumstances.

JULIE. What circumstances?

JEAN. Like those in question. The last time . . .

JULIE, *rising*. Stop. I don't want to hear any more.

JEAN. Nor did *she*—curiously enough. May I go to bed now please?

JULIE, *gently*. Go to bed on Midsummer Eve?

JEAN. Yes. Dancing with that crowd doesn't really amuse me.

JULIE. Get the key of the boathouse and row me out on the lake. I want to see the sun rise.

JEAN. Would that be wise?

JULIE. You sound as though you're frightened for your reputation.

JEAN. Why not? I don't want to be made a fool of, nor to be sent packing without a character when I'm trying to better myself. Besides, I have Kristin to consider.

JULIE. So now it's Kristin.

JEAN. Yes, but it's you I'm thinking about too. Take my advice and go to bed.

JULIE. Am I to take orders from you?

JEAN. Just this once, for your own sake. Please. It's very late and sleepiness goes to one's head and makes one rash. Go to bed. What's more, if my ears don't deceive me, I hear people coming this way. They'll be looking for me, and if they find us here, you're done for.

The CHORUS *approaches, singing. During the following dialogue the song is heard in snatches, and in full when the peasants enter.*

> *Out of the wood two women came,*
> *Tridiri-ralla, tridiri-ra.*
> *The feet of one were bare and cold,*
> *Tridiri-ralla-la.*
>
> *The other talked of bags of gold,*
> *Tridiri-ralla, tridiri-ra.*
> *But neither had a sou to her name,*
> *Tridiri-ralla-la.*
>
> *The bridal wreath I give to you,*
> *Tridiri-ralla, tridiri-ra.*
> *But to another I'll be true,*
> *Tridiri-ralla-la.*

JULIE. I know our people and I love them, just as they do me. Let them come. You'll see.

JEAN. No, Miss Julie, they don't love you. They take your food, then spit at it. You must believe me. Listen to them, just listen to what they're singing . . . No, don't listen.

JULIE, *listening*. What are they singing?

JEAN. They're mocking—you and me.

JULIE. Oh no! How horrible! What cowards!

JEAN. A pack like that's always cowardly. But against such odds there's nothing we can do but run away.

JULIE. Run away? Where to? We can't get out and we can't go into Kristin's room.

JEAN. Into mine then. Necessity knows no rules. And you can trust me. I really am your true and devoted friend.

JULIE. But supposing . . . supposing they were to look for you in there?

JEAN. I'll bolt the door, and if they try to break in I'll shoot. Come on. *Pleading*. Please come.

JULIE, *tensely*. Do you promise . . . ?

JEAN. I swear!

> JULIE *goes quickly into his room and he excitedly follows her.*
> Led by the fiddler, the peasants enter in festive attire with flowers in their hats. They put a barrel of beer and a keg of spirits, garlanded with leaves, on the table, fetch glasses and begin to carouse. The scene becomes a ballet. They form a ring and dance and sing and mime: "Out of the wood two women came." Finally they go out, still singing.*
> JULIE *comes in alone. She looks at the havoc in the kitchen, wrings her hands, then takes out her powder puff and powders her face.*
> JEAN *enters in high spirits.*

JEAN. Now you see! And you heard, didn't you? Do you still think it's possible for us to stay here?

JULIE. No, I don't. But what can we do?

JEAN. Run away. Far away. Take a journey.

JULIE. Journey? But where to?

JEAN. Switzerland. The Italian lakes. Ever been there?

JULIE. No. Is it nice?

JEAN. Ah! Eternal summer, oranges, evergreens . . . ah!

JULIE. But what would we do there?

JEAN. I'll start a hotel. First-class accommodation and first-class customers.

JULIE. Hotel?

JEAN. There's life for you. New faces all the time, new languages—no time for nerves or worries, no need to look for something to do—work rolling up of its own accord. Bells ringing night and day, trains whistling, buses coming and going, and all the time gold pieces rolling on to the counter. There's life for you!

JULIE. For *you*. And I?

JEAN. Mistress of the house, ornament of the firm. With your looks, and your style . . . oh, it's bound to be a success! Terrific! You'll sit like a queen in the office and set your slaves in motion by pressing an electric button. The guests will file past your throne and nervously lay their treasure on your table. You've no idea the way people tremble when they get their bills. I'll salt the bills and you'll sugar them with your sweetest smiles. Ah, let's get away from here! *Produces a time-table.* At once, by the next train. We shall be at Malmö at six-thirty, Hamburg eight-forty next morning, Frankfurt-Basle the following day, and Como by the St. Gothard pass in—let's see—three days. Three days!

JULIE. That's all very well. But Jean, you must give me courage. Tell me you love me. Come and take me in your arms.

JEAN, *reluctantly.* I'd like to, but I daren't. Not again in this house. I love you—that goes without saying. You can't doubt that, Miss Julie, can you?

JULIE, *shyly, very feminine.* Miss? Call me Julie. There aren't any barriers between us now. Call me Julie.

JEAN, *uneasily.* I can't. As long as we're in this house, there *are* barriers between us. There's the past and there's the Count. I've never been so servile to anyone as I am to him. I've only got to see his gloves on a chair to feel small. I've only to hear his bell and I shy like a horse. Even now, when I look at his boots, standing there so proud and stiff,

I feel my back beginning to bend. *Kicks the boots.* It's those old, narrow-minded notions drummed into us as children . . . but they can soon be forgotten. You've only got to get to another country, a republic, and people will bend themselves double before my porter's livery. Yes, double they'll bend themselves, but I shan't. I wasn't born to bend. I've got guts, I've got character, and once I reach that first branch, you'll watch me climb. Today I'm valet, next year I'll be proprietor, in ten years I'll have made a fortune, and then I'll go to Roumania, get myself decorated and I may, I only say *may*, mind you, end up as a Count.

JULIE, *sadly.* That would be very nice.

JEAN. You see in Roumania one can buy a title, and then you'll be a Countess after all. My Countess.

JULIE. What do I care about all that? I'm putting those things behind me. Tell me you love me, because if you don't . . . if you don't, what am I?

JEAN. I'll tell you a thousand times over—later. But not here. No sentimentality now or everything will be lost. We must consider this thing calmly like reasonable people. *Takes a cigar, cuts and lights it.* You sit down there and I'll sit here and we'll talk as if nothing has happened.

JULIE. My God, have you no feelings at all?

JEAN. Nobody has more. But I know how to control them.

JULIE. A short time ago you were kissing my shoe. And now . . .

JEAN, *harshly.* Yes, that was then. Now we have something else to think about.

JULIE. Don't speak to me so brutally.

JEAN. I'm not. Just sensibly. One folly's been committed, don't let's have more. The Count will be back at any moment and we've got to settle our future before that. Now, what do you think of my plans? Do you approve?

JULIE. It seems a very good idea—but just one thing. Such a big undertaking would need a lot of capital. Have you got any?

JEAN, *chewing his cigar*. I certainly have. I've got my professional skill, my wide experience and my knowledge of foreign languages. That's capital worth having, it seems to me.

JULIE. But it won't buy even one railway ticket.

JEAN. Quite true. That's why I need a backer to advance some ready cash.

JULIE. How could you get that at a moment's notice?

JEAN. You must get it, if you want to be my partner.

JULIE. I can't. I haven't any money of my own. *Pause.*

JEAN. Then the whole thing's off.

JULIE. And . . . ?

JEAN. We go on as we are.

JULIE. Do you think I'm going to stay under this roof as your mistress? With everyone pointing at me. Do you think I can face my father after this? No. Take me away from here, away from this shame, this humiliation. Oh my God, what have I done? My God, my God! *Weeps.*

JEAN. So that's the tune now, is it? What have you done? Same as many before you.

JULIE, *hysterically*. And now you despise me. I'm falling, I'm falling.

JEAN. Fall as far as me and I'll lift you up again.

JULIE. Why was I so terribly attracted to you? The weak to the strong, the falling to the rising? Or was it love? Is that love? Do you know what love is?

JEAN. Do I? You bet I do. Do you think I never had a girl before?

JULIE. The things you say, the things you think!

JEAN. That's what life's taught me, and that's what I am. It's no good getting hysterical or giving yourself airs. We're both in the same boat now. Here, my dear girl, let me give you a glass of something special. *Opens the drawer, takes out the bottle of wine and fills two used glasses.*

JULIE. Where did you get that wine?

JEAN. From the cellar.

JULIE. My father's burgundy.

JEAN. Why not, for his son-in-law?

JULIE. And I drink beer.

JEAN. That only shows your taste's not so good as mine.

JULIE. Thief!

JEAN. Are you going to tell on me?

JULIE. Oh God! The accomplice of a petty thief! Was I blind drunk? Have I dreamt this whole night? Midsummer Eve, the night for innocent merrymaking.

JEAN. Innocent, eh?

JULIE. Is anyone on earth as wretched as I am now?

JEAN. Why should *you* be? After such a conquest. What about Kristin in there? Don't you think she has any feelings?

JULIE. I did think so, but I don't any longer. No. A menial is a menial . . .

JEAN. And a whore is a whore.

JULIE, *falling to her knees, her hands clasped.* O God in heaven, put an end to my miserable life! Lift me out of this filth in which I'm sinking. Save me! Save me!

JEAN. I must admit I'm sorry for you. When I was in the onion bed and saw you up there among the roses, I . . . yes, I'll tell you now . . . I had the same dirty thoughts as all boys.

JULIE. You, who wanted to die because of me?

JEAN. In the oats-bin? That was just talk.

JULIE. Lies, you mean.

JEAN, *getting sleepy.* More or less. I think I read a story in some paper about a chimney-sweep who shut himself up in a chest full of lilac because he'd been summonsed for not supporting some brat . . .

JULIE. So this is what you're like.

JEAN. I had to think up something. It's always the fancy stuff that catches the women.

JULIE. Beast!

JEAN. Merde!

JULIE. Now you have seen the falcon's back.

JEAN. Not exactly its *back*.

JULIE. I was to be the first branch.

JEAN. But the branch was rotten.

JULIE. I was to be a hotel sign.

JEAN. And I the hotel.

JULIE. Sit at your counter, attract your clients and cook their accounts.

JEAN. I'd have done that myself.

JULIE. That any human being can be so steeped in filth!

JEAN. Clean it up then.

JULIE. Menial! Lackey! Stand up when I speak to you.

JEAN. Menial's whore, lackey's harlot, shut your mouth and get out of here! Are you the one to lecture me for being coarse? Nobody of my kind would ever be as coarse as you were tonight. Do you think any servant girl would throw herself at a man that way? Have you ever seen a girl of my class asking for it like that? I haven't. Only animals and prostitutes.

JULIE, *broken*. Go on. Hit me, trample on me—it's all I deserve. I'm rotten. But help me! If there's any way out at all, help me.

JEAN, *more gently*. I'm not denying myself a share in the honour of seducing you, but do you think anybody in my place would have dared look in your direction if you yourself hadn't asked for it? I'm still amazed . . .

JULIE. And proud.

JEAN. Why not? Though I must admit the victory was too easy to make me lose my head.

JULIE. Go on hitting me.

JEAN, *rising*. No. On the contrary I apologise for what I've said. I don't hit a person who's down—least of all a woman. I can't deny there's a certain satisfaction in finding that what dazzled one below was just moonshine, that that falcon's back is grey after all, that there's powder on the lovely cheek, that polished nails can have black tips,

that the handkerchief is dirty although it smells of scent.
On the other hand it hurts to find that what I was strug-
gling to reach wasn't high and isn't real. It hurts to see
you fallen so low you're far lower than your own cook.
Hurts like when you see the last flowers of summer lashed
to pieces by rain and turned to mud.

JULIE. You're talking as if you're already my superior.

JEAN. I am. I might make you a Countess, but you could
never make me a Count, you know.

JULIE. But I am the child of a Count, and you could never be
that.

JEAN. True, but I might be the father of Counts if . . .

JULIE. You're a thief. I'm not.

JEAN. There are worse things than being a thief—much lower.
Besides, when I'm in a place I regard myself as a member of the family to some extent, as one of the children.
You don't call it stealing when children pinch a berry
from overladen bushes. *His passion is roused again.* Miss
Julie, you're a glorious woman, far too good for a man
like me. You were carried away by some kind of madness,
and now you're trying to cover up your mistake by per-
suading yourself you're in love with me. You're not,
although you may find me physically attractive, which
means your love's no better than mine. But I wouldn't
be satisfied with being nothing but an animal for you,
and I could never make you love me.

JULIE. Are you sure?

JEAN. You think there's a chance? Of my loving you, yes, of
course. You're beautiful, refined—*takes her hand*—educated, and you can be nice when you want to be. The fire
you kindle in a man isn't likely to go out. *Puts his arm
round her.* You're like mulled wine, full of spices, and
your kisses . . . *He tries to pull her to him, but she
breaks away.*

JULIE. Let go of me! You won't win me that way.

JEAN. Not that way, how then? Not by kisses and fine
speeches, not by planning the future and saving you from
shame? How then?

JULIE. How? How? I don't know. There isn't any way. I loathe you—loathe you as I loathe rats, but I can't escape from you.

JEAN. Escape with me.

JULIE, *pulling herself together*. Escape? Yes, we must escape. But I'm so tired. Give me a glass of wine. *He pours it out. She looks at her watch.* First we must talk. We still have a little time. *Empties the glass and holds it out for more.*

JEAN. Don't drink like that. You'll get tipsy.

JULIE. What's that matter?

JEAN. What's it matter? It's vulgar to get drunk. Well, what have you got to say?

JULIE. We've got to run away, but we must talk first—or rather, I must, for so far you've done all the talking. You've told me about your life, now I want to tell you about mine, so that we really know each other before we begin this journey together.

JEAN. Wait. Excuse my saying so, but don't you think you may be sorry afterwards if you give away your secrets to me?

JULIE. Aren't you my friend?

JEAN. On the whole. But don't rely on me.

JULIE. You can't mean that. But anyway everyone knows my secrets. Listen. My mother wasn't well-born; she came of quite humble people, and was brought up with all those new ideas of sex-equality and women's rights and so on. She thought marriage was quite wrong. So when my father proposed to her, she said she would never become his *wife* . . . but in the end she did. I came into the world, as far as I can make out, against my mother's will, and I was left to run wild, but I had to do all the things a boy does—to prove women are as good as men. I had to wear boys' clothes; I was taught to handle horses—and I wasn't allowed in the dairy. She made me groom and harness and go out hunting; I even had to try to plough. All the men on the estate were given the women's jobs, and the women the men's, until the whole place went to rack and ruin and we were the laughing-stock of the neighbourhood. At last my father seems to have come to his senses and rebelled. He changed everything and ran the place his own way. My mother got ill—I don't know what was the matter with her, but she used to have strange attacks and hide herself in the attic or the garden. Sometimes she stayed out all night. Then came the great fire which you have heard people talking about. The house and the stables and the barns—the whole place burnt to the ground. In very suspicious circumstances. Because the accident happened the very day the insurance had to be renewed, and my father had sent the new premium, but through some carelessness of the messenger it arrived too late. *Refills her glass and drinks.*

JEAN. Don't drink any more.

JULIE. Oh, what does it matter? We were destitute and had to sleep in the carriages. My father didn't know how to get money to rebuild, and then my mother suggested he should borrow from an old friend of hers, a local brick manufacturer. My father got the loan and, to his surprise, without having to pay interest. So the place was rebuilt. *Drinks.* Do you know who set fire to it?

JEAN. Your lady mother.

JULIE. Do you know who the brick manufacturer was?

JEAN. Your mother's lover?

JULIE. Do you know whose the money was?

JEAN. Wait . . . no, I don't know that.

JULIE. It was my mother's.

JEAN. In other words the Count's, unless there was a settlement.

JULIE. There wasn't any settlement. My mother had a little money of her own which she didn't want my father to control, so she invested it with her—friend.

JEAN. Who grabbed it.

JULIE. Exactly. He appropriated it. My father came to know all this. He couldn't bring an action, couldn't pay his wife's lover, nor prove it was his wife's money. That was my mother's revenge because he made himself master in his own house. He nearly shot himself then—at least there's a rumour he tried and didn't bring it off. So he went on living, and my mother had to pay dearly for what she'd done. Imagine what those five years were like for me. My natural sympathies were with my father, yet I took my mother's side, because I didn't know the facts. I'd learnt from her to hate and distrust men—you know how she loathed the whole male sex. And I swore to her I'd never become the slave of any man.

JEAN. And so you got engaged to that attorney.

JULIE. So that he should be my slave.

JEAN. But he wouldn't be.

JULIE. Oh yes, he wanted to be, but he didn't have the chance. I got bored with him.

JEAN. Is that what I saw—in the stable-yard?

JULIE. What did you see?

JEAN. What I saw was him breaking off the engagement.

JULIE. That's a lie. It was I who broke it off. Did he say it was him? The cad.

JEAN. He's not a cad. Do you hate men, Miss Julie?

JULIE. Yes . . . most of the time. But when that weakness comes, oh . . . the shame!

JEAN. Then do you hate me?

JULIE. Beyond words. I'd gladly have you killed like an animal.

JEAN. Quick as you'd shoot a mad dog, eh?

JULIE. Yes.

JEAN. But there's nothing here to shoot with—and there isn't a dog. So what do we do now?

JULIE. Go abroad.

JEAN. To make each other miserable for the rest of our lives?

JULIE. No, to enjoy ourselves for a day or two, for a week, for as long as enjoyment lasts, and then—to die . . .

JEAN. Die? How silly! I think it would be far better to start a hotel.

JULIE, *without listening* . . . die on the shores of Lake

Como, where the sun always shines and at Christmas time there are green trees and glowing oranges.

JEAN. Lake Como's a rainy hole and I didn't see any oranges outside the shops. But it's a good place for tourists. Plenty of villas to be rented by—er—honeymoon couples. Profitable business that. Know why? Because they all sign a lease for six months and all leave after three weeks.

JULIE, *naïvely.* After three weeks? Why?

JEAN. They quarrel, of course. But the rent has to be paid just the same. And then it's let again. So it goes on and on, for there's plenty of love although it doesn't last long.

JULIE. You don't want to die with me?

JEAN. I don't want to die at all. For one thing I like living and for another I consider suicide's a sin against the Creator who gave us life.

JULIE. You believe in God—*you?*

JEAN. Yes, of course. And I go to church every Sunday. Look here, I'm tired of all this. I'm going to bed.

JULIE. Indeed! And do you think I'm going to leave things like this? Don't you know what you owe the woman you've ruined?

JEAN, *taking out his purse and throwing a silver coin on the table.* There you are. I don't want to be in anybody's debt.

JULIE, *pretending not to notice the insult.* Don't you know what the law is?

JEAN. There's no law unfortunately that punishes a woman for seducing a man.

JULIE. But can you see anything for it but to go abroad, get married and then divorce?

JEAN. What if I refuse this mésalliance?

JULIE. Mésalliance?

JEAN. Yes, for me. I'm better bred than you, see! Nobody in my family committed arson.

JULIE. How do you know?

JEAN. Well, you can't prove otherwise, because we haven't any family records outside the Registrar's office. But I've seen your family tree in that book on the drawing-room table. Do you know who the founder of your family was? A miller who let his wife sleep with the King one night during the Danish war. I haven't any ancestors like that. I haven't any ancestors at all, but I might become one.

JULIE. This what I get for confiding in someone so low, for sacrificing my family honour . . .

JEAN. Dishonour! Well, I told you so. One shouldn't drink, because then one talks. And one shouldn't talk.

JULIE. Oh, how ashamed I am, how bitterly ashamed! If at least you loved me!

JEAN. Look here—for the last time—what do you want? Am I to burst into tears? Am I to jump over your riding whip? Shall I kiss you and carry you off to Lake Como for three weeks, after which . . . What am I to do? What do you want? This is getting unbearable, but that's what comes of playing around with women. Miss Julie, I can see how miserable you are; I know you're going through hell, but I don't understand you. We don't have scenes like this; we don't go in for hating each other. We make love for fun in our spare time, but we haven't all day and all night for it like you. I think you must be ill. I'm sure you're ill.

JULIE. Then you must be kind to me. You sound almost human now.

JEAN. Well, be human yourself. You spit at me, then won't let me wipe it off—on you.

JULIE. Help me, help me! Tell me what to do, where to go.

JEAN. Jesus, as if I knew!

JULIE. I've been mad, raving mad, but there must be a way out.

JEAN. Stay here and keep quiet. Nobody knows anything.

JULIE. I can't. People do know. Kristin knows.

JEAN. They don't know and they wouldn't believe such a thing.

JULIE, *hesitating*. But—it might happen again.

JEAN. That's true.

JULIE. And there might be—consequences.

JEAN, *in panic*. Consequences! Fool that I am I never thought of that. Yes, there's nothing for it but to go. At once. I can't come with you. That would be a complete give-away. You must go alone—abroad—anywhere.

JULIE. Alone? Where to? I can't.

JEAN. You must. And before the Count gets back. If you stay, we know what will happen. Once you've sinned you feel you might as well go on, as the harm's done. Then you get more and more reckless and in the end you're found out. No. You must go abroad. Then write to the Count and tell him everything, except that it was me. He'll never guess that—and I don't think he'll want to.

JULIE. I'll go if you come with me.

JEAN. Are you crazy, woman? "Miss Julie elopes with valet." Next day it would be in the headlines, and the Count would never live it down.

JULIE. I can't go. I can't stay. I'm so tired, so completely worn out. Give me orders. Set me going. I can't think any more, can't act . . .

JEAN. You see what weaklings you are. Why do you give yourselves airs and turn up your noses as if you're the lords of creation? Very well, I'll give you your orders. Go upstairs and dress. Get money for the journey and come down here again.

JULIE, *softly*. Come up with me.

JEAN. To your room? Now you've gone crazy again. *Hesitates a moment.* No! Go along at once. *Takes her hand and pulls her to the door.*

JULIE, *as she goes*. Speak kindly to me, Jean.

JEAN. Orders always sound unkind. Now you know. Now you know.

Left alone, JEAN *sighs with relief, sits down at the table, takes out a note-book and pencil and adds up figures, now and then aloud. Dawn begins to break.* KRISTIN *enters dressed for church, carrying his white dickey and tie.*

KRISTIN. Lord Jesus, look at the state the place is in! What have you been up to? *Turns out the lamp.*

JEAN. Oh, Miss Julie invited the crowd in. Did you sleep through it? Didn't you hear anything?

KRISTIN. I slept like a log.

JEAN. And dressed for church already.

KRISTIN. Yes, you promised to come to Communion with me today.

JEAN. Why, so I did. And you've got my bib and tucker, I see. Come on then. *Sits.* KRISTIN *begins to put his things on. Pause. Sleepily.* What's the lesson today?

KRISTIN. It's about the beheading of John the Baptist, I think.

JEAN. That's sure to be horribly long. Hi, you're choking me! Oh Lord, I'm so sleepy, so sleepy!

KRISTIN. Yes, what have you been doing up all night? You look absolutely green.

JEAN. Just sitting here talking with Miss Julie.

KRISTIN. She doesn't know what's proper, that one. *Pause.*

JEAN. I say, Kristin.

KRISTIN. What?

JEAN. It's queer really, isn't it, when you come to think of it? Her.

KRISTIN. What's queer?

JEAN. The whole thing. *Pause.*

KRISTIN, *looking at the half-filled glasses on the table.* Have you been drinking together too?

JEAN. Yes.

KRISTIN. More shame you. Look me straight in the face.

JEAN. Yes.

KRISTIN. Is it possible? Is it possible?

JEAN, *after a moment.* Yes, it is.

KRISTIN. Oh! This I would never have believed. How low!

JEAN. You're not jealous of her, surely?

KRISTIN. No, I'm not. If it had been Clara or Sophie I'd have scratched your eyes out. But not of her. I don't know why; that's how it is though. But it's disgusting.

JEAN. You're angry with her then.

KRISTIN. No. With you. It was wicked of you, very very wicked. Poor girl. And, mark my words, I won't stay here any longer now—in a place where one can't respect one's employers.

JEAN. Why should one respect them?

KRISTIN. You should know since you're so smart. But you don't want to stay in the service of people who aren't respectable, do you? I wouldn't demean myself.

JEAN. But it's rather a comfort to find out they're no better than us.

KRISTIN. I don't think so. If they're no better there's nothing for us to live up to. Oh and think of the Count! Think of him. He's been through so much already. No, I won't stay in the place any longer. A fellow like you too! If it had been that attorney now or somebody of her own class . . .

JEAN. Why, what's wrong with . . .

KRISTIN. Oh, you're all right in your own way, but when all's said and done there is a difference between one class and another. No, this is something I'll never be able to stomach. That our young lady who was so proud and so down on men you'd never believe she'd let one come near her should go and give herself to one like you. She who wanted to have poor Diana shot for running after the lodge-keeper's pug. No, I must say. . . ! Well, I won't stay here any longer. On the twenty-fourth of October I quit.

JEAN. And then?

KRISTIN. Well, since you mention it, it's about time you began to look around, if we're ever going to get married.

JEAN. But what am I to look for? I shan't get a place like this when I'm married.

KRISTIN. I know you won't. But you might get a job as porter or caretaker in some public institution. Government rations are small but sure, and there's a pension for the widow and children.

JEAN. That's all very fine, but it's not in my line to start thinking at once about dying for my wife and children. I must say I had rather bigger ideas.

KRISTIN. You and your ideas! You've got obligations too, and you'd better start thinking about them.

JEAN. Don't *you* start pestering me about obligations. I've had enough of that. *Listens to a sound upstairs.* Anyway we've plenty of time to work things out. Go and get ready now and we'll be off to church.

KRISTIN. Who's that walking about upstairs?

JEAN. Don't know—unless it's Clara.

KRISTIN, *going.* You don't think the Count could have come back without our hearing him?

JEAN, *scared.* The Count? No, he can't have. He'd have rung for me.

KRISTIN. God help us! I've never known such goings on.
Exit.

The sun has now risen and is shining on the treetops. The light gradually changes until it slants in through the windows. JEAN *goes to the door and beckons.* JULIE *enters in travelling clothes, carrying a small bird-cage covered with a cloth which she puts on a chair.*

JULIE. I'm ready.

JEAN. Hush! Kristin's up.

JULIE, *in a very nervous state.* Does she suspect anything?

JEAN. Not a thing. But, my God, what a sight you are!

JULIE. Sight? What do you mean?

JEAN. You're white as a corpse and—pardon me—your face is dirty.

JULIE. Let me wash then. *Goes to the sink and washes her face and hands.* There. Give me a towel. Oh! The sun is rising!

JEAN. And that breaks the spell.

JULIE. Yes. The spell of Midsummer Eve . . . But listen, Jean. Come with me. I've got the money.

JEAN, *sceptically.* Enough?

JULIE. Enough to start with. Come with me. I can't travel alone today. It's Midsummer Day, remember. I'd be packed into a suffocating train among crowds of people who'd all stare at me. And it would stop at every station while I yearned for wings. No, I can't do that, I simply can't. There will be memories too; memories of Midsummer Days when I was little. The leafy church—birch and lilac—the gaily spread dinner table, relatives, friends— evening in the park—dancing and music and flowers and fun. Oh, however far you run away—there'll always be memories in the baggage car—and remorse and guilt.

JEAN. I will come with you, but quickly now then, before it's too late. At once.

JULIE. Put on your things. *Picks up the cage.*

JEAN. No luggage mind. That would give us away.

JULIE. No, only what we can take with us in the carriage.

JEAN, *fetching his hat.* What on earth have you got there? What is it?

JULIE. Only my greenfinch. I don't want to leave it behind.

JEAN. Well, I'll be damned! We're to take a bird-cage along, are we? You're crazy. Put that cage down.

JULIE. It's the only thing I'm taking from my home. The only living creature who cares for me since Diana went off like that. Don't be cruel. Let me take it.

JEAN. Put that cage down, I tell you—and don't talk so loud. Kristin will hear.

JULIE. No, I won't leave it in strange hands. I'd rather you killed it.

JEAN. Give the little beast here then and I'll wring its neck.

JULIE. But don't hurt it, don't . . . no, I can't.

JEAN. Give it here. I *can.*

JULIE, *taking the bird out of the cage and kissing it.* Dear little Serena, must you die and leave your mistress?

JEAN. Please don't make a scene. It's *your* life and future we're worrying about. Come on, quick now!

He snatches the bird from her, puts it on a board and picks up a chopper. JULIE *turns away.*

You should have learnt how to kill chickens instead of target-shooting. Then you wouldn't faint at a drop of blood.

JULIE, *screaming.* Kill me too! Kill me! You who can butcher an innocent creature without a quiver. Oh, how I hate you, how I loathe you! There is blood between us now. I curse the hour I first saw you. I curse the hour I was conceived in my mother's womb.

JEAN. What's the use of cursing. Let's go.

JULIE, *going to the chopping-block as if drawn against her will.* No, I won't go yet. I can't . . . I must look. Listen! There's a carriage. *Listens without taking her eyes off the board and chopper.* You don't think I can bear the sight of blood. You think I'm so weak. Oh, how I should like to see your blood and your brains on a chopping-block! I'd like to see the whole of your sex swimming like that in a sea of blood. I think I could drink out of your skull, bathe my feet in your broken breast and eat your heart roasted whole. You think I'm weak. You think I love you, that my womb yearned for your seed and I want to carry your offspring under my heart and nourish it with my blood. You think I want to bear your child and take your name. By the way, what is your name? I've never heard your surname. I don't suppose you've got one. I should be "Mrs. Hovel" or "Madam Dunghill." You dog wearing my collar, you lackey with my crest on your buttons! I share you with my cook; I'm my own servant's rival! Oh! Oh! Oh! . . . You think I'm a coward and will run away. No, now I'm going to stay—and let the storm break. My father will come back . . . find his desk broken open . . . his money gone. Then he'll ring that bell—twice for the valet —and then he'll send for the police . . . and I shall tell everything. Everything. Oh how wonderful to make an end of it all—a real end! He has a stroke and dies and

that's the end of all of us. Just peace and quietness . . .
eternal rest. The coat of arms broken on the coffin and
the Count's line extinct . . . But the valet's line goes on
in an orphanage, wins laurels in the gutter and ends in
jail.

JEAN. There speaks the noble blood! Bravo, Miss Julie. But
now, don't let the cat out of the bag.

KRISTIN *enters dressed for church, carrying a prayer-book.*
JULIE *rushes to her and flings herself into her arms for
protection.*

JULIE. Help me, Kristin! Protect me from this man!

KRISTIN, *unmoved and cold.* What goings-on for a feast day
morning! *Sees the board.* And what a filthy mess. What's
it all about? Why are you screaming and carrying on so?

JULIE. Kristin, you're a woman and my friend. Beware of that
scoundrel!

JEAN, *embarrassed.* While you ladies are talking things over,
I'll go and shave. *Slips into his room.*

JULIE. You must understand. You must listen to me.

KRISTIN. I certainly don't understand such loose ways. Where
are you off to in those travelling clothes? And he had his
hat on, didn't he, eh?

JULIE. Listen, Kristin. Listen, I'll tell you everything.

KRISTIN. I don't want to know anything.

JULIE. You must listen.

KRISTIN. What to? Your nonsense with Jean? I don't care a
rap about that; it's nothing to do with me. But if you're
thinking of getting him to run off with you, we'll soon put
a stop to that.

JULIE, *very nervously.* Please try to be calm, Kristin, and
listen. I can't stay here, nor can Jean—so we must go
abroad.

KRISTIN. Hm, hm!

JULIE, *brightening.* But you see, I've had an idea. Supposing
we all three go—abroad—to Switzerland and start a hotel
together . . . I've got some money, you see . . . and

Jean and I could run the whole thing—and I thought you would take charge of the kitchen. Wouldn't that be splendid? Say yes, do. If you come with us everything will be fine. Oh do say yes! *Puts her arms round* KRISTIN.

KRISTIN, *coolly thinking.* Hm, hm.

JULIE, *presto tempo.* You've never travelled, Kristin. You should go abroad and see the world. You've no idea how nice it is travelling by train—new faces all the time and new countries. On our way through Hamburg we'll go to the zoo—you'll love that—and we'll go to the theatre and the opera too . . . and when we get to Munich there'll be the museums, dear, and pictures by Rubens and Raphael—the great painters, you know . . . You've heard of Munich, haven't you? Where King Ludwig lived— you know, the king who went mad. . . . We'll see his castles—some of his castles are still just like in fairy-tales . . . and from there it's not far to Switzerland—and the Alps. Think of the Alps, Kristin dear, covered with snow in the middle of summer . . . and there are oranges there and trees that are green the whole year round . . . JEAN *is seen in the door of his room, sharpening his razor on a strop which he holds with his teeth and his left hand. He listens to the talk with satisfaction and now and then nods approval.* JULIE *continues, tempo prestissimo.*

And then we'll get a hotel . . . and I'll sit at the desk, while Jean receives the guests and goes out marketing and writes letters . . . There's life for you! Trains whistling, buses driving up, bells ringing upstairs and downstairs . . . and I shall make out the bills—and I shall cook them too . . . you've no idea how nervous travellers are when it comes to paying their bills. And you—you'll sit like a queen in the kitchen . . . of course there won't be any standing at the stove for you. You'll always have to be nicely dressed and ready to be seen, and with your looks—no, I'm not flattering you—one fine day you'll catch yourself a husband . . . some rich Englishman, I shouldn't wonder—they're the ones who are easy—*slowing down*—to catch . . . and then we'll get rich and build ourselves a villa on Lake Como . . . of course it rains there a little now and then—but—*dully*—the sun must shine there too sometimes—even though it seems gloomy—and if not—then we can come home again—come back—*pause*—here—or somewhere else . . .

KRISTIN. Look here, Miss Julie, do you believe all that yourself?

JULIE, *exhausted*. Do I believe it?

KRISTIN. Yes.

JULIE, *wearily*. I don't know. I don't believe anything any more. *Sinks down on the bench; her head in her arms on the table*. Nothing. Nothing at all.

KRISTIN, *turning to* JEAN. So you meant to beat it, did you?

JEAN, *disconcerted, putting the razor on the table*. Beat it? What are you talking about? You've heard Miss Julie's plan, and though she's tired now with being up all night, it's a perfectly sound plan.

KRISTIN. Oh, is it? If you thought I'd work for that . . .

JEAN, *interrupting*. Kindly use decent language in front of your mistress. Do you hear?

KRISTIN. Mistress?

JEAN. Yes.

KRISTIN. Well, well, just listen to that!

JEAN. Yes, it would be a good thing if you did listen and talked less. Miss Julie is your mistress and what's made you lose your respect for her now ought to make you feel the same about yourself.

KRISTIN. I've always had enough self-respect——

JEAN. To despise other people.

KRISTIN. —not to go below my own station. Has the Count's cook ever gone with the groom or the swineherd? Tell me that.

JEAN. No, you were lucky enough to have a high-class chap for your beau.

KRISTIN. High-class all right—selling the oats out of the Count's stable.

JEAN. You're a fine one to talk—taking a commission on the groceries and bribes from the butcher.

KRISTIN. What the devil . . . ?

JEAN. And now you can't feel any respect for your employers. You, you!

KRISTIN. Are you coming to church with me? I should think you need a good sermon after your fine deeds.

JEAN. No, I'm not going to church today. You can go alone and confess your own sins.

KRISTIN. Yes, I'll do that and bring back enough forgiveness to cover yours too. The Saviour suffered and died on the cross for all our sins, and if we go to Him with faith and a penitent heart, He takes all our sins upon Himself.

JEAN. Even grocery thefts?

JULIE. Do you believe that, Kristin?

KRISTIN. That is my living faith, as sure as I stand here. The faith I learnt as a child and have kept ever since, Miss Julie. "But where sin abounded, grace did much more abound."

JULIE. Oh, if I had your faith! Oh, if . . .

KRISTIN. But you see you can't have it without God's special grace, and it's not given to all to have that.

JULIE. Who is it given to then?

KRISTIN. That's the great secret of the workings of grace, Miss Julie. God is no respecter of persons, and with Him the last shall be first . . .

JULIE. Then I suppose He does respect the last.

KRISTIN, *continuing* . . . and it is easier for a camel to go through the eye of a needle than for a rich man to enter into the kingdom of God. That's how it is, Miss Julie. Now I'm going—alone, and on my way I shall tell the groom not to let any of the horses out, in case anyone should want to leave before the Count gets back. Goodbye.
   Exit.

JEAN. What a devil! And all on account of a greenfinch.

JULIE, *wearily.* Never mind the greenfinch. Do you see any way out of this, any end to it?

JEAN, *pondering.* No.

JULIE. If you were in my place, what would you do?

JEAN. In your place? Wait a bit. If I was a woman—a lady of rank who had—fallen. I don't know. Yes, I do know now.

JULIE, *picking up the razor and making a gesture.* This?

JEAN. Yes. But *I* wouldn't do it, you know. There's a difference between us.

JULIE. Because you're a man and I'm a woman? What is the difference?

JEAN. The usual difference—between man and woman.

JULIE, *holding the razor.* I'd like to. But I can't. My father couldn't either, that time he wanted to.

JEAN. No, he didn't want to. He had to be revenged first.

JULIE. And now my mother is revenged again, through me.

JEAN. Didn't you ever love your father, Miss Julie?

JULIE. Deeply, but I must have hated him too—unconsciously. And he let me be brought up to despise my own sex, to be half woman, half man. Whose fault is what's happened? My father's, my mother's or my own? My own? I haven't anything that's my own. I haven't one single thought that I didn't get from my father, one emotion that didn't come from my mother, and as for this last idea—about all people being equal—I got that from him, my fiancé—that's why I call him a cad. How can it be my fault? Push the responsibility on to Jesus, like Kristin does? No, I'm too proud and —thanks to my father's teaching—too intelligent. As for all that about a rich person not being able to get into heaven, it's just a lie, but Kristin, who has money in the savings-bank, will certainly not get in. Whose fault is it? What does it matter whose fault it is? In any case I must take the blame and bear the consequences.

JEAN. Yes, but . . . *There are two sharp rings on the bell.* JULIE *jumps to her feet.* JEAN *changes into his livery.* The Count is back. Supposing Kristin . . . *Goes to the speaking-tube, presses it and listens.*

JULIE. Has he been to his desk yet?

JEAN. This is Jean, sir. *Listens.* Yes, sir. *Listens.* Yes, sir, very good, sir. *Listens.* At once, sir? *Listens.* Very good, sir. In half an hour.

JULIE, *in panic.* What did he say? My God, what did he say?

JEAN. He ordered his boots and his coffee in half an hour.

JULIE. Then there's half an hour . . . Oh, I'm so tired! I can't do anything. Can't be sorry, can't run away, can't stay, can't live—can't die. Help me. Order me, and I'll obey like a dog. Do me this last service—save my honour, save his name. You know what I ought to do, but haven't the strength to do. Use your strength and order me to do it.

JEAN. I don't know why—I can't now—I don't understand . . . It's just as if this coat made me—I can't give you orders— and now that the Count has spoken to me—I can't quite explain, but . . . well, that devil of a lackey is bending my back again. I believe if the Count came down now and ordered me to cut my throat, I'd do it on the spot.

JULIE. Then pretend you're him and I'm you. You did some fine acting before, when you knelt to me and played the aristocrat. Or . . . Have you ever seen a hypnotist at the theatre? *He nods.* He says to the person "Take the broom," and he takes it. He says "Sweep," and he sweeps . . .

JEAN. But the person has to be asleep.

JULIE, *as if in a trance.* I am asleep already . . . the whole room has turned to smoke—and you look like a stove—a stove like a man in black with a tall hat—your eyes are glowing like coals when the fire is low—and your face is a white patch like ashes. *The sunlight has now reached the floor and lights up* JEAN. How nice and warm it is! *She holds out her hands as though warming them at a fire.* And so light—and so peaceful.

JEAN, *putting the razor in her hand.* Here is the broom. Go now while it's light—out to the barn—and . . . *Whispers in her ear.*

JULIE, *waking.* Thank you. I am going now—to rest. But just tell me that even the first can receive the gift of grace.

JEAN. The first? No, I can't tell you that. But wait . . . Miss Julie, I've got it! You aren't one of the first any longer. You're one of the last.

JULIE. That's true. I'm one of the very last. I *am* the last. Oh! . . . But now I can't go. Tell me again to go.

JEAN. No, I can't now either. I can't.

JULIE. And the first shall be last.

JEAN. Don't think, don't think. You're taking my strength away too and making me a coward. What's that? I thought I saw the bell move . . . To be so frightened of a bell! Yes, but it's not just a bell. There's somebody behind it— a hand moving it—and something else moving the hand— and if you stop your ears—if you stop your ears—yes, then it rings louder than ever. Rings and rings until you answer —and then it's too late. Then the police come and . . . and . . . *The bell rings twice loudly.* JEAN *flinches, then straightens himself up.* It's horrible. But there's no other way to end it . . . Go!

JULIE *walks firmly out through the door.*

CURTAIN

THE STRONGER

by

AUGUST STRINDBERG

THE STRONGER was written in 1889, when Strindberg was still writing plays for Antoine's Théâtre Libre, and hoping to form an experimental theatre of his own in Stockholm. This project was not realised until 1907, when THE STRONGER had its première with one of Strindberg's new Chamber Plays, THE BURNED SITE. Since then it has been performed often and in many countries, and is acclaimed as a jewel among monologues.

E. S.

Characters

MRS. X., *actress, married*
MISS Y., *actress, unmarried*
A WAITRESS

Scene: A corner of a ladies' café (in Stockholm in the eighteen eighties). Two small wrought-iron tables, a red plush settee and a few chairs.

MISS Y. is sitting with a half-empty bottle of beer on the table before her, reading an illustrated weekly which from time to time she exchanges for another.

MRS. X. enters, wearing a winter hat and coat and carrying a decorative Japanese basket.

MRS. X. Why, Millie, my dear, how are you? Sitting here all alone on Christmas Eve like some poor bachelor.

MISS Y. *looks up from her magazine, nods, and continues to read.*

MRS. X. You know it makes me feel really sad to see you. Alone. Alone in a café and on Christmas Eve of all times. It makes me feel as sad as when once in Paris I saw a wedding party at a restaurant. The bride was reading a comic paper and the bridegroom playing billiards with the witnesses. Ah me, I said to myself, with such a beginning how will it go, and how will it end? He was playing billiards on his wedding day! And she, you were going to say, was reading a comic paper on hers. But that's not quite the same.

A WAITRESS brings a cup of chocolate to MRS. X. and goes out.

MRS. X. Do you know, Amelia, I really believe now you would have done better to stick to him. Don't forget I was the first who told you to forgive him. Do you remember? Then you would be married now and have a home. Think how happy you were that Christmas when you stayed with your fiancé's people in the country. How warmly you spoke of domestic happiness! You really quite longed to

Note: Translator's addition to scene bracketed. First mention of Miss Y. and Mrs. X. reversed.

be out of the theatre. Yes, Amelia dear, home is best—next best to the stage, and as for children—but you couldn't know anything about that.

MISS Y.'s *expression is disdainful.* MRS. X. *sips a few spoonfuls of chocolate, then opens her basket and displays some Christmas presents.*

MRS. X. Now you must see what I have bought for my little chicks. *Takes out a doll.* Look at this. That's for Lisa. Do you see how she can roll her eyes and turn her head. Isn't she lovely? And here's a toy pistol for Maja.* *She loads the pistol and shoots it at* MISS Y. *who appears frightened.*

MRS. X. Were you scared? Did you think I was going to shoot you? Really, I didn't think you'd believe that of me. Now if *you* were to shoot *me* it wouldn't be so surprising, for after all I did get in your way, and I know you never forget it—although I was entirely innocent. You still think I intrigued to get you out of the Grand Theatre, but I didn't. I didn't, however much you think I did. Well, it's no good talking, you will believe it was me . . . *Takes out a pair of embroidered slippers.* And these are for my old man, with tulips on them that I embroidered myself. As a matter of fact I hate tulips, but he has to have tulips on everything.

MISS Y. *looks up, irony and curiosity in her face.*

MRS. X., *putting one hand in each slipper.* Look what small feet Bob has, hasn't he? And you ought to see the charming way he walks—you've never seen him in slippers, have you?

MISS Y. *laughs.*

MRS. X. Look, I'll show you. *She makes the slippers walk across the table, and* MISS Y. *laughs again.*

MRS. X. But when he gets angry, look, he stamps his foot like this. "Those damn girls who can never learn how to make coffee! Blast! That silly idiot hasn't trimmed the lamp properly!" Then there's a draught under the door and his

*Pronounced Maya.

feet get cold. "Hell, it's freezing, and the damn fools can't even keep the stove going!" *She rubs the sole of one slipper against the instep of the other.* MISS Y. *roars with laughter.*

MRS. X. And then he comes home and has to hunt for his slippers, which Mary has pushed under the bureau . . . Well, perhaps it's not right to make fun of one's husband like this. He's sweet anyhow, and a good, dear husband. You ought to have had a husband like him, Amelia. What are you laughing at? What is it? Eh? And, you see, I know he is faithful to me. Yes, I know it. He told me himself— what *are* you giggling at?—that while I was on tour in Norway that horrible Frederica came and tried to seduce him. Can you imagine anything more abominable? *Pause.* I'd have scratched her eyes out if she had come around while I was at home. *Pause.* I'm glad Bob told me about it himself, so I didn't just hear it from gossip. *Pause.* And, as a matter of fact, Frederica wasn't the only one. I can't think why, but all the women in the Company* seem to be crazy about my husband. They must think his position gives him some say in who is engaged at the Theatre. Perhaps you have run after him yourself? I don't trust you very far, but I know he has never been attracted by you, and you always seemed to have some sort of grudge against him, or so I felt. *Pause. They look at one another guardedly.*

MRS. X. Do come and spend Christmas Eve with us tonight, Amelia—just to show that you're not offended with us, or anyhow not with me. I don't know why, but it seems specially unpleasant not to be friends with you. Perhaps it's because I did get in your way that time . . . *slowly* or—I don't know—really, I don't know at all why it is. *Pause.* MISS Y. *gazes curiously at* MRS. X.

MRS. X., *thoughtfully.* It was so strange when we were getting to know one another. Do you know, when we first met, I was frightened of you, so frightened I didn't dare let you out of my sight. I arranged all my goings and

*"In the Company" translator's addition.

comings to be near you. I dared not be your enemy, so I became your friend. But when you came to our home, I always had an uneasy feeling, because I saw my husband didn't like you, and that irritated me—like when a dress doesn't fit. I did all I could to make him be nice to you, but it was no good—until you went and got engaged. Then you became such tremendous friends that at first it looked as if you only dared show your real feelings then —when you were safe. And then, let me see, how was it after that? I wasn't jealous—that's queer. And I remember at the christening, when you were the godmother, I told him to kiss you. He did, and you were so upset . . . As a matter of fact I didn't notice that then . . . I didn't think about it afterwards either . . . I've never thought about it—until *now! Rises abruptly.* Why don't you say something? You haven't said a word all this time. You've just let me go on talking. You have sat there with your eyes drawing all these thoughts out of me—they were there in me like silk in a cocoon—thoughts . . . Mistaken thoughts? Let me think. Why did you break off your engagement? Why did you never come to our house after that? Why don't you want to come to us tonight?

MISS Y. *makes a motion, as if about to speak.*

MRS. X. No. You don't need to say anything, for now I see it all. That was why—and why—and why. Yes. Yes, that's why it was. Yes, yes, all the pieces fit together now. That's it. I won't sit at the same table as you. *Moves her things to the other table.* That's why I have to embroider tulips, which I loathe, on his slippers—because you liked tulips. *Throws the slippers on the floor.* That's why we have to spend the summer on the lake—because you couldn't bear the seaside. That's why my son had to be called Eskil— because it was your father's name. That's why I had to wear your colours, read your books, eat the dishes you liked, drink your drinks—your chocolate, for instance. That's why—oh my God, it's terrible to think of, terrible! Everything, everything came to me from you—even your passions. Your soul bored into mine like a worm into an apple, and ate and ate and burrowed and burrowed, till nothing was left but the skin and a little black mould. I wanted to fly from you, but I couldn't. You were there like a snake, your black eyes fascinating me. When I spread my wings, they only dragged me down. I lay in the water with my feet tied together, and the harder I worked my arms, the deeper I sank—down, down, till I reached the bottom, where you lay in waiting like a giant crab to catch me in your claws—and now here I am. Oh how I hate you! I hate you, I hate you! And you just go on sitting there, silent, calm, indifferent, not caring whether the moon is new or full, if it's Christmas or New Year, if other people are happy or unhappy. You don't know how to hate or to love. You just sit there without moving—like a cat* at a mouse-hole. You can't drag your prey out, you can't chase it, but you can out-stay it. Here you sit in your corner—you know they call it the rat-trap after you—reading the papers to see if anyone's ruined or wretched or been thrown out of the Company. Here you sit sizing up your victims and weighing your chances—like a pilot his shipwrecks for the salvage. *Pause.* Poor Amelia! Do you know, I couldn't be more sorry for you. I know you are miserable, miserable like some wounded creature, and vicious because you are wounded. I can't be angry with you. I should like to be, but after all you are the small one—and as for your affair with Bob, that doesn't worry me in the least. Why should it matter to me? And if you, or somebody else taught me to drink chocolate, what's the difference? *Drinks a spoonful. Smugly.* Chocolate is very wholesome anyhow. And if I learnt from you how to dress, *tant mieux!*—that only gave me a stronger hold over my husband, and you have lost what I gained. Yes, to judge from various signs, I think you have now lost him. Of course, you meant me to walk out, as you once did, and which you're now regretting. But I won't do that, you may be sure. One shouldn't be narrow-minded, you know. And why should nobody else want what I have? *Pause.* Perhaps, my dear, taking everything into consideration, at this moment it is I who

*In Swedish, "stork."

am the stronger. You never got anything from me, you just gave away—from yourself. And now, like the thief in the night, when you woke up I had what you had lost. Why was it then that everything you touched became worthless and sterile? You couldn't keep a man's love—for all your tulips and your passions—but I could. You couldn't learn the art of living from your books—but I learnt it. You bore no little Eskil, although that was your father's name. *Pause.* And why is it you are silent—everywhere, always silent? Yes, I used to think this was strength, but perhaps it was because you hadn't anything to say, because you couldn't think of anything. *Rises and picks up the slippers.* Now I am going home, taking the tulips with me—*your* tulips. You couldn't learn from others, you couldn't bend, and so you broke like a dry stick. I did not. Thank you, Amelia, for all your good lessons. Thank you for teaching my husband how to love. Now I am going home—to love him.

Exit.

EASTER

A Play in Three Acts
by

AUGUST STRINDBERG

Copyright, 1949, by Elizabeth Sprigge

INTRODUCTION

EASTER has long been a favourite among Strindberg's plays, both in Sweden and in England. The small cast of six characters and the single set of a verandah furnished as a living-room, put it within the scope of the smallest theatre, while the opportunities for fine acting and imaginative production are large. Nor in this modern Mystery or Morality Play is there any of the grim tragedy found in many of Strindberg's dramas. It is tender, sensitive and has a haunting quality of goodness.

Strindberg tells us that the mood of Easter was suggested by Haydn's *Sieben Worte des Erlösers* ("The Seven Words of the Redeemer"), and its form by the three poignant days of the Christian calendar—Maundy Thursday, Good Friday and Easter Eve. The Christian message is woven into that of Nature herself, as spring comes to the frozen north, and man's pride cracks with the melting ice.

The Heyst family is seen in a provincial university town, where the father is serving a term of imprisonment for embezzling trust funds. His wife displays a fanatical belief in his innocence, and Elis, the schoolmaster son, is weighed down with shame, for in addition to his father's dishonour and debts, Eleanora, the young daughter, has been sent away to a mental hospital. Kristina, Elis's fiancée, and Benjamin, one of his pupils whose inheritance was purloined by the father, make up the household.

Maundy Thursday brings further difficulties and disappointments, and Lindkvist, the Heysts' heaviest creditor, comes to live across the road and remind them by his presence that he can sell up their home whenever he pleases. But it also brings Eleanora, half child, half angel, to breathe peace among them in spite of her own trouble.

Good Friday is dark indeed. Elis is forced to go vainly through all the reports of his father's case again, and he believes he has lost Kristina to a friend who has already played him false. Eleanora fears that she may be arrested for taking a daffodil from a closed shop, and over the whole family looms the shadow of the Creditor.

On Easter Eve the clouds gradually lift, until at the end the Creditor comes not as ogre, but as guardian angel, and the future promises fair for the little family which has gone through "the school of suffering."

The theme is slight, but the play is rich in imagery, of which the producer could make far better use than is usually made. Some of the characters, such as Mrs. Heyst and Kristina the fiancée, are shadowily sketched and need plenty of invention to bring them into the round. Elis, on the other hand, is fully drawn—a portrait of young, frustrated manhood, blinded by self pity; and so is Eleanora, the "Easter Girl"—one of the strangest and most poetic of Strindberg's creations. Simple, child-like, clairvoyant, she can hear the language of flowers and read the hearts of human beings, and the words of the Scriptures pour unpremeditated from her lips, because God is her friend.

All Strindberg's work is, in some degree, autobiographical, and it is a help to the interpretation of this play to notice some of the threads woven into it. EASTER was written in Stockholm in the autumn of 1900, when the dramatist, at the age of fifty-one, had returned to his own country and to the theatre after a long absence. While recovering from a prolonged nervous breakdown he lived at Lund, the University town in the South of Sweden which, as a Stockholmer with an adoration for the skerries and the Mälar Lake, he did not like. He therefore chose this town as the purgatory of the Heyst family. While he was there his sister Elisabeth was sent into a mental hospital. Strindberg believed that she had taken the sins of their whole family on her shoulders and she was never out of his mind as he modelled his "Easter Girl." Eleanora was also influenced by Balzac's Séraphita, and Strindberg endowed her with all his own hypersensitiveness and clairvoyance, and gave her into the bargain the flower-like patience in suffering he could never achieve himself. To Elis he gave much of his own pride, his moodiness, jealousy and timidity, and his own detested days both as schoolmaster and pupil are reflected in the play. Here too we find the garden of the Deaf and Dumb which one of his lodgings in Paris overlooked, and some of the phenomena of birds and flowers he had gathered up on his travels for a Book of Miracles. EASTER also contains some of Strindberg's favourite themes, to be found in many of his works, such as the law of recurrence—"everything happens again," and the doctrine of crime as punishment.

Here and there a little knowledge of Swedish life helps to explain the action. The examination, for instance, in which, in the first act, Benjamin knows himself to have failed, is the annual Student Examination, which bestows the right to enter a university. The students usually make a rough copy of their papers, and this is what Benjamin shows Elis. The disappointment of failing to pass at the right age (16–17) would be heavy in any case, but for Benjamin his failure involves a further year of living in the home of the man who stole his inheritance. Then, again, when a Swedish graduate presents his thesis for a Doctor's degree in any subject, the thesis is printed and distributed, and its author is called upon to defend his work in a public debate. In Act One Peter Holmblad has just done this, and is giving a dinner to celebrate his success. The Lenten Birch, ancient symbol of penance, decorates many Swedish homes at this season, its original grimness disguised with bright ribbons and tassels.

The Swedish Church is, of course, Lutheran, and Strindberg was brought up as a Pietist, a strict sect of this denomination. Although he broke away, a puritanical influence remained; but it is essential that the religious message of EASTER should not obscure the Northerner's passion for spring itself. The taking down of double windows and the laying aside of heavy winter clothing are poignant expressions of release from the long imprisonment of winter, and although the whole play takes place within a verandah, Nature plays an important part in the action.

Strindberg's stage directions are always capricious. He brings characters on and omits to take them off again; he instructs them to stand up when it seems unlikely that they would have been sitting, and often gives no indication at all when one is most anxious to see the action through his eyes. The same with properties. Some object is suddenly presented as important, when we have never heard of it before. Take, for instance, the pendulum clock in Act Two. This was the family possession that Eleanora

loved best of all. Would she then not have looked for it
in Act One, when she came back from the asylum, "bare
and white as a bathroom", to the dear familiarity of her
home? And the piano that is mentioned just once, when
Eleanora describes the bad clock that always began to
strike when Elis played, should this not be used too?
Might not Elis in one of his moods—perhaps when he
thinks Kristina has deserted him—be heard playing that
piano?—another precious possession, by the way, that the
Creditor has the power to seize. Then there is the birch,
symbol of "the school of suffering" through which the
family is passing. It comes as a present to Elis, to warn
him of his pride—just as his own voice on the telephone
tries to warn him to stand the test to which Kristina is
compelled to put him. The Lenten Birch and the Lenten
Lily, symbol of healing, dominate the play. Elis hears
the galoshes of the Creditor swishing like the birch in use
and works himself up into a frenzy of flagellation. Yet
he has simply stuck the birch behind the mirror, where
Strindberg leaves it to speak for itself. There are many
more such instances of the dramatist's reliance on the
imagination of his producer, and in return we should
remember two things. First that Strindberg often criticised
a producer's lack of boldness, and second that he was a
pioneer of Expressionism. He is essentially a twentieth
century, not a nineteenth century writer. He was bent on
breaking the bourgeois tradition of the theatre of his age,
and should never be limited by the dates of his life. His
plays, whether historical or contemporary, are not period
pieces; they all have a quality of timelessness.

This translation was made while two different amateur
companies were putting the play on, and I had the benefit
of constantly hearing the lines spoken. I have taken a
few liberties with the original text, but only, of course,
in the matter of stage directions, based on the experience
of these productions. I have, for example, left the placing
of the furniture to the discretion of the producer, and
omitted the indications "Left" or "Right" in entrances
or exits. Apropos, it is interesting to note that when
Lindkvist makes his only entrance in Act Three, Strindberg has him coming from the side. Much emphasis is
laid in Act One on the open front door in the centre of
the back wall, and in Act Two on the gigantic shadow of

the Creditor thrown right across the back, a device actually suggested to Strindberg by a Shadow Play of *The Giant of the Skinflint Mountains*. But when at last Lindkvist enters in the flesh, his creator slips him in at the side. The only reason for this would seem to be that Mrs. Heyst should see Lindkvist first in the kitchen, as she describes his appearance to Elis; but this reason is refuted as Lindkvist himself shortly afterwards wonders if Mrs. Heyst is at home. When the Uppsala students performed the play in England, they followed Strindberg's direction, but it was certainly an anti-climax, robbing Lindkvist of a most dramatic entry and Elis of scope for reaction. And so, occasionally, I have left out Strindberg's stage directions, and where I felt it was quite necessary to make his meaning clear, I have added to them.

The world première of EASTER was at Frankfurt in March 1901, and the first Swedish performance followed at the Dramatic Theatre in Stockholm on Maundy Thursday of the same year, with Harriet Bosse, the talented young Norwegian actress who was shortly to become Strindberg's third wife, creating the part of Eleanora. It was revived next in 1908 for Strindberg's own Intimate Theatre when it had an outstanding success, and since then has been very often played in Sweden. The first English performance appears to have been by a small experimental theatre group in 1924, and it is interesting to remember that in 1928 it was produced at the Arts Theatre Club with John Gielgud and Peggy Ashcroft in the principal parts.

E. S.

Characters

The whole play takes place inside the glass verandah of a house in a small university town in the south of Sweden, furnished as the living-room of a middle-class family.

In the centre of the back wall is the front door leading into a garden, with a fence and a gate to the street. Across the street which, like the house, is on a height, can be seen another low fence round a garden sloping down to the town. The trees in this garden are breaking into leaf, and beyond them are a church tower and the imposing gable of a house. In the street is a lamp post with an incandescent lamp.

The glass windows of the verandah, stretching across the back and two sides of the stage, are hung with curtains of a pale yellow flowery material which can be drawn. On one side of the front door hangs a mirror with a calendar below it.

There are two other doors, one leading to the kitchen, the other to the rest of the house.

The furniture consists of a big porcelain stove with mica panes, a dining-table, a sideboard, a large writing table on which stand books, writing materials and a telephone, and a sewing table, arm chairs, lamps, etc.

ACT ONE

MAUNDY THURSDAY

Musical Prelude: Haydn: The Seven Words of the Redeemer. Introduction: Maestoso Adagio.

A shaft of sunlight falls across the room, reaching one of the arm chairs by the sewing-table. In the other chair, out of the sun, sits KRISTINA, *threading a tape through a pair of freshly ironed white curtains.*

ELIS *enters, leaving the front door open. He is wearing his winter overcoat, unbuttoned, and carries a bundle of papers. He and* KRISTINA *greet one another affectionately.*

ELIS. My dear!

KRISTINA. Ah Elis, here you are!

ELIS *flings down the papers and they embrace. Then, as he takes off his coat, he gazes round the room in delight.*

ELIS. The double windows have been taken down—oh, and the floor has been scrubbed and fresh curtains put up! Yes, it's spring again. They have hacked up the ice in the street, and down by the river the willows are in leaf. Yes, it's spring again—and I can put away my winter overcoat. *He weighs the coat in his hands, and his mood quickly changes to bitterness.* Look how heavy it is. As if it had soaked up all the hardships of winter—the sweat of anguish, and the dust of school. *He throws the coat down on a chair.*

KRISTINA, *soothing him.* But now you have a holiday.

ELIS. Yes, the Easter Holiday. Five glorious days to make the most of—to breathe and forget. *He takes her hands and they sit down together.* Look, the sun has come back. It went away in November. I remember the very day when it disappeared over there behind the brewery. Oh, what a winter, what an endless winter!

KRISTINA, *anxiously, indicating the kitchen door.* Hush!

ELIS. Don't worry my dear. I'm going to be quite calm. It's just that I'm so glad it's over. Ah, this good sun! *He springs up.* I want to wash myself in sunshine. I want to bathe myself in light after all this filth and darkness.

KRISTINA, *again glancing anxiously towards the kitchen.* Hush, Elis, hush.

ELIS, *recovering.* But you know I really believe peace is on the way—that our misfortunes are wearing themselves out at last.

KRISTINA. What makes you think that?

ELIS. Well . . . partly because just now as I was passing the cathedral, a white dove came flying by. It swooped down to the pavement and dropped the twig it was carrying in its beak right at my feet.

KRISTINA. Did you see what kind of twig it was?

ELIS. I suppose it couldn't really have been an olive branch, but I feel sure it was a sign of peace. And now at this moment, I feel such a saving, sunlit calm . . . *With sudden anxiety.* Where is Mother?

KRISTINA. In the kitchen.

ELIS, *reassured, closes his eyes, smiles and speaks softly and happily.* I *hear* that it is spring. I hear that the double windows have been taken out. Do you know what tells me? *Pause.* First, the creaking of the cart-wheels . . . And now what's that? The chatter of the chaffinch. And they're hammering in the shipyard . . . and there's a smell of paint . . . the red-lead paint they are using for the steamers.

KRISTINA. Can you get all that here?

ELIS. Here? *He opens his eyes and his smile fades.* Yes, true enough, we are—*here. With growing misery.* But I was *there,* far away up north where our home is. Why did we ever come to this odious town where people all hate each other, and one is always lonely? Yes, it was to get our daily bread, but the bread was spread with calamities—with Father's crime and my little sister's sickness. *Pause.*

Do you know if Mother got permission to see Father in prison?

KRISTINA. As a matter of fact I believe she was there today.

ELIS. What did she say about it?

KRISTINA. Not a word. She talked about other things.

ELIS. All the same something has been achieved. After the verdict, there was an end of suspense. There was even a kind of strange calm once the papers had dropped the subject. And now one year is over. In another year he will be out, and then we can make a new start.

KRISTINA. I admire your patience in suffering.

ELIS. Don't. Don't admire anything about me, for I am nothing but faults. Now you know—and you'll have to believe me.

KRISTINA. It's not as if it were your own faults you're suffering for. It's other people's.

ELIS, *to change the subject.* What's that you're making?

KRISTINA. Curtains for the kitchen, dear.

ELIS. They look like a bridal veil . . . In the autumn, Kristina, you will be my bride.

KRISTINA. Yes . . . But we have the summer to look forward to first.

ELIS, *excited.* Yes, the summer. *He fetches his bank book from the writing table and shows it to her.* Look how much money I have saved already. As soon as term is over we will set out for the north, for our own country, for the Mälar Lake. The cottage stands there waiting, just as it was when we were children. The lime trees are there —and the boat moored under the willows. Ah, that it were summer now and I could bathe in the lake! This family disgrace has smeared me all over—body and soul, so that I pine for a lake to wash myself in.

KRISTINA. Have you heard at all from your sister?

ELIS. Yes. Poor little Eleanora. She's miserable and she writes letters that make my heart bleed. Naturally she begs to be let out and allowed to come home. But you see, the Principal of the Institution dare not let her go, because

she does things which might land her in prison. All the
same I sometimes feel conscience-stricken for having
given my consent to her being shut up there.

KRISTINA. You blame yourself for everything, dearest, but
surely—as things were—it was a mercy to have her properly taken care of, poor little thing.

ELIS. You are perfectly right, and I know very well how
much better things are this way. Yes, she is as well off
there as she could possibly be anywhere. And when I
think of the shadow she threw over any glimmer of happiness when she was here, of how her condition weighed
on us like a nightmare, tormenting us past bearing, I am
selfish enough to feel such relief that it is almost happiness. The worst misfortune I can imagine at this moment
would be to see her come through that door. What a
wretch I am!

KRISTINA. How human you are.

ELIS. But all the same I'm tormented. Tormented by the
thought of her misery and my father's.

KRISTINA. It's as if some people were born to suffering.

ELIS. Poor you—to come into a family doomed from the beginning . . . and damned.

KRISTINA. Elis, you can't tell whether all this is a punishment
or just a kind of test.

ELIS. I don't know what it can be for you. You, of all people,
are free from guilt.

KRISTINA. Well, there's the saying "tears in the morning,
laughter at eve." Dearest, perhaps I can help you to get
through . . .

ELIS. Do you think Mother has a clean white tie for me?

KRISTINA, *uneasily*. Are you going out?

ELIS. Yes. You know, Peter presented his thesis yesterday,
and tonight he's giving a dinner to celebrate getting his
doctor's degree.

KRISTINA. Do you want to go to it?

ELIS. You mean I ought to stay away, considering what an
ungrateful pupil he has turned out.

KRISTINA. I admit I'm shocked by his disloyalty—promising to quote your work, and then lifting whole passages from it without acknowledgment.

ELIS. Oh, that's always the way. And I get a certain satisfaction from knowing it's really my own work.

KRISTINA. Has he invited you?

ELIS, *surprised.* Come to think of it, he hasn't. That's really most extraordinary, for he's been talking about this dinner for years, as if I were certain to be there—and I've talked about it too, to other people. If now I'm not invited it's a public insult. No matter, it's not the first I've had, nor will it be the last. *Pause.*

KRISTINA. Benjamin's late. Do you think he'll have passed?

ELIS. I certainly hope so—with a credit in Latin.

KRISTINA. He's a nice boy, Benjamin.

ELIS. Uncommonly nice, although he does rather brood over things . . . Kristina, I suppose you know why he is living here with us?

KRISTINA, *hesitating.* Is it because . . . ?

ELIS, *harshly.* Because, as in the case of so many others, my father embezzled the money that was in trust for the boy. That's what's so horrible, Kristina. In school I have to see all these fatherless children whom my father robbed and who now have the humiliation of being charity pupils. And you can imagine how they look at me. I have to go on reminding myself of the miserable plight they are in so as to forgive their cruelty.

KRISTINA. I believe your father is really better off than you are.

ELIS. Undoubtedly.

KRISTINA. Elis, we must think of the summer, and not of the past.

ELIS. Yes, of the summer. Do you know, last night I was woken up by students singing the song that goes "Yes, I am coming. Happy winds, go tell the earth, tell the birds I love them. Tell the birches and limes, the mountains and lakes, I long to see them once again—to see them as

when I was a child."* Shall I "see them once again?"
Shall I ever escape from this dreadful town—from Ebal,
the mount of curses, and behold Gerizim once more?

KRISTINA. —Yes, yes, you will.

ELIS. But even then, shall I see my birches and limes as I saw
them when I was a child? Won't the same black veil
cling to them that clings to all nature—*He moves as if
trying to free his body from this terrible clinging gloom*
—that has clung to life itself ever since that day . . . *He
breaks off and points to the arm chair which is now in
shadow.* Look, the sun has gone?

KRISTINA. It will come again, and next time it will stay longer.

ELIS. That's true. The days are lengthening, and the shadows
growing shorter.

KRISTINA. We are moving towards the light, Elis—believe me.

ELIS. Sometimes I do believe it. When I think of past days
and compare them with these now, I am happy. Last year
you were not sitting there. You had left me—you had
broken off our engagement. You know, for me that was
the darkest time of all. I literally died, bit by bit—but
when you came back, I came to life again. Why did you
go away? KRISTINA *shakes her head.* Can't you remember?

KRISTINA. No, I don't remember. It seems now as if there was
no real reason. I just felt I was being told to go, and so I
went—as if I were walking in my sleep. When I saw you
again, I woke up and was happy.

ELIS. And now we will never part again. If you left me now,
I really should die . . . Here's Mother. Don't say anything. Let her go on living in her world of illusion, believing that Father is a martyr and all his victims are swindlers. MRS. HEYST *comes in from the kitchen, wearing an
apron and peeling an apple. She speaks in a kindly, absent-
minded way.*

MRS. HEYST. Good evening, children. Would you like your
apple sauce† cold or hot?

*Lines from a well-known student song.
†Soup in the original.

ELIS. Cold, Mother dear.

MRS. HEYST. That's right, my son. You always know what you want and say so. You can't do that, Kristina. Elis learnt it from his father. He always knew what he wanted and what he was about. People can't stand that, and so things went badly for him. But his day will come, when he will be proved right and the others wrong. Now, wait a minute, what was it I wanted to tell you? . . . Oh yes. Have you heard that Lindkvist has come to town? Lindkvist, the greatest swindler of them all.

ELIS, *agitated.* He has come here?

MRS. HEYST. Yes, he's living just across the street.

ELIS. Then we're bound to see him passing every day. That too!

MRS. HEYST. Just let me have a word with him, and he'll never show his face again, for I know a thing or two about him . . . Well, Elis, how did Peter get on with his thesis?

ELIS. Very well.

MRS. HEYST. I can quite believe it. And when are you going to present your thesis?

ELIS. When I can afford to, Mother.

MRS. HEYST. When I can afford to—that's no answer. And Benjamin? Has he got through his exam?

ELIS. We don't know yet, but he'll be in soon.

MRS. HEYST. I see. You know, I'm not sure I quite like Benjamin. He goes round giving himself airs, as if he had some claim on us, but we'll cure him of that, he's a nice boy really. Oh yes, there's a parcel for you, Elis. *She goes out to the kitchen.*

ELIS. You know, Mother doesn't miss much. I sometimes think she's not so simple as she makes out.

MRS. HEYST, *coming in and handing* ELIS *a parcel.* Here it is. Lina took it in.

ELIS. A present? I'm afraid of presents, since that day I was sent a box of stones. *He puts it down.*

MRS. HEYST. I'm going back to the kitchen. *She looks anx-*

iously at the front door, as if fearing an intruder. Isn't it too cold with that door open?

ELIS. No no, not at all, Mother.

MRS. HEYST. Elis, you shouldn't leave your overcoat there—it looks so untidy. Well, Kristina, are my curtains nearly ready?

KRISTINA. Yes, Mother, in just a few minutes. *She begins to work again.*

MRS. HEYST. You know I like that Peter—he's rather a favourite of mine . . . Aren't you going to his dinner, Elis?

ELIS. Yes, yes—why, certainly—of course.

MRS. HEYST. Then why did you say you wanted your apple sauce cold, if you're going out? You're so vague, Elis. But Peter isn't. Shut the door if there's a draught, so you don't catch cold. *She goes out to the kitchen.*

ELIS. Poor dear Mother. And it's always Peter. What's her idea? Is she trying to tease you about Peter?

KRISTINA. Me?

ELIS. Well, you know the queer notions old women get.

KRISTINA. What is your present?

ELIS *opens the parcel and slowly draws out a bundle of birch twigs tied together.*

ELIS. A Lenten birch.

KRISTINA. Who's it from?

ELIS. It doesn't say. Well, it's harmless enough. I shall put it in water and it will blossom like Aaron's rod. *Then suddenly he cuts the air with it and speaks cynically.* "Birch . . . as when I was a child" . . . And as for limes—Lindkvist—the twig of lime*—has come here.

KRISTINA. Why does it matter so much?

ELIS, *laying down the birch.* We owe him more money than all the rest.

KRISTINA. But surely *you* don't owe him anything?

*Lindkvist means in Swedish "Twig of Lime." I have added these words after his name to give point to "birches and limes," etc., otherwise lost in English.

ELIS. *We* do. We are all in this together. The family name is dishonoured so long as one debt remains.

KRISTINA. Change your name.

ELIS. Kristina!

KRISTINA. Thank you, Elis. I only wanted to test you.

ELIS. But you mustn't tempt me. Lindkvist is a poor man. He needs what belongs to him. Wherever my father went, the place became like a battlefield strewn with dead and wounded. Yet my mother believes he is the victim. *Pause.* Would you like to come for a walk?

KRISTINA. And find the sun? With all my heart.

ELIS, *thinking it out.* Do you understand this, Kristina? The Redeemer suffered for our sins, yet we have to go on paying. No one is paying for me.

KRISTINA. But if someone *were* paying for you, would you understand then?

ELIS. Yes, of course, then I should understand. . . . *Listening.* Here comes Benjamin. Can you see if he is looking cheerful?

KRISTINA, *looking out.* He's walking very slowly . . . and now he's stopping at the fountain, and bathing his eyes.

ELIS. That too.

KRISTINA. Wait a little. . . .

ELIS. Tears, tears!

KRISTINA. Be patient.

BENJAMIN *comes in, polite but sad. . . . He is carrying some books and a satchel.*

ELIS. Well, how did the Latin go?

BENJAMIN. Badly.

ELIS. May I see your notes? What went wrong?

BENJAMIN. I used "ut" with the indicative where I knew it should be the subjunctive.

ELIS. Then you're done for. But what on earth made you do such a thing?

BENJAMIN, *humbly.* I can't make it out. I knew how it ought to go, and I wanted to write it that way—but I wrote it wrong.

A long pause, while ELIS *looks through the papers.* BENJAMIN *slumps down at the table.*

ELIS. Yes, here it is, the indicative. O Lord!

KRISTINA, *to* BENJAMIN. Well, better luck next time. Life is long, terribly long.

BENJAMIN, *bitterly.* Yes, it certainly is.

ELIS, *sadly, but without bitterness.* That everything should happen at once like this. You were my best pupil, so what can I expect of the others? My reputation as a teacher will be ruined. I shall get no more tutoring and so—well, everything's gone to pieces. *Seeing* BENJAMIN's *distress* . . . Don't take it so hard, it's not your fault.

KRISTINA, *urgently.* Elis, for heaven's sake, have courage.

ELIS. Where am I to find it?

KRISTINA. Where you found it before.

ELIS. This isn't the same as before. I seem to have fallen from grace.

KRISTINA. It is a sign of grace to suffer when you are innocent. Don't be tempted to impatience. Stand the test—for this is only a test. I feel sure of that.

ELIS. Can the year Benjamin must go through now be less than 365 days?

KRISTINA. Yes, a cheerful heart makes time go quickly.

ELIS, *ironically.* Blow on the sore and make it better—that's what they tell children.

KRISTINA, *to* ELIS *gently.* Be a child then, and I'll comfort you like one. Think of your mother, how she bears it all.

ELIS. Give me your hand, I am sinking. KRISTINA *gives him her hand.* Your hand is trembling.

KRISTINA. I don't feel it.

ELIS. You're not so strong as you make out.

KRISTINA. I don't feel any weakness.

ELIS. Then why can't you give me strength?

KRISTINA. I have none to spare.

ELIS, *turns to the window. Pause.* Look who's coming—the Creditor!

KRISTINA, *looking out of the window too.* This is too much.

ELIS, *hysterically.* The Creditor. The man who can take all our furniture, everything we own, whenever he pleases. Lindkvist, who has come here to sit like a spider in the centre of his web and watch the flies.

KRISTINA, *catching hold of him and pointing to the kitchen.* Go away.

ELIS. No, I won't. Just now when you grew weak, I grew strong. Now he's coming up the street. He has already cast his evil eye on his prey.

KRISTINA. At least keep out of his sight.

ELIS. No, now I find him amusing. He seems to be gloating over his quarry caught in the trap. Come on, my friend! He's measuring the distance to the gate. He sees by the open door that we are at home . . . But now he has met someone. He's stopping to talk. They're talking about us—he's glancing this way.

KRISTINA. So long as he doesn't meet Mother. If she gives him the sharp edge of her tongue, there'll be no hope at all. Don't let that happen, Elis.

ELIS. Now he's shaking his stick, as if to declare that in this case mercy shall not take the place of justice. He's unbuttoning his overcoat to show that at least we've left him the clothes he stands up in. I can see by his lips what he's saying. What shall I answer? Sir, you are right. Take everything, it belongs to you?

KRISTINA. That's all you can say.

ELIS. Now he's laughing. *Pause. Surprised.* But it's a kind laugh, not a cruel one. Perhaps he's not so cruel after all, even if he does want his money. I wish he'd come on in and stop that blessed chatter. *Watches.* Now he's waving his stick again—they always have sticks—those creditors that come to dun you—and galoshes that go "swish, swish";—like a cane through the air. *He holds Kristina's hand against his heart.* Feel how my heart is pounding. There's a throbbing in my right ear like an ocean liner. Ah, now he's saying goodbye. And here come the galoshes "swish, swish" like the Lenten birch. But he has a watch chain, with trinkets dangling from it—so he's not quite destitute. They always wear trinkets made of cornelian—like chunks of flesh cut off their neighbour's backs. Listen to the galoshes. *Working himself up into a flagellating frenzy.* Swish, swish, beast, beasts, hard, harder, harder! Swish, swish!* Look out! He's seen me, he's seen me! *Bows towards the street.* He bowed to me first. He's smiling. He's waving his hand—and . . . he has gone the other way. *He collapses at the writing table.*

KRISTINA. Thank God.

ELIS. He has gone away, but he will come again. *Long pause.* Let us go out into the sun.

KRISTINA. But what about Peter's dinner?

ELIS. As I haven't been invited, I'm not going. Anyhow, what have I to do with people celebrating? Why go to meet a disloyal friend? I should suffer just the same, but blame it all on him.

KRISTINA. So you're going to stay at home with us. Oh thank you!

ELIS. You know very well that's what I want to do. Shall we go?

KRISTINA. Yes—this way. *She goes out to the kitchen.*

ELIS *begins to follow her, but stops to pick up the birch. As he passes* BENJAMIN, *he puts a hand on his head.*

ELIS. Courage, boy! BENJAMIN *hides his face.* ELIS *puts the birch behind the mirror. Sadly.* It was no olive branch the dove brought, but a birch.

He goes out.

Pause. The Haydn is heard from the Church.

*In the original this is "vargar, vargar, argar, argare" . . . meaning "wolves, angry, angrier," etc. As it is impossible to reproduce the rhyme, I have simply chosen words to produce a plausible sound and meaning.

Eleanora comes in from the street. She looks about sixteen, has her hair in plaits, and wears the plain dress of an institution. She carries a yellow daffodil in a pot. Without seeming to see BENJAMIN, *she puts the daffodil on the side-board and waters it, then looks lovingly round her familiar home. Then she moves the flower to the dining-table, sits down opposite* BENJAMIN, *watches him and mimics his movements. He looks up at her in amazement.*

ELEANORA, *pointing to the daffodil.* Do you know what that is?

BENJAMIN, *boyishly.* Of course I do, it's a daffodil. But who are you?

ELEANORA, *echoes, sadly and gently.* Yes, who are you?

BENJAMIN. I am called Benjamin, and I'm boarding here at Mrs. Heyst's.

ELEANORA. I see. I am called Eleanora and I'm the daughter of the house.

BENJAMIN. How queer! They've never talked about you.

ELEANORA. One doesn't talk about the dead.

BENJAMIN. The dead?

ELEANORA. In the eyes of the world I am dead, for I have done something very wicked.

BENJAMIN. You?

ELEANORA. Yes, I embezzled trust funds— Of course that doesn't matter very much—for ill-gotten gains never prosper. But my old father was blamed for it and put in prison, and that, you see, can never be forgiven.

BENJAMIN. How strangely and beautifully you speak. It never occurred to me that my inheritance might have been ill-gotten.

ELEANORA. We should not bind people but set them free.

BENJAMIN. Yes, you have set me free—from the shame of feeling myself cheated.

ELEANORA. So you're being brought up by guardians, too.

BENJAMIN. Yes, it's my miserable fate to be kept here by these unhappy people—serving a sentence for their crime.

ELEANORA, *shrinking*. You mustn't use hard words, or I shall go away. I am so soft I can't bear anything hard. *Pause.* But you—are you bearing all this because of me?

BENJAMIN. Because of your father.

ELEANORA. It's all one, for he and I are one and the same person. *Pause.* I have been very ill . . . Why are you so sad?

BENJAMIN. Oh, I've had rather a blow.

ELEANORA. Why be sad about that? "The rod and reproof give wisdom, and he that hateth correction shall die." What was the blow?

BENJAMIN. I failed in my Latin exam—when I was absolutely sure I'd get through.

ELEANORA. I see. So sure, so cocksure, that you'd have even bet your pocket money on it.

BENJAMIN. Yes—I did.

ELEANORA. I thought so. Don't you see it happened like that just because you were so sure?

BENJAMIN. Do you think that was the reason?

ELEANORA. Of course it was. Pride goes before a fall.

BENJAMIN, *smiling*. Well, I'll remember that next time.

ELEANORA. Good. And a sacrifice acceptable to God is a broken spirit.

BENJAMIN, *boyishly*. Are you religious?

ELEANORA. Yes, I am religious.

BENJAMIN. Really? A believer, I mean?

ELEANORA. Yes, that's what I mean. So if you say anything bad about God, who is my friend, I won't sit at the same table with you.

BENJAMIN. How old are you?

ELEANORA. For me there is neither time nor space. I am everywhere and of all times. I am in my father's prison and in my brother's schoolroom, I am in my mother's kitchen, and in my sister's shop, far away in America. When sales are good I share her joy, when they aren't I'm sorry, but not so sorry as when she does something bad.

Benjamin—you are called Benjamin because you are
the youngest of my friends—yes, all human beings are my
friends—Benjamin, if you trust yourself to me, I will suffer
for you too.

BENJAMIN. I don't really understand your words, but I seem
to know what you mean all the same—and so I'll do whatever you want me to.

ELEANORA. Then, to begin with, stop judging people—even
those who are convicted of sin.

BENJAMIN. Yes, but I must have a reason for that. You see,
I've studied philosophy.

ELEANORA. Oh, have you? Then you can help me to understand these words of a great philosopher. He says "He
who hateth the righteous shall himself become a sinner."

BENJAMIN. By all the laws of logic that means that man can be
foredoomed to sin.

ELEANORA. And the sin itself is punishment.

BENJAMIN. That's really deep. One could take it for Kant or
Schopenhauer.

ELEANORA. I don't know them.

BENJAMIN. Where did you read that?

ELEANORA. In the Holy Scriptures.

BENJAMIN. Really? Are there things like that in them?

ELEANORA. How ignorant you are! You've been neglected. If
only I could bring you up.

BENJAMIN, *laughing.* You're very sweet.

ELEANORA. But it's clear there's nothing bad in you. In fact
you look very good to me. What's the name of your Latin
Master?

BENJAMIN. Dr. Algren.*

*According to Swedish authorities Strindberg originally
meant to give Dr. Algren the part of Lindkvist. As it is,
he is twice mentioned in the text, but this leads to nothing.
He can well be cut in production, specially as the men-
tioning of him is inconsistent with Elis's vexation that *his*
best pupil should fail in the examination.

ELEANORA. I shall remember that. *Pause. . . . Then she gets up and cries out in agony.* Oh, now my father is in great trouble! They're being cruel to him. *She stands still, listening.* Do you hear how the telephone wires are wailing? That's because of the hard words the beautiful soft red copper can't bear. When people speak ill of one another on the telephone the copper wails and wails. *Sternly.* And every word is written in the Book, and at the end of time will come the reckoning.

BENJAMIN. How stern you are!

ELEANORA. I? Oh, no, no! How would I dare be? I, I! *Her mood changes. She becomes quiet and crafty, looks round, tiptoes to the stove, opens the door and takes out several torn-up pieces of white note-paper.* BENJAMIN *goes over to watch as she pieces the letter together on the sewing table.* How careless people are—leaving their secrets in stoves! Wherever I am I go straight to the stove. But I never misuse anything I find. I wouldn't dare. If I did, something awful would happen to me . . . Now what's this? *Reads.*

BENJAMIN. It's Mr. Peter writing to Kristina to ask her to meet him . . . I've been expecting this for some time.

ELEANORA, *putting her hand over the papers.* Oh you, what have you been expecting? You wicked creature, always thinking the worst of people. This letter has nothing but good in it. I know Kristina—she is going to be my sister-in-law. This meeting will prevent a misfortune to my brother Elis. Benjamin, will you promise not to say a word about this?

BENJAMIN. I wouldn't dare talk about it.

ELEANORA. It's wrong of people to have secrets. They think themselves wise and are fools. *She gathers up the pieces and puts them back in the stove.* Now what made me do that?

BENJAMIN. Yes, why are you so inquisitive?

ELEANORA. You see, that's my sickness. I must know everything. I can't rest until I do.

BENJAMIN. Know everything?

ELEANORA, *sadly*. Yes, it's a fault I can't overcome. *Gaily*. Anyhow, I know what the starlings say.

BENJAMIN. Can they talk?

ELEANORA. Haven't you heard of starlings being taught to speak?

BENJAMIN. Yes, taught.

ELEANORA. Well then, they can learn. And there are some that teach themselves. They sit and listen—without our knowing, of course—and then they mimic us. Just now as I came along, I heard a couple chatting in the walnut tree.

BENJAMIN. What fun you are! What did they say?

ELEANORA. Well, one said "Peter!" and the other said "Judas!" "Much of a muchness," said the first, "Fie, fie, fie!" said the second. And have you noticed the only place the nightingales sing is over there in the garden of the Deaf and Dumb.

BENJAMIN. Yes, everybody knows that. Why is it?

ELEANORA. Because those who have hearing don't hear what the nightingales say, but the deaf and dumb people do hear it. *Pause*.

BENJAMIN. Tell me some more fairy tales.

ELEANORA. I will if you're kind to me.

BENJAMIN. How do you mean—kind?

ELEANORA. Well you must never hold me to my words—never say "then you said that, and now you say this." See? . . . Now I'll tell you some more about birds. There is a bad one called the rat-buzzard because he feeds on rats. Because he's bad it's made hard for him to catch them. He can only say one word and that sounds like a cat's "miaow." So when the buzzard says "miaow," the rats run away and hide. But the buzzard doesn't understand what he's saying—so he goes without food very often. Do you want to hear any more? Or shall I tell you about flowers? You see, when I was ill I had to take some medicine with henbane in it. That turns your eye into a magnifying glass —just the opposite of belladonna, which makes you see

everything small. So now I can see further than other
people. I can see the stars in daylight.

BENJAMIN. The stars aren't up then.

ELEANORA. Silly! The stars are always up. Why at this moment I'm sitting facing north and looking at Cassiopea
like a W in the middle of the Milky Way. Can you see it?

BENJAMIN. No, I can't.

ELEANORA. There you are—one person can see what another
can't. So don't be so cocksure. Now I'll tell you about this
flower on the table. It's a Lenten Lily, and its home is in
Switzerland. It has a chalice, full of sunlight—that's why
it's yellow—and it has the power of soothing pain. *Pause.*
I passed a flower shop on my way, and saw it. *Tenderly.*
I wanted it—to give my brother Elis. I went up to the
door, but the shop was shut—of course because it's Confirmation Day. So as I had to have the flower, I took out
my keys and tried them. And what do you think? My
latchkey fitted—and I went in. *Pause.* Oh, if only you understood the silent language of flowers! Every scent says
so many things. I was quite overwhelmed. And with my
magnifying eye I looked right into their works which no
one else sees, and they told me how they suffered at the
hands of the careless gardener—I don't say cruel, for he
is only thoughtless. Then I put a coin on the counter with
my card, took the flower and came away.

BENJAMIN. But how rash of you. Suppose they miss the
flower and don't find the money.

ELEANORA. That's true. You're right.

BENJAMIN. A coin gets lost so easily, and if they only find
your card, you're done for.

ELEANORA. But surely no one would believe I'd just take
something?

BENJAMIN, *looking hard at her.* Wouldn't they?

ELEANORA, *hurt.* Oh, I know what you mean! Like father, like
child. How thoughtless of me! *For a moment she is silent,
then depression changes to resignation.* Oh, well, what
must be, must be . . . That's all there is to it.

BENJAMIN. Can't we do something to put it right?

ELEANORA. Hush . . . Let's talk about something else. Dr. Algren. Poor Elis . . . poor all of us. But this is Easter, and we must suffer. There'll be the Easter Concert tomorrow, won't there? They'll play Haydn's "Seven Words of the Redeemer"—"Mother, behold thy son!" *She weeps.*

BENJAMIN, *after a long pause.* What sort of illness was it you had?

ELEANORA. My illness is not sickness unto death, but unto the honour of God. I expected good and evil came; I expected light and darkness came . . . What was *your* childhood like, Benjamin?

BENJAMIN. Oh, I don't know—pretty miserable. And yours?

ELEANORA. I never had one. I was born old . . . I knew everything when I was born, and when I learnt anything, it was just like remembering. I knew all about people— their blindness and folly—when I was four years old. That's why they were unkind to me.

BENJAMIN. Everything you say I seem to have thought myself.

ELEANORA. I expect you have. What made you think the coin I left in the flower shop would get lost?

BENJAMIN. Because that annoying sort of thing always does happen.

ELEANORA. So you've found that too . . . Hush, someone's coming! *She listens.* I can hear . . . that it's Elis. Oh, how lovely! My one and only friend on earth. *Her happiness vanishes.* But he's not expecting me. And he won't be glad to see me. Of course he won't . . . Benjamin, Benjamin, be friendly and look happy when my poor brother comes in. I'll go, and you must break it to him that I'm here. But no hard words, remember, they hurt me so. Give me your hand. *He does so and she kisses him on the head.* Now you're my dear brother too. God bless you and keep you. *As she passes* ELIS's *overcoat she pats the sleeve affectionately. . . .* BENJAMIN *watches her.* Poor Elis. ELEANORA *goes into the house. . . .* ELIS *comes in from the street, looking troubled and goes to the writ-*

ing table. Before BENJAMIN *can tell him of the arrival,* MRS. HEYST *enters from the kitchen.*

ELIS. Ah, there you are, Mother!

MRS. HEYST. Was that you? I thought I heard a strange voice.

ELIS, *brusquely.* I've got some news. I met our lawyer in the street.

MRS. HEYST. Yes?

ELIS. The case is going to the Court of Appeal, and to save time I've got to read through the whole report of the proceedings. *He pulls some documents from a drawer.*

MRS. HEYST. Well, that won't take you long.

ELIS. Oh, I thought all that was over, and now I have to go through it all again—that long tale of suffering—with all the accusations, all the witnesses, all the evidence . . . the whole thing over again.

MRS. HEYST. Yes. But then he'll be acquitted by the Court of Appeal.

ELIS. No, he won't, Mother. You know he confessed.

MRS. HEYST. But there may be some legal error. That was the last thing the lawyer said to me.

ELIS. He only said it to comfort you.

MRS. HEYST. Oughtn't you to be off to that dinner?

ELIS. No.

MRS. HEYST. Now you've changed your mind again.

ELIS. I know.

MRS. HEYST. You shouldn't do that.

ELIS. I can't help it. I'm tossed about like drift-wood in a storm.

MRS. HEYST. I was quite sure I heard a strange voice that I recognized—but I must have been wrong. *Points to the overcoat.* That coat shouldn't be left there, as I said before. *She goes out to the kitchen.*

ELIS, *catching sight of the daffodil, to* BENJAMIN. Where did that flower come from?

BENJAMIN. A young lady brought it.

ELIS. Young lady? What's happened now? Who was it?

BENJAMIN. It was . . .

ELIS. Was it . . . my sister?

BENJAMIN. Yes. ELIS *sits down at the table. Pause.*

ELIS. Did you speak to her?

BENJAMIN. Oh yes!

ELIS. My God, is there no end to it? Did she . . . behave badly?

BENJAMIN. Oh no! She was very, very nice.

ELIS. How extraordinary! Did she mention me? Is she very angry with me?

BENJAMIN. On the contrary. She said you were her one and only friend on earth.

ELIS. What an amazing change!

BENJAMIN. And when she left she patted that coat of yours on the sleeve.

ELIS. Left? Where did she go?

BENJAMIN, *pointing.* In there.

ELIS. You mean she's there now?

BENJAMIN. Yes.

ELIS. You look so happy and friendly, Benjamin.

BENJAMIN. She talked so beautifully.

ELIS. What did she talk about?

BENJAMIN. She told me fairy tales—and then there was a lot about religion.

ELIS, *rising.* And that made you happy? BENJAMIN *nods.* Poor Eleanora she's so unhappy herself, and yet she can make others happy. *Reluctantly he goes towards the door to face the ordeal of meeting* ELEANORA. God help me!

ACT TWO

GOOD FRIDAY

Musical Prelude: Haydn: The Seven Words of the Re-deemer. Largo No. 1 Pater dimitte illis.

The scene is the same, but the curtains are drawn and light comes through them from the lamp in the street. The hanging lamp is lighted and also a small lamp on the table. A fire is burning in the stove.

ELIS and KRISTINA are sitting by the sewing-table, talking. ELEANORA and BENJAMIN are sitting opposite one another at the dining-table, with the lamp between them. ELEANORA is reading the Bible and BENJAMIN has some books. The weather is cold. ELEANORA has a wrap over her shoulders. All are dressed in black. ELIS and BENJAMIN are wearing white ties. The writing table is strewn with legal documents. The daffodil stands on the sewing-table. On the dining-table is an old pendulum clock.

From time to time the shadow of someone passing in the street falls on the curtains. The organ can be heard in the distance, playing the Haydn Largo.

ELIS, *to* KRISTINA, *low*. Good Friday . . . yes, Long Friday,* as they call it—and how terribly long! The snow lies in the streets like the straw they spread outside the houses of the dying. Every sound is blotted out—except for the deep notes of the organ, which one can catch even in here.

KRISTINA. I suppose Mother went to evening service.

ELIS. Yes. She couldn't bear to go in the morning. She's so hurt by the way people look at her.

KRISTINA. They are extraordinary, those people. They seem to expect us all to keep out of sight, as if that was the correct way for us to behave.

*The Swedish for Good Friday.

ELIS. Perhaps they're right.

KRISTINA. One person makes a false step, and the whole family is ostracized.

ELIS. Yes, that's how it is.

ELEANORA *pushes the lamp towards* BENJAMIN *so that he shall see better.*

ELIS, *indicating* ELEANORA *and* BENJAMIN. Look at those two.

KRISTINA, *low.* Isn't it a charming sight? They get on so well together.

ELIS. It is such a mercy Eleanora's so calm. If only it would last.

KRISTINA. Why shouldn't it?

ELIS. Because . . . well, good times don't usually last long. And today I'm afraid of everything.

BENJAMIN, *smiling, pushes the lamp back to* ELEANORA.

KRISTINA. Look at them.

ELIS. Have you noticed how changed Benjamin is? That sulky defiance has quite gone. He's so gentle and willing.

KRISTINA. There is something exquisite about her whole nature. Even the word "beautiful" isn't quite right.

ELEANORA *begins to cry silently as she reads.*

ELIS. Yes, she has brought an angel of peace with her, who walks unseen and breathes repose. Even Mother was curiously calm when she saw Eleanora, and that I didn't expect.

KRISTINA. Do you think she's cured?

ELIS. I would think so, if it were not for that oversensitiveness. Look, she can't help weeping as she reads the story of Christ's passion.

KRISTINA. Well I remember doing the same thing—at school on Ash Wednesdays.

ELIS. Don't talk so loud; she'll hear.

KRISTINA. No. At the moment she's too far away.

ELIS. Have you noticed that something dignified—almost noble —has come into Benjamin's face?

KRISTINA. Suffering has done that. Pleasure makes things commonplace.

ELIS. Or perhaps it's rather love. Do you think those two young creatures . . . ?

KRISTINA. Ssh, ssh! Don't touch the butterfly's wings or it will fly away.

ELIS. They are looking at each other now, and only pretending to read. I can't hear any pages being turned.

KRISTINA. Hush!

ELEANORA *gets up and puts her wrap round* BENJAMIN'S *shoulders . . . He demurs mildly, then gives in. She sits down, and pushes the lamp towards him again.*

ELIS, *during this action.* She can't help doing these things.

KRISTINA. Poor Eleanora, she has no idea how good she is.

ELIS, *rising.* I must get back to my documents.

KRISTINA. Do you see any point in reading all that?

ELIS. Only one—to keep hope alive for Mother. But though I too only pretend to read, the words prick my eyes like thorns. *Picks up documents.* The evidence of the witnesses, the rows of figures, Father's admissions—as, for example, "the accused confessed with tears" . . . So many tears, so many tears. *Displays documents.* And the documents themselves, stamped like counterfeit money, or prison bars. And the strings . . . and the red seals like the five wounds of Jesus . . . and the sentences that run on for ever . . . endless torture. This is Good Friday Penance. Yesterday the sun shone, yesterday our imagination carried us out into the countryside. Kristina, suppose we had to stay here all the summer.

KRISTINA. Well, we should save a lot of money, but it would be sad.

ELIS. I couldn't bear it. I've spent three summers here and it's like a tomb. Mid-day—and one sees the long grey street winding like an unending trench. Not a man, not a horse, not a dog. Only the rats coming out of the sewers because the cats are on holiday. And the few people left

sit at their window mirrors,* spying on their neighbours'
clothes, prying on their down-at-heel boots and shabby
ways. "Look, that fellow's wearing his winter suit!" And
cripples, who had hidden, creep out from the slums, and
people without noses and ears—miserable, evil people.
There they sit on the promenade, sunning themselves, just
as if they had taken the town by storm. There, where a
little while before, pretty, well-dressed children played—
encouraged with tender words by their lovely mothers—
now a crowd of ragged hooligans swarm, cursing and
tormenting each other. I remember one midsummer day
two years ago . . .

KRISTINA. Elis, Elis, you must look to the future.

ELIS. Is it brighter there?

KRISTINA. Let us believe it is.

ELIS. If only it were not snowing. Then we could go out and
walk.

KRISTINA. Oh, my dear, only yesterday evening you wanted
the darkness to return so as to hide us from people's
glances. "The darkness is so good, so blessed," you said,
"it's like drawing the blankets up over one's head."

ELIS. Well, there you are—the misery's as great either way.
Picks up documents. The worst part of these proceedings
is the impertinent questions about my father's way of
living. It says here that we gave grand parties. One witness declares that Father drank. It's too much. I can't go
on. And yet I must—to the bitter end. *He shivers.* Aren't
you cold?

KRISTINA. No, but it's not exactly warm. Isn't Lina in?

ELIS. You know very well she went to Church.†

KRISTINA. Surely Mother will be back soon.

ELIS. I'm always terrified when she comes back from the
town. She hears so much, and sees so much—and all of it's
wrong.

*Mirrors set at an angle inside windows so that one can
see who is approaching in the street. They appear in
several of Strindberg's plays.
†Literally Communion.

KRISTINA. There's a queer, melancholy strain in your family.

ELIS. That's why only melancholy people have anything to do with us. The happy ones avoid us.

KRISTINA. There's Mother coming in now—by the kitchen door.

ELIS. Don't be impatient with her, Kristina.

KRISTINA. Of course not. It's harder for her than for any of us. But I don't understand her.

ELIS. She hides her shame as best she can—and that makes her difficult. Poor Mother.
MRS. HEYST *comes in. . . . She is dressed in black and carries a prayer book and a handkerchief.*

MRS. HEYST. Good evening, my dears. *All greet her affectionately, except* BENJAMIN *who only bows.* You're all in black—as if you were in mourning. *Silence.*

ELIS. Is it still snowing?

MRS. HEYST. Yes, great wet flakes. It's cold in here. *Goes over to* ELEANORA *and caresses her.* Well, my chick, at your studies I see. *To* BENJAMIN. But you're not studying much, are you?

ELEANORA *holds her mother's hand against her face and kisses it.* MRS. HEYST *tries to hide her emotion.*

MRS. HEYST. There, my pet, there, there.

ELIS. So you've been to evening service, Mother.

MRS. HEYST. Yes, the Vicar took it, and I don't like him.

ELIS. Did you meet anyone you know?

MRS. HEYST, *sitting down by the sewing table.* It would have been better if I hadn't.

ELIS. Then I have no doubt who . . .

MRS. HEYST, *nodding.* Lindkvist—and he came straight up to me . . .

ELIS. How cruel, how very cruel!

MRS. HEYST. And asked me how we were. And then . . . you can imagine what a shock it was to me—he asked if he might call on us this evening.

ELIS. Good Friday evening!

MRS. HEYST. I couldn't speak. And he took my silence for consent. *Pause.* He'll be here any moment.

ELIS. Here? Now?

MRS. HEYST, *vaguely.* He said he wanted to leave a paper, and it was urgent.

ELIS. He's going to take the furniture.

MRS. HEYST. His manner was so odd, I didn't know what to make of it.

ELIS. Let him come then. He has the law on his side and we must submit. *To them all.* We must receive him correctly when he comes.

MRS. HEYST. If only I needn't see him.

ELIS. Well, you can stay in your room.

MRS. HEYST. But he mustn't take the furniture. How shall we manage if he takes everything away? We can't live in empty rooms, can we?

ELIS. The foxes have holes and the birds have nests. Some homeless people live in the woods.

MRS. HEYST. That's the right place for swindlers, not honest people.

ELIS, *sits down at the writing table.* I must get on with this reading, Mother.

MRS. HEYST. Have you found an error yet?

ELIS. No, I don't believe there is one.

MRS. HEYST. But I met the Notary just now. He says we ought to be able to find something—an unqualified witness or an unproved statement—or some contradiction. You can't be reading carefully enough.

ELIS. Of course I am, Mother—but it's very painful.

MRS. HEYST. Listen, I did meet the Notary just now—it was quite true what I said. And he also told me about a case of shop-breaking. In the town, yesterday, in broad daylight.

ELEANORA *and* BENJAMIN *prick up their ears.*

ELIS. Shop-breaking? Here, in the town? Where?

MRS. HEYST. It was at the flower shop in Convent Street. The whole thing was very odd. This is what seems to have happened. The shopkeeper locked up the shop so as to go to the church where his son—or perhaps it was his daughter—was being confirmed. When he came back at three o'clock—or perhaps it was four—but that doesn't make any difference—what do you think? The shop door was open and his flowers had vanished—masses of them, and in particular—and this was the first thing he missed—a yellow tulip.

ELIS. A tulip! If it had been a daffodil I should have been worried.

MRS. HEYST. No, it was a tulip. That's quite definite. However, the police are investigating. ELEANORA *rises as if to speak, but* BENJAMIN *pulls her back and whispers to her.* Just think, shop-breaking on Maundy Thursday while the children were being confirmed. Nothing but swindlers, the whole town. And then they have to put innocent people in prison.

ELIS. Have they any notion who did it?

MRS. HEYST. No. But it was a peculiar kind of thief, because he didn't take any money from the till.

KRISTINA. Oh, that this day were over!

MRS. HEYST. I wish Lina would come in . . . By the way, everyone was talking about Peter's dinner last night. The Governor was there.

ELIS. Was he? That surprises me. Peter's always been opposed to the Governor's policy.

MRS. HEYST. Then he must have changed.

ELIS. He isn't called Peter for nothing it seems.

MRS. HEYST. What have you got against the Governor?

ELIS. He's an obstructionist. He obstructs everything. He fought against the workers' colleges and military training for the boys. He even wanted to prohibit perfectly harmless bicycles—not to speak of those splendid summer camps. And he has always been against me.

MRS. HEYST. I don't know anything about that, but it doesn't matter. The point is that the Governor made a speech, and Peter thanked him.

ELIS. With emotion, I suppose. And denied his teacher and said "I know not the man." And the cock crew a second time. Isn't the Governor called Pontius, with the surname Pilate?

ELEANORA *rises again as if to speak, but controls herself.*

MRS. HEYST. You shouldn't be so bitter, Elis. Men are human, and one must take them as they are.

ELIS. Ssh. I can hear Lindkvist coming.

MRS. HEYST. Can you hear him in the snow?

ELIS. I hear his stick tapping the pavement . . . and his galoshes . . . You had better go away, Mother.

MRS. HEYST. No, I've decided to stay and give him a piece of my mind.

ELIS. Mother dear, please go. This is intolerable.

MRS. HEYST, *rising in great agitation.* May the day I was born be blotted out!

KRISTINA. Oh don't blaspheme!

MRS. HEYST, *passionately.* Were it not more just that the unrighteous should suffer this anguish and the evil doer this tribulation?

ELEANORA, *with a cry of agony.* Mother!

MRS. HEYST. My God, why hast Thou forsaken me—and my children? *She goes out.*

ELIS, *listening.* He has stopped. Perhaps he realises it's not correct to call on Good Friday. Or perhaps he thinks it's too cruel. But of course he wouldn't think that, or he couldn't write such terrible letters. They were always on blue note-paper. I've never been able to see a blue letter since without trembling.

KRISTINA. What are you going to say? What will you suggest to him?

ELIS. I don't know. I can't think clearly any more. Shall I fall

on my knees and beg for mercy? Can you hear him? All
I can hear now is the blood singing in my ears.

KRISTINA. Let's be prepared for the worst. Suppose he does
take everything?

ELIS. Then the landlord will come and ask for a guarantee,
which I shall be unable to give him. He'll want a guarantee because the furniture will no longer be a security for
the rent.

KRISTINA, *looking through the curtains.* He's not there. He
must have gone.

ELIS *gives a long sigh of relief. Pause.*

ELIS. You know Mother's apathy troubles me far more than
these outbursts.

KRISTINA. That apathy's not real. It's put on to deceive us or
herself. There was something of the roaring of the lioness
in her last words. Did you see how she grew—how big
she became?

ELIS. Do you know, just then, as I was thinking about Lindkvist, I saw him as a good-natured giant who does nothing
worse than frighten children. I wonder what made me
think of that just then.

KRISTINA. Thoughts come and go.

ELIS. It was a good thing I wasn't at that dinner yesterday.
I should have made a speech against the Governor, and
that would have ruined everything, for myself and for us
all. Yes, it really was a good thing.

KRISTINA. You see?

ELIS. Thanks for the advice. So you knew your Peter.

KRISTINA. *My* Peter?

ELIS. I meant—mine. Look, here he is again. Mercy upon us!
*Against the curtains appears the shadow of a man draw-
ing nearer and nearer. It grows steadily until it is gigantic.* *

The giant! Look at the giant who is coming to devour us.

*This is where the shadow appears in the Swedish text,
but surely it should be seen by the audience when Elis
says the earlier lines about the giant.

KRISTINA. This is something to smile at—a kind of fairy tale.

ELIS. I don't know how to smile any more. *The shadow crosses the back until it disappears.*

KRISTINA. Look at his stick and you'll have to laugh.

ELIS. He's gone. Now I can breathe again. He won't come again now—until tomorrow. *He sighs with relief.*

KRISTINA. And tomorrow the sun will shine, for it is the eve of the Resurrection. The snow will have melted and the birds will sing.

ELIS, *closing his eyes.* Go on talking like that. I can see all that you're saying.

KRISTINA. Oh, if only you could see into my heart, could see my thoughts, my real purpose, my fervent prayer, when now I . . . *Breaks off.* Elis, Elis . . .

ELIS. When what?

KRISTINA. When now I ask something of you.

ELIS. Go on.

KRISTINA. It's a test. Remember that, Elis, please—it's a test.

ELIS. Test? Well, what is it?

KRISTINA. Let me . . . no, I daren't . . . it might not work.
ELEANORA *grows alert.*

ELIS. Why do you torment me?

KRISTINA. I shall regret it I know . . . but it must be said. Elis, let me go to that concert this evening.

ELIS. What concert?

KRISTINA. In the cathedral—Haydn's "Seven Words."

ELIS. Who with?

KRISTINA. With Alice . . .

ELIS. And?

KRISTINA. Peter.

ELIS. With Peter?

KRISTINA: There—you are angry. I regret it already—but it's too late.

ELIS. Yes, it is rather late. But you had better explain.

KRISTINA. I've been trying to warn you that I can't explain. That's why I want you to trust me completely.

ELIS, *softly*. Go then. I do trust you, but all the same it is an agony to me that you should choose the company of that traitor.

KRISTINA. I know it is—but it's only a test.

ELIS. One which I can't stand.

KRISTINA. You will.

ELIS. I want to, but I can't. But anyhow you shall go.

KRISTINA. Give me your hand.

ELIS, *giving it to her*. There.

The telephone rings.

ELIS, *at telephone*. Hullo! . . . No answer . . . Hullo . . . My own voice is answering . . . Who is it? . . . How extraordinary! . . . I hear my own words like an echo.

KRISTINA. That does sometimes happen.

ELIS. Hullo! How uncanny! *Rings off*. Go now, Kristina, without explanations, without fuss. I shall stand the test.

KRISTINA. If you do, then all will be well with us.

ELIS. I will. KRISTINA *moves towards the kitchen*. Why are you going that way?

KRISTINA. My coat is out there. Well then, goodbye for the moment. *She goes out.*

ELIS. Goodbye, my dear. *Pause*. For ever! *He rushes out the other way.*

ELEANORA. Oh heavens! And what have I done? The police are looking for the thief, and if I am discovered, poor Mother, poor Elis!

BENJAMIN, *boyishly*. Eleanora, you must say I did it.

ELEANORA. You're only a child. How could you bear another's guilt?

BENJAMIN. That's easy when one knows one's innocent.

ELEANORA. But we mustn't deceive people.

BENJAMIN. Then let me telephone the flower shop and explain what happened.

ELEANORA. No. I did wrong, and I must be punished with this anxiety. I've woken their fear of burglars, so I have to be frightened too.

BENJAMIN. But if the police come?

ELEANORA. It will be terrible. But if they do, that's how it's to be. Oh, that this day were over! *Draws the pendulum clock on the table towards her and moves the hands.* Dear clock, please go a little faster. Tick, tock, ping, ping, ping. Now it's eight. Ping, ping, ping. Now it's nine. Ten. Eleven . . . Twelve Now it's Easter eve. Soon the sun will be rising, and we shall write on the Easter eggs. I shall write this: "The Adversary hath desired to have you that he may sift you as wheat, but I have prayed for thee."

BENJAMIN. Why do you give yourself such a bad time, Eleanora?

ELEANORA. A *bad* time? Me? *She shakes her head.* Benjamin, think of all the flowers that have come out—the anemones and snowdrops that have to stand in the snow the whole day long—and all through the night, too, freezing in the darkness. Think how they suffer. The night's the worst, because then it's dark, and they are afraid of the dark and can't run away. They just stand and wait for the day to come.* Everything, everything suffers, but the flowers most of all. And the birds who have already come back from the South—where will they sleep tonight?

BENJAMIN. In hollow trees, of course.

ELEANORA. There aren't enough hollow trees for them all. I've only seen two in the gardens here, and owls live in those. They kill little birds. *Pause.* Poor Elis. He thinks Kristina has left him, but I know she'll come back.

BENJAMIN. If you knew, why didn't you say so?

ELEANORA. Because Elis must suffer. Everyone has to suffer today, Good Friday, so as to remember Christ's suffering on the cross. *A whistle is heard outside.* ELEANORA *starts.* What was that?

BENJAMIN, *rising.* Don't you know?

*Unconsciously thinking of herself in the asylum.

ELEANORA. No.

BENJAMIN. It's the police.

ELEANORA. The police! Oh! Yes, that was the sound when they came to take Father away. And then I was ill. And now they're coming to take me. BENJAMIN *takes his stand between* ELEANORA *and the door.*

BENJAMIN. No, they shan't take you. I will defend you, Eleanora.

ELEANORA. That's fine of you, Benjamin, but you mustn't.

BENJAMIN, *peeping through the curtains.* There are two of them. ELEANORA *tries to take his place. He resists.* Not you, Eleanora. I wouldn't want to go on living if anything happened to you.

ELEANORA, *firmly.* Benjamin, go and sit down—in that chair. Go on. BENJAMIN *obeys as if hypnotised.* ELEANORA *draws back the curtains and looks boldly out of the window.* It's just a couple of boys. Oh, we of little faith! How could we believe God would be so cruel, when I've done nothing wicked, only acted thoughtlessly? It serves me right. Why did I doubt?

BENJAMIN. All the same, there's still that man coming tomorrow to take away the furniture.

ELEANORA. Yes. He must come—and we must go. And leave everything behind—all the old furniture Father collected for our home, and which I've known ever since I was little. *She goes round touching the furniture.* We should have nothing to bind us to earth. We must climb the stony paths that wound our feet and weary us so.

BENJAMIN. Now you're tormenting yourself again, Eleanora.

ELEANORA. Let me. But do you know what I shall find it hardest to part from? It's this clock. It was there when I was born. It measured all my hours and all my days. *She lifts the clock up.* Do you hear it beating like a heart? Exactly like a heart. It stopped just at the hour my grandfather died—we had it even then. Goodbye, little clock. Please stop again soon . . . Do you know, Benjamin, this clock had a way of going faster when there was bad luck

in the house, as if it wanted to hurry over the trouble—
for our sakes, of course. But when things were going well
it slowed down to let us enjoy them longer. This was the
good clock—but we had a bad one too. It's hanging in the
kitchen still. It couldn't bear music. As soon as Elis began
to play the piano it started to strike. We all noticed it,
not only I. That's why it was put in the kitchen, because
it was so naughty. But Lina doesn't like it either. It won't
keep quiet at night, and one can't cook eggs by it. They're
always hard-boiled, Lina says . . . Now you're laughing.

BENJAMIN. How can I help it?

ELEANORA. You're a nice boy, Benjamin, but you must be
serious. Think of the birch there behind the mirror.

BENJAMIN. But they're such fun, the things you say. I can't
help smiling. And why should we cry all the time?

ELEANORA. If we don't weep here in this vale of tears, where
shall we weep?

BENJAMIN. Hm!

ELEANORA. You'd like to smile all day, that's why you got into
trouble. But I only really like you when you're serious.
Don't forget that.

BENJAMIN. Eleanora, do you think we'll ever get out of all
this?

ELEANORA. Yes. Most of it will clear up once Good Friday is
over—although not everything. Today the birch, tomorrow Easter eggs. Today snow, tomorrow thaw. Today
death, tomorrow resurrection.

BENJAMIN. You're very wise.

ELEANORA. I can feel already that it's clearing up into lovely
weather. The snow is melting—there's the smell of melting
snow in here already . . . Tomorrow the violets will be
out against the south wall. The clouds have lifted—I can
feel it as I breathe. Oh, I know so well when the heavens
are open! Benjamin pull back the curtains. I want God to
see us. BENJAMIN *obeys. The room is flooded with moonlight.* Look at the full moon. The Easter moon. And, you
know, the sun is there—although the moon is giving us the
light.

ACT THREE

EASTER EVE

*Musical Prelude: Haydn: Seven Words of The Redeemer.
No. 5 Adagio.*

*The curtains are drawn back, disclosing grey misty
weather. The door to the street is closed. The stove is
alight, and* ELEANORA *sits beside it holding a bunch of
hepatica.* BENJAMIN *comes in from the kitchen.*

ELEANORA. Where have you been all this time, Benjamin?

BENJAMIN. It wasn't long.

ELEANORA. I missed you.

BENJAMIN. Well, where have *you* been, Eleanora?

ELEANORA. I went to the market and bought these flowers.
Now I'm warming them—they were frozen, poor things.

BENJAMIN. And where's your sun now?

ELEANORA. Behind the mist. There are no clouds today—only
mist from the sea. It smells of salt.

BENJAMIN. Did you see if the birds were still alive?

ELEANORA. Yes. Not a single one can fall to the ground unless
God wills it. But in the market there were dead birds.

ELIS *comes in.*

ELIS. Has the paper come?

ELEANORA. No, Elis.

ELIS *crosses the verandah. When he's half way,* KRISTINA
comes in from the other side and ignores him.

KRISTINA, *to* ELEANORA. Has the paper come?

ELEANORA. No, not yet.

ELIS *and* KRISTINA, *paying no attention to one another,
cross and go out.*

ELEANORA. Oh, how cold it has grown! Hate has come into the house. While there was love one could bear it all. But now, oh dear, it's so cold!

BENJAMIN. Why do they want the paper?

ELEANORA. Don't you realize? It will be in it.

BENJAMIN. What will?

ELEANORA. Everything. The shop-breaking, the police—and more too.

MRS. HEYST, *entering from the kitchen.* Has the paper come?

ELEANORA. No, Mother dear.

MRS. HEYST, *going back to the kitchen.* When it comes, let me know first.

ELEANORA. The paper, the paper. Oh, that the printing press had broken down, or the editor gone sick! No, one mustn't wish such things. Do you know, I was with Father last night.

BENJAMIN. Last night?

ELEANORA. Yes, in my sleep. And I was in America, too, with my sister. On Thursday she sold something for thirty dollars and made five dollars profit.

BENJAMIN. Is that a lot or a little?

ELEANORA. Quite a lot.

BENJAMIN, *artfully.* Did you meet anyone you knew in the market?

ELEANORA. Why do you ask me that? You mustn't pry, Benjamin. You want to know my secrets, but you can't.

BENJAMIN. But you expect to find out mine.

ELEANORA. Listen to the telephone wires humming. So now the paper has come out, and people are ringing each other up. "Have you read about it?" "Yes I've read it." "Isn't it frightful?"

BENJAMIN. What's frightful?

ELEANORA. Everything. The whole of life is frightful—but we have to accept it all the same. Look at Elis and Kristina. They're so fond of one another, yet they hate each other —so much that the thermometer drops when they walk through the room. Yesterday Kristina went to the concert, and today they aren't speaking. Why? Why?

BENJAMIN. Because your brother's jealous.

ELEANORA. Don't say that word. What do we know about it, anyway, except that it's an illness and therefore a punishment? One mustn't touch evil, or one may catch it. Look at Elis. Have you noticed how changed he is since he began reading those documents?

BENJAMIN. About the trial?

ELEANORA, *going over to the writing table*. Yes. It's as if the evil in them had got right into his soul, and flamed out in his face and eyes. Kristina feels it—and so as not to catch his evil, she's put on an armour of ice. Oh, these documents! If only I could burn them. Cruelty and lies and revenge pour out of them. That's why you must keep evil and dirty things away from you, Benjamin—away from your lips and your heart too.

BENJAMIN. What a lot you see in everything.

ELEANORA, *after a pause*. Do you know what's in store for me, if Elis and the others find out it was I who bought the daffodil in such an odd way?

BENJAMIN. What will they do to you?

ELEANORA. I shall be sent back . . . back to that place I came from. Where the sun doesn't shine, where the walls are white and bare like a bathroom. Where you hear only weeping and wailing. Where I have lost a whole year of my life.

BENJAMIN. Where do you mean?

ELEANORA. Where you are tortured worse than in prison, where the damned dwell, where unrest has its home, where despair keeps watch day and night. A place from which no one ever returns.

BENJAMIN. Did you say worse than prison?

ELEANORA. In prison you are condemned, but there you are doomed. In prison you are examined and heard, there you are unheard. Poor daffodil, the cause of it all. I meant so well and did so badly.

BENJAMIN. But why don't you go to the flower shop and explain how it happened. You're just like a lamb going to the slaughter.

ELEANORA. When it knows it has to be slaughtered it doesn't complain or try to run away. There's nothing it can do.

ELIS *enters, a letter in his hand.*

ELIS. Hasn't the paper come yet?

ELEANORA. No, brother.

ELIS, *calling into the kitchen.* Lina, go and get a paper!

MRS. HEYST *comes in from the kitchen. At the look of her* ELEANORA *and* BENJAMIN *are frightened.*

MRS. HEYST. Children, will you go away for a few minutes please. *They go out.* You've had a letter?

ELIS. Yes.

MRS. HEYST. From the asylum?

ELIS. Yes.

MRS. HEYST. What do they say?

ELIS. They want Eleanora back.

MRS. HEYST. They shan't have her. She's my child.

ELIS. My sister.

MRS. HEYST. What do you mean by that?

ELIS. I don't know. I can't think any more.

MRS. HEYST. But I can. Eleanora, this child of sorrow, has brought us joy. Not of this world, it is true—but her unrest has been changed into a peace she shares with us all. Sane or not, for me she is wise—for she knows how to bear life's burdens better than I do, better than any of us. What's more, Elis, if I am sane now, was I sane when I believed my husband innocent? I knew very well he was convicted on factual tangible evidence—and that he had confessed. *Pause.* And you, Elis, are you in your right mind when you can't see that Kristina loves you—when you go on thinking she hates you?

ELIS. It's a queer way of loving.

MRS. HEYST. No. Your coldness freezes her heart. It is you

who are doing the hating. But you're wrong—and so you're suffering.

ELIS. How can I be wrong? Didn't she go out last night with the friend who played me false?

MRS. HEYST. Yes, she did. And with your knowledge. But why did she go? You ought to be able to see why.

ELIS. Well, I can't.

MRS. HEYST. In that case you deserve what you get.

The kitchen door opens; MRS. HEYST *goes to it and returns with the newspaper which she hands to* ELIS.

ELIS. That was the worst blow of all. With her I could have borne the rest. Now my last support has gone, and I am falling.

MRS. HEYST. Fall then, but fall in the right way—so you can get up again. Well, what is there in the paper?

ELIS. I don't know. I'm afraid of the paper today.

MRS. HEYST. Give it to me. I'll read it.

ELIS. No, give me time!

MRS. HEYST. What are you afraid of? What are you expecting?

ELIS. The worst possible.

MRS. HEYST. That's happened so many times already. Oh my child, if you only knew my life, if you had been there while I was watching your father going step by step to his destruction—without my being able to warn all those people he was ruining. When the crash came, I knew I was guilty too, for I was fully aware of the crime. If the judge had not been a man of understanding, who saw how difficult my position was as wife, I should have been punished too.

ELIS. What really caused Father's downfall? I've never understood.

MRS. HEYST. Pride, as with us all.

ELIS. But why should we who are innocent suffer for his fault?

MRS. HEYST. Oh, be quiet! *She takes the paper and reads.* ELIS *stands in apprehension, then paces up and down.*

What's this? Didn't I say that among the flowers stolen from that shop was a yellow tulip?

ELIS. Yes, I remembered that distinctly.

MRS. HEYST. But here it says a daffodil.

ELIS, *shocked.* Does it say that?

MRS. HEYST. It was Eleanora. Oh my God, my God! *She collapses into a chair.*

ELIS. So the worst was still to come.

MRS. HEYST. Prison or asylum.

ELIS. It's impossible that she did it, impossible.

MRS. HEYST. Now the family name will be dragged in the mud again.

ELIS. Do they suspect her?

MRS. HEYST, *reading.* It says—clues point in a certain direction. It's pretty clear where.

ELIS. I'll talk to her.

MRS. HEYST, *rising.* Be gentle with her. I can't bear any more. She is lost, found and lost again. Yes, talk to her. *She goes out to the kitchen.* ELIS *looks at the paper, groans, then goes to the other door and calls.*

ELIS. Eleanora, my child, will you come in here a minute? I want to speak to you.

ELEANORA, *off.* I'm just doing my hair.

ELIS. Never mind. Leave it as it is. ELEANORA *comes in with her hair loose.* Tell me, dear. Where did you get that flower?

ELEANORA. I took it.

ELIS. Oh my God!

ELEANORA. But I left the money there.

ELIS. You paid for it?

ELEANORA. Yes and no. Oh, it's always so difficult. But I didn't do anything wrong. I meant to do something nice. You do believe me, don't you?

ELIS. I believe you, my dear—but the newspaper doesn't know you're innocent.

ELEANORA. Oh, Elis, so I must go through that too! What will they do to me? *She hangs her head.* Well—so be it. *Her hair falls over her face.* BENJAMIN *rushes in beside himself.*

BENJAMIN. You mustn't touch her. She's done nothing wrong. I know, because I did it. It was I, I, I who did it.

ELEANORA. Don't believe a word he's saying. It was I.

ELIS. What shall I believe? Which of you shall I believe?

BENJAMIN. Me, me! *He is almost in tears at the thought of* ELEANORA's *peril.*

ELEANORA. Me, me!

BENJAMIN. Let me go to the police.

ELIS. Come now, be quiet!

BENJAMIN. I must go. I will go.

ELEANORA. No, no!

ELIS. Be quiet, both of you! Mother's coming.

MRS. HEYST *comes in, much moved, takes* ELEANORA *in her arms and kisses her.*

MRS. HEYST. Child, child—you are my beloved child and you are to stay with me.

ELEANORA. You're kissing me, Mother. You haven't done that for years. Why now?

MRS. HEYST. Because . . . because . . . My dear, the shop-keeper has come to apologise for causing so much trouble. The lost money has been found with your card.

ELEANORA *leaps into* ELIS's *arms and kisses him, then hugs* BENJAMIN.

ELEANORA. Dear Benjamin, wanting to go through all that for me. Why did you?

BENJAMIN, *shyly, boyishly.* Because I like you so much, Eleanora.

MRS. HEYST. You'd better put your things on, children, and go out into the garden. It's clearing up.

ELEANORA, *happily.* Oh, it's clearing up! Come along, Benjamin. *She takes his hand and pulls him out.*

ELIS. Now can we put the birch on the fire?

MRS. HEYST. Not yet. There's still one thing more.

ELIS. You mean Lindkvist?

MRS. HEYST. He's standing outside. He looks very odd—almost gentle in spite of himself. It's a pity he's so garrulous and will talk so much about himself.

ELIS. Now I've seen a ray of light I'm not afraid to meet the giant. Let him come.

MRS. HEYST. But don't provoke him. Providence has put our fate in his hands. Blessed are the meek . . . and you know only too well what happens to the proud.

ELIS, *impatiently*. Yes, I know all that. Listen to the galoshes. Swish, swish, beast, beasts! Does he intend to come in here with them on? Why not? These are his carpets and his furniture.

MRS. HEYST. Elis, think of us all.

ELIS. I do, Mother.

MRS. HEYST *goes out to the kitchen.*
ELIS *opens the front door, and* LINDKVIST *is framed in it. He is an elderly man of fierce appearance with grey hair, black bushy eyebrows, black whiskers and round black-rimmed spectacles. Large cornelian trinkets hang from his watch-chain. A cane is in his hand with which he was about to knock on the door. He wears a black overcoat with a fur collar and large pockets stuffed with papers. He carries a top hat. His galoshes squeak. As he enters he looks piercingly at* ELIS. *Both men bow formally.*

LINDKVIST. My name is Lindkvist.

ELIS, *stiffly*. Mine is Heyst . . . Won't you sit down?

LINDKVIST *sits by the sewing table and stares at* ELIS. *Pause.*

ELIS. What can I do for you?

LINDKVIST, *formally*. Hm! I had the honour to announce my intention to call yesterday evening, but on second thoughts I decided it was not fitting to talk business on Good Friday.

ELIS. We are very grateful.

LINDKVIST, *sharply*. We are not grateful. *Pause*. However . . .
On Thursday I happened to pay a visit to the Governor.
Pauses, and watches to see the impression this makes on
ELIS. Do you know the Governor?

ELIS, *casually*. I have not that honour.

LINDKVIST. Then you shall have that honour. We talked about
your father.

ELIS. I can well believe it.

LINDKVIST, *putting a white document on the table*. And I got
this paper from him.

ELIS. I've been expecting this for a long time. But before we
go further, may I take the liberty of asking a question?

LINDKVIST, *curtly*. Certainly.

ELIS. Why don't you deliver this order to the official receiver,
so that at least we may be spared this long and painful
execution?

LINDKVIST. So that's the line, young man.

ELIS. Young or not, I don't ask for mercy, only for justice.

LINDKVIST, *balancing the paper on the rim of the table*. So
that's the line. No mercy . . . no mercy. You see this
paper—balancing here on the edge of the table? Now I
take it back. Justice, you say, nothing but justice. Now
listen, my friend—once upon a time I was robbed—robbed
in an unpleasant way of my money. When I wrote politely
asking you when it would be convenient for you to settle,
you answered me rudely. You treated me as if I were an
usurer, bent on robbing the widowed and fatherless—
whereas it was I who was robbed, and your people were
the robbers. But, since I have some sense, I was content
to answer your rude abuse civilly, though sharply. You
know my blue note-paper, eh? I can get it officially
stamped too when I wish—but I don't always wish. *Looks
round the room*.

ELIS. If you please—the furniture is at your disposal.

LINDKVIST. I wasn't looking at the furniture. I was wondering if your mother was in. I presume she loves justice just as much as you do.

ELIS. I hope so.

LINDKVIST. Good. Do you realise that if the justice which you esteem so highly had taken its course, your mother, as an accessory to the crime, would have been convicted under common law?

ELIS. Oh no!

LINDKVIST. Oh yes! And it's not too late even now. *He takes another paper, a blue one, from his pocket and puts it on the table.*

ELIS. My mother!

LINDKVIST. Look. Now I'm balancing *this* paper on the edge—it's certainly blue—but it's not stamped yet.

ELIS. Almighty God, my Mother! It's happening all over again.

LINDKVIST. Yes, my young lover of justice, everything happens all over again. That's how it is. *Pause.* If I were now to ask myself this question: "You, Andrew John Lindkvist, born in poverty and brought up in toil and privation, is it right that you, in your old age, should deprive yourself and your children—mark that, your children—of the means of support which you by your industry, foresight, and self-denial—mark that, self-denial—have saved up, farthing by farthing? What are you to do, Andrew John Lindkvist, if you want to be just? You robbed nobody, yet if you object to having been robbed—you'll have to leave town. Nobody will have anything to do with the hardhearted man who demanded his own back." *Pause.* But you see, there is a charity which runs counter to the law and is above it . . . That is mercy.

ELIS. You're right. Take everything. It belongs to you.

LINDKVIST. I have the right, but I dare not exercise it.

ELIS. I will think of your children and not complain.

LINDKVIST, *putting the paper away in his coat pocket.* Good, then we'll put this blue paper back too. Now, we'll go a step further.

ELIS. Excuse me, do they really mean to prosecute my mother?

LINDKVIST. We will go a step further first. So you don't know
the Governor personally?

ELIS. No, and don't want to.

LINDKVIST, *taking the blue paper out again and waving it.*
Come, come! You see, in their young days, the Governor
and your father were friends, and he would like to make
your acquaintance. Everything happens again, everything.
Won't you call on him?

ELIS. No!

LINDKVIST. The Governor . . .

ELIS, *rising impatiently.* Can't we talk about something else?

LINDKVIST. You must be polite to me. I'm defenceless—you
have public opinion on your side and I have nothing but—
justice. What have you got against the Governor? He
doesn't like bicycles and working people's colleges—that's
one of his little eccentricities. We needn't exactly admire
people's eccentricities, but we can get over them, get over
them and keep to essentials. We're all human, and in life's
crises we must take one another as we are with all our
faults and weaknesses—swallow each other neck and crop.
Go to the Governor!

ELIS. Never.

LINDKVIST. Is that the kind of man you are?

ELIS. Yes, that's the kind.

LINDKVIST, *rising and walking across the room, his galoshes
swishing and waving the blue paper.* Worse and worse!
. . . I'll begin again from the other end . . . A re-
vengeful person intends to bring a charge against your
mother. This you can prevent.

ELIS. How?

LINDKVIST. By going to the Governor.

ELIS. No!

LINDKVIST, *taking hold of* ELIS *by the shoulders.* Then you are
the most contemptible creature I've ever met in my life.
Now I shall go to your mother.

ELIS. No, don't do that.

LINDKVIST. Then will you go to the Governor?

ELIS, *murmurs.* Yes.

LINDKVIST. Say that again, louder.

ELIS. Yes.

LINDKVIST. Then that's settled. *Puts down the blue paper beside* ELIS. There's that paper. ELIS *takes the paper without reading it.* Now we come to number two, which *was* number one. Shall we sit down? *They sit as before.* You see, if only we go to meet each other, the road is just half as long. Number two—my claim on your household effects . . . Have no illusions, for I neither can nor will give away what is the property of my family. I shall extort my claim to the last farthing.

ELIS. I understand that.

LINDKVIST, *sharply.* Oh you understand, do you?

ELIS. I didn't mean to be offensive.

LINDKVIST. No. I quite realise that. *He puts on his spectacles and glares at* ELIS. Beast, angry beast, swish, swish! And the cornelian charms the colour of flesh. The giant from the Skinflint Mountain who doesn't eat children, only frightens them. I'll frighten you, I will, I'll frighten you out of your wits. I'll have the value of every stick of furniture. The inventory's here in my pocket, and if a single item is missing, you'll be clapped into gaol where the sun never shines—nor Cassiopaea. Yes, I can eat children and widows too when I'm provoked. Public opinion? Bah! I'll just move to another town, that's all. ELIS *is speechless.* You had a friend called Peter. Peter Holmblad. He was a linguist—and your pupil in languages. But you wanted to set him up as a sort of prophet . . . Very well, Peter denied you. And the cock crew twice. Isn't that so? ELIS *is silent.* You can't rely on human nature, any more than on the nature of matter or of thought. Peter *was* faithless, I don't deny it—and I don't defend him. Not on that point. But the human heart is fathomless—it has layers of gold—and dross. Peter was a faithless friend, but a friend all the same.

ELIS. A faithless one.

LINDKVIST. A faithless one, yes. But a friend none the less. Unknown to you this faithless friend has done you a great service.

ELIS. That too!

LINDKVIST. Everything happens again, everything.

ELIS. Everything evil, yes. And good is rewarded with evil.

LINDKVIST. Not always. The good comes again too, believe me.

ELIS. I suppose I must believe you, or else you'll torture the life out of me.

LINDKVIST. Not the life, but the pride and wickedness I shall squeeze out of you.

ELIS. Go on then.

LINDKVIST. Peter has done you a service, I tell you.

ELIS. I don't want any services from that fellow.

LINDKVIST. So we're back there, are we? Now listen to this. Through the intervention of your friend Peter, the Governor has been induced to intercede for your mother. So you must write a letter to Peter and thank him. Promise you will.

ELIS. No. To anyone else in the world, but not to him.

LINDKVIST, *pouncing on him.* Then I must squeeze you some more. You've got some money in the bank, haven't you?

ELIS. What's that got to do with you? I'm not responsible for my father's debts, am I?

LINDKVIST. Aren't you? Aren't you? Weren't you here eating and drinking while my children's money was being squandered in this house? Answer me that.

ELIS. I can't deny it.

LINDKVIST. And since the furniture does not suffice to pay the debt, you will now make out a cheque for the balance— you know the amount.

ELIS, *devastated.* That too!

LINDKVIST. That too. Be so good as to write it. ELIS *rises, takes out his cheque book, and sits at the writing-table.* Make it payable to self or bearer.

ELIS. It won't be enough anyhow.

LINDKVIST. Then you must borrow the rest . . . every farthing of it.

ELIS, *handing the cheque to* LINDKVIST. There you are. This is
all I possess. It is my summer and my bride. I have no
more to give.

LINDKVIST. Then, as I say, you must go and borrow it.

ELIS. I can't do that.

LINDKVIST. Then you must find a guarantor.

ELIS. No one will guarantee a Heyst.

LINDKVIST. I shall now, as my ultimatum, present you with
two alternatives—thank Peter or pay up.

ELIS. I'll have nothing to do with Peter.

LINDKVIST. Then you're the most contemptible creature I've
ever known. By a simple act of courtesy you can save
your mother's home and your own marriage, and you
won't do it. There must be some reason you won't admit.
Why do you hate Peter?

ELIS. Kill me, but don't torture me any more.

LINDKVIST. You're jealous. So that's the situation. *Walks about
the room, thinking.* Have you read today's paper?

ELIS. Yes, worse luck.

LINDKVIST. All of it?

ELIS. No, not all.

LINDKVIST. I see . . . Then . . . er . . . perhaps you don't
know that Peter has announced his engagement?

ELIS, *startled.* I didn't know that.

LINDKVIST. And who to? Can you guess?

ELIS. I . . .

LINDKVIST. He is engaged to Miss Alice. It was arranged at a
certain concert last night—with the aid of your fiancée.

ELIS. Then why all this secrecy?

LINDKVIST. Haven't two young people the right to keep the
secrets of their hearts from you?

ELIS. And I had to suffer this agony for their happiness?

LINDKVIST. Yes. And these have suffered to prepare the way
for *your* happiness—your mother, your father, your sweetheart, your sister. Sit down. I want to tell you a story.
Quite a short one. ELIS *sits reluctantly. Outside the
weather is growing steadily brighter.* It was about forty
years ago. I came to town to look for a job. Young, alone,
unknown. I had next to no money, and it was a dark night.
As I knew of no cheap lodging, I asked the passers-by, but
no one would tell me. When I was absolutely desperate, a
man came up to me and asked why I was weeping—I
was actually in tears. I told him my predicament. Then he
turned aside from his own way, took me to a lodging and
comforted me with kind words. Just as I was going in, a
shop door was flung open and a pane of glass broke
against my elbow. The furious shopkeeper grabbed hold
of me and said I must pay or he'd call the police. Imagine
my despair. A night on the street before me. My unknown
benefactor, who had seen what happened, took the
trouble of calling the police himself—and saved me. That
man was your father. So—everything happens again, the
good things too. For your father's sake I have renounced
my claim. So take this paper—*hands him the first white
paper*—and keep your cheque. *Rising as* ELIS *struggles
with his emotions.* As you find it difficult to say thank
you, I'll take my leave, specially as I find it painful to be
thanked. *As he reaches the street door.* Instead, go in
now to your mother and set her mind at rest. *Waves* ELIS
back as he tries to approach him. Go on. ELIS *rushes into
the kitchen. Pause. As* LINDKVIST *turns to go, the front
door is quietly opened by* ELEANORA *and* BENJAMIN. *Seeing* LINDKVIST *they start back in alarm.* Well, youngsters,
come along in. Don't be frightened. *They enter.* Do you
know who I am? *Growls.* I'm the giant of the Skinflint
Mountain, who frightens children. Yum, yum, yum! *In
his natural voice.* But I'm not really so dangerous. Come
here, Eleanora. *Takes her head between his hands and
looks into her eyes.* You have your father's good eyes, and
he was a good man—although weak. *Kisses her on the
forehead.* That's how it was.

ELEANORA. Oh, he's speaking well of Father! Can anyone think well of him?

LINDKVIST. I can. Ask your brother Elis.

ELEANORA. Then you can't want to hurt us.

LINDKVIST. No, no, dear child.

ELEANORA. Then help us!

LINDKVIST. Child, I can't help your father to escape his punishment. *Looking kindly at* BENJAMIN. Nor Benjamin to get through his Latin examination. But the other help has already been given. Life won't give us everything—and nothing gratis. So you must help me too. Will you?

ELEANORA. How can I, who have nothing, help you?

LINDKVIST. What's the date today? Look and see.

ELEANORA, *taking down the calendar.* It's the sixteenth.

LINDKVIST. Very well. Before the twentieth you must get your brother to call on the Governor and to write a letter to Peter.

ELEANORA. Is that all?

LINDKVIST. Oh, child! But if he doesn't do those things, the giant will come again with his yum, yum, yum!

ELEANORA. Why does the giant come and frighten children?

LINDKVIST. To make 'em good.

ELEANORA. Yes, of course. And he's quite right. *Rubs her cheek against the sleeve of his coat.* Thank you, kind giant.

BENJAMIN. You ought to call him Mr. Lindkvist, you know.

ELEANORA. Oh no, that's far too ordinary.

LINDKVIST. Well—goodbye, children. Now you can throw the birch on the fire.

ELEANORA *goes towards the birch then stops and smiles.*

ELEANORA. No, it had better stay there—children are so forgetful.

LINDKVIST, *gently.* How well you know children, little one. *The children show him out and wave as he goes down the street.*

ELEANORA. Oh, Benjamin, just think, we shall be able to go

to the country! In two months. Oh, may they pass quickly!
*She tears the sheets off the calendar and strews them in
the sunlight now streaming into the room.* KRISTINA *enters
and stands watching.* Look how the days are passing!
April . . . May . . . June . . . And the sun is shining
on them all—see? *She pulls him to the window and stands
gazing up.* Now you must thank God for helping us to get
to the country.

BENJAMIN, *shyly.* Can't I say it silently?

ELIS *and* MRS. HEYST *come quietly in from the kitchen.*
ELIS *and* KRISTINA *look tenderly at one another.*

ELEANORA. Yes, you can say it silently, for now the clouds
have lifted, and we can be heard up there.

For a moment all are motionless, then KRISTINA *and* ELIS
*move towards each other, but the curtain falls before
they meet.*

A DREAM PLAY

by

AUGUST STRINDBERG

INTRODUCTION

A DREAM PLAY was begun in 1901 shortly after Strindberg's marriage at the age of fifty-two to his third wife,
the young Norwegian actress Harriet Bosse.

He had emerged now from the long "Inferno" period in
which he had wrestled with his soul and written no plays,
only scientific and alchemical treatises. He had been born
again into a period of "new productivity, with faith, hope
and charity regained—and absolute conviction," and as he
had changed, so must his drama, for Strindberg's life and
writings are inseparable. In earlier years, although he was
"born with a nostalgia for heaven," and had clairvoyant
gifts, he chose materialism and forced himself to explain
everything by natural phenomena. The last brilliant fruits
of that phase were his two Naturalist plays THE FATHER
and MISS JULIE, although even then his creation was larger
than life. Now, convinced at last of the truth of his poetic
vision, he invited spirits to play upon his stage and ig-
nored every restricting convention.

After choosing Harriet Bosse to play The Lady in TO
DAMASCUS, the first of his visionary plays, a rôle for which
she was really too young, Strindberg, at the time of their
betrothal, designed the part of Eleanora in EASTER specially for her. Indra's Daughter, the heavenly visitor in A
DREAM PLAY is, Strindberg tells us, Eleanora grown up.
The same pity for human suffering and the same horror
of ugliness and sin are found in both characters, but
whereas Eleanora has vicarious experience of the joys
and sorrows of other people, the Daughter of Indra must
live through these things herself, in order to achieve a
wider comprehension and a deeper compassion.

In spite of his marriage and the fact that Harriet Bosse
shortly bore him a child—parenthood was to him the most
moving of all human experiences—when Strindberg wrote
A DREAM PLAY he was not happy. Although he was no
longer persecuted by invisible enemies, his ordeal had left
him frail and more sensitive even than before. His wife

often went away for weeks at a time; he felt the gulf of age between them, and theatre too, which they both loved so well, conspired to take her from him. A terrible anticipation of new loneliness hung over him, aggravated by fear of losing this child as, in two divorces, he had lost the others. He often felt as if his whole life were a dream, in which everything that had happened was happening again; the idea grew into an obsession, and from it came the seed of this play.

His first title for it was PRISONERS, since it was clear to him that this world which looked so fair was either a prison or a lunatic asylum, then he changed the name to ALLEY DRAMA, after the alley leading to the stage door of the theatre in Stockholm where, night after night, he had waited for Harriet Bosse, and where his fancy had been struck by a mysterious door with an airhole shaped like a four-leafed clover. In this play that door conceals the secret of existence, which turns out to be nothing, since out of nothing God made life. His next title was THE GROWING CASTLE, suggested by the domed roof of the cavalry barracks which he could see from the window of his study, flashing gold above the trees. Everything struggled upwards away from earth's filth, so why not a castle too?

Finally he brought all these ideas together and called the work A DREAM PLAY, explaining in a foreword that it continued the experiment of TO DAMASCUS in reproducing the disconnected yet apparently logical form of a dream. Far ahead of his time, he explored the workings of the subconscious during sleep and saw how the personality of the single dreamer sometimes split into many seemingly different characters.

To the Daughter of Indra (Harriet Bosse's dark beauty influenced the choice this time of a Hindu goddess), Strindberg gave his own agony at being earth-bound, chained within life's limitations. The Officer undergoes Strindberg's own punishment of being endlessly sent back to school to learn the same lessons again; to the Officer too is given his eternal waiting for the perfect love which never came. Then there is the Lawyer, the young idealist, trapped and broken and mirroring in his own ugliness the evil and suffering of the world, and finally the Poet appears, the man who is closest to the heavens, who takes mud-baths to harden his skin, and whose imperfect words, telling of man's plight, the Daughter of Indra promises to interpret to the Gods. All these characters, and that too of the Quarantine Master, wearing a mask so as to appear a shade blacker than he really is, are facets of the dreamer—of Strindberg himself.

There is more poetry both in form and language in A DREAM PLAY than in TO DAMASCUS, and it is filled with imagery. Nor are the images always tormented. Although Kristin pastes man up in his prison and the Lawyer twists the squeaking door handle, which is at the same time the heart of his love, although the rich are tortured on the hell-racks of their gymnasium, Earth itself stretches heavenward, the Castle grows up out of the manure, the giant hollyhocks climb to the light, and man himself ascends by the ladder of suffering. There is much sadness in the play, but no despair. As the Daughter of Indra returns to heaven, the Castle blazes up in an all-purging fire, and although the faces of mankind still mirror agony, the bud on the summit of the Castle, a symbol of faith, bursts at last into a gigantic chrysanthemum. Strindberg believed that if the old pattern were destroyed, a new world would rise, and the golden age of the poet and the dreamer yet be reached.

A DREAM PLAY was first produced in Stockholm in 1907 with Harriet Bosse, now divorced from Strindberg but still his friend, creating the part of Indra's Daughter. Strindberg considered that the Director, Ranft, was not daring enough in his production. In any case the play, called by the critics an interesting experiment, closed after twelve performances.

Since then this play has been little performed except in Germany, until recently Sweden's leading director, Olaf Molander, started a Strindberg renaissance. He has directed several productions of A DREAM PLAY in Scandinavia, each different. To have seen one of these, and to have worked on the London broadcast of my earlier translation, has confirmed my belief that this, in spite of the unevenness which prevents it from being great, is a wonderful piece of work. Had they been written later, A DREAM PLAY, and still more THE GHOST SONATA, might have been called surrealist, but however one classifies these plays, it is clear that Strindberg's dramatic vision was in advance of his own times and is still ahead of ours. He should never be restricted by the convention of any period, and for this reason his work, specially his late poetic drama, invites imaginative and adventurous interpretation.

In Molander's productions and, I feel sure, in earlier ones, no visual resemblance was made between the Officer, the Lawyer, and the Poet; but as these three characters are all facets of one Dreamer I think they should not be quite unlike. The Poet, by Swedish convention, usually resembles Strindberg. The Director of the B.B.C. production, interested in the link between the characters, gave all three parts to one actor, but I myself think this was going too far. Strindberg wrote three characters, not one, although they are seldom on the stage together. Incidentally a number of other characters may be doubled with good effect.

The theme line of the play: "Det är synd om människorna," repeated many times by Indra's Daughter, is exceedingly difficult to translate. "Mankind is pitiable," or "pitiful," "Human beings are to be pitied," are all fair versions of the Swedish, but there is also a suggestion of "it's a shame about human beings." The Daughter, however, is dominated by compassion not contempt, and whenever she says this line one must feel the link between her and her heavenly father Indra, who has sent her down to earth to find out if human complaint is justified. Strindberg never once alters the Daughter's phrase, but after long consideration I have made an occasional slight variation in English, in order that the meaning may be more exact.

Another translation problem is the term: "Alla Rätttänkande," the people who refuse the Lawyer his laurels because he has defended the poor, who fight all reform, and who, the Poet tells the Daughter, crucified the Saviour because He came to liberate. Literally, of course, the term means "right-thinking," but as this does not work easily into the English text, in this version I have used "Righteous," not in the biblical sense, but as having nowadays a flavour "self-righteous" and implying the respectable citizen.

Strindberg's stage directions, even for taking characters on or off the stage, are erratic, and where I have judged necessary I have added a direction, such additions marked by square brackets. I have also occasionally omitted directions such as "Left" or "Right," when they restrict rather than aid visual imagination. Writing in the era of painted backcloths and drops, Strindberg uses these words in his sets. I have substituted "background," and written "the scene changes," rather than "the backdrop rises," as more undated terms. I have also sometimes altered the order of stage directions to make them clearer, but in every other way this text follows the Swedish as closely as possible.

The play needs skilful cutting for production; the Mediterranean scene, for instance, is completely out of date, and no translation can prevent the young lover's song in the Foulstrand scene from tedious sentimentality. Arranging the play for the theatre is not the translator's job but the director's, but I find myself dreaming this fascinating ever-changing dream upon the stage, and I have had both audience and reader in mind while working on the text. A realistic presentation is not only very costly but very cumbersome. What an opportunity for an ingenious use of light and modern methods and materials, and what a film the play would make!

E. S.

AUTHOR'S NOTE

In this dream play, as in his former dream play TO DAMASCUS, the Author has sought to reproduce the disconnected but apparently logical form of a dream. Anything can happen; everything is possible and probable. Time and space do not exist; on a slight groundwork of reality, imagination spins and weaves new patterns made up of memories, experiences, unfettered fancies, absurdities and improvisations.

The characters are split, double and multiply; they evaporate, crystallise, scatter and converge. But a single consciousness holds sway over them all—that of the dreamer. For him there are no secrets, no incongruities, no scruples and no law. He neither condemns nor acquits, but only relates, and since on the whole, there is more pain than pleasure in the dream, a tone of melancholy, and of compassion for all living things, runs through the swaying narrative. Sleep, the liberator, often appears as a torturer, but when the pain is at its worst, the sufferer awakes—and is thus reconciled with reality. For however agonising real life may be, at this moment, compared with the tormenting dream, it is a joy.

Dramatis Personæ*

(*The voice of*) FATHER INDRA
INDRA'S DAUGHTER
THE GLAZIER
THE OFFICER
THE FATHER
THE MOTHER
LINA
THE DOORKEEPER
THE BILLSTICKER
THE PROMPTER
THE POLICEMAN
THE LAWYER
THE DEAN OF PHILOSOPHY
THE DEAN OF THEOLOGY
THE DEAN OF MEDICINE
THE DEAN OF LAW
THE CHANCELLOR
KRISTIN
THE QUARANTINE MASTER
THE ELDERLY FOP
THE COQUETTE
THE FRIEND
THE POET
HE
SHE (*doubles with Victoria's voice*)
THE PENSIONER
UGLY EDITH
EDITH'S MOTHER
THE NAVAL OFFICER

*There is no list of characters in the original. E. S.

ALICE

THE SCHOOLMASTER

NILS

THE HUSBAND

THE WIFE

THE BLIND MAN

1ST COAL HEAVER

2ND COAL HEAVER

THE GENTLEMAN

THE LADY

SINGERS AND DANCERS (*Members of the Opera Company*)

CLERKS, GRADUATES, MAIDS, SCHOOLBOYS,

CHILDREN, CREW, RIGHTEOUS PEOPLE.

PROLOGUE

*An impression of clouds, crumbling cliffs, ruins of castles
and fortresses.*
*The constellations Leo, Virgo and Libra are seen, with
the planet Jupiter shining brightly among them.*
On the highest cloud-peak stands THE DAUGHTER OF
INDRA. INDRA'S VOICE *is heard from above.*

INDRA'S VOICE. *Where art thou, Daughter?*

DAUGHTER. *Here, Father, here!*

INDRA'S VOICE. *Thou hast strayed, my child.*
Take heed, thou sinkest.
How cam'st thou here?

DAUGHTER. *Borne on a cloud, I followed the lightning's
blazing trail from the ethereal heights.*
But the cloud sank, and still is falling.
*Tell me, great Father Indra, to what region
am I come? The air's so dense, so hard to breathe.*

INDRA'S VOICE. *Leaving the second world thou camest to the
third.*
*From Cuora, Star of the Morning,
Far art thou come and enterest
Earth's atmosphere. Mark there
The Sun's Seventh House that's called the Scales.
The Morning Star is at the autumn weighing,
When day and night are equal.*

DAUGHTER. *Thou speak'st of Earth. Is that the dark
and heavy world the moon lights up?*

INDRA'S VOICE. *It is the darkest and the heaviest
of all the spheres that swing in space.*

DAUGHTER. *Does not the sun shine there?*

INDRA'S VOICE. *It shines, but not unceasingly.*

DAUGHTER. *Now the clouds part, and I can see . . .*

INDRA'S VOICE. *What see'st thou, child?*

DAUGHTER. *I see . . . that Earth is fair . . . It has green woods,*
blue waters, white mountains, yellow fields.

INDRA'S VOICE. *Yes, it is fair, as all that Brahma shaped,*
yet in the dawn of time
was fairer still. Then came a change,
a shifting of the orbit, maybe of more.
Revolt followed by crime which had to be suppressed.

DAUGHTER. *Now I hear sounds arising . . .*
What kind of creatures dwell down there?

INDRA'S VOICE. *Go down and see. The Creator's children I would not decry,*
but it's their language that thou hearest.

DAUGHTER. *It sounds as if . . . it has no cheerful ring.*

INDRA'S VOICE. *So I believe. Their mother-tongue*
is called Complaint. Truly a discontented,
thankless race is this of Earth.

DAUGHTER. *Ah, say not so! Now I hear shouts of joy,*
and blare and boom. I see the lightning flash.
Now bells are pealing and the fires are lit.
A thousand thousand voices rise,
singing their praise and thanks to heaven.
Pause.

Thy judgment is too hard on them, my Father.

INDRA. *Descend and see, and hear, then come again*
and tell me if their lamentations
and complaint are justified.

DAUGHTER. *So be it. I descend. Come with me, Father!*

INDRA. *No. I cannot breathe their air.*

DAUGHTER. *Now the cloud sinks. It's growing dense. I suffocate!*
This is not air, but smoke and water that I breathe,
so heavy that it drags me down and down.
And now I clearly feel its reeling!
This third is surely not the highest world.

INDRA. *Neither the highest, truly, nor the lowest.*
It is called Dust, and whirls with all the rest,

And so at times its people, struck with dizziness,
live on the borderline of folly and insanity . . .
Courage, my child, for this is but a test!

DAUGHTER, *on her knees as the cloud descends.*
I am sinking!

[*The curtain rises on* THE GROWING CASTLE.]

The background shows a forest of giant hollyhocks in
bloom: white, pink, crimson, sulphur-yellow and violet.
Above this rises the gilded roof of a castle with a flower-
bud crowning its summit. Under the walls of the castle
lie heaps of straw and stable-muck.
On each side of the stage are stylised representations
of interiors, architecture and landscape which remain
unchanged throughout the play.

The GLAZIER *and the* DAUGHTER *enter together.*

DAUGHTER. The castle keeps on growing up out of the earth.
Do you see how it has grown since last year?

GLAZIER, *to himself.* I've never seen that castle before—and
I've never heard of a castle growing . . . but . . . *to*
the DAUGHTER *with conviction.* Yes, it's grown six feet, but
that's because they've manured it. And if you look carefully, you'll see it's put out a wing on the sunny side.

DAUGHTER. Ought it not to blossom soon? We are already
halfway through the summer.

GLAZIER. Don't you see the flower up there?

DAUGHTER, *joyfully.* Yes, I see it. Father, tell me something.
Why do flowers grow out of dirt?

GLAZIER. They don't like the dirt, so they shoot up as fast as
they can into the light—to blossom and to die.

DAUGHTER. Do you know who lives in the castle?

GLAZIER. I used to know, but I've forgotten.

DAUGHTER. I believe there is a prisoner inside, waiting for me
to set him free.

GLAZIER. What will you get if you do?

DAUGHTER. Ones does not bargain about what one has to do.
Let us go into the castle.

GLAZIER. Very well, we will.

> *They go towards the background which slowly vanishes to the sides, disclosing a simple bare room with a table and a few chairs. A screen cuts the stage in two [the other half unlighted].* A YOUNG OFFICER *in an unconventional modern uniform sits rocking his chair and striking the table with his sword.*

> [*The* DAUGHTER *and the* GLAZIER *enter.*]

> *She goes up to the* OFFICER *and gently takes the sword from his hands.*

DAUGHTER. No, no, you mustn't do that.

OFFICER. Please, Agnes, let me keep my sword.

DAUGHTER. But you are cutting the table to pieces. *To the* GLAZIER. Father, you go down to the harness room and put in that window pane, and we will meet later.

> *Exit* GLAZIER.

DAUGHTER. You are a prisoner in your own room. I have come to set you free.

OFFICER. I have been waiting for this, but I wasn't sure you would want to.

DAUGHTER. The castle is strong—it has seven walls—but it shall be done. Do you want to be set free—or not?

OFFICER. To tell the truth, I don't know. Either way I'll suffer. Every joy has to be paid for twice over with sorrow. It's wretched here, but I'd have to endure three times the agony for the joys of freedom . . . Agnes, I'll bear it, if only I may see you.

DAUGHTER. What do you see in me?

OFFICER. The beautiful, which is the harmony of the universe. There are lines in your form which I have only found in the movement of the stars, in the melody of strings, in the vibrations of light. You are a child of heaven.

DAUGHTER. So are you.

OFFICER. Then why do I have to groom horses, clean stables and have the muck removed?

DAUGHTER. So that you may long to get away.

OFFICER. I do. But it's so hard to pull oneself out of it all.

DAUGHTER. It is one's duty to seek freedom in the light.

OFFICER. Duty? Life has not done its duty by me.

DAUGHTER. You feel wronged by life?

OFFICER. Yes. It has been unjust. . . .

Voices are now heard from behind the dividing screen, which is drawn aside [as the lights go up on the other set: a homely living-room]. The OFFICER *and the* DAUGHTER *stand watching, gestures and expression held. The* MOTHER, *an invalid, sits at a table. In front of her is a lighted candle, which from time to time she trims with snuffers. On the table are piles of new underclothing, which she is marking with a quill pen. Beyond is a brown cupboard.*

The FATHER *brings her a silk shawl.*

FATHER, *gently.* I have brought you this.

MOTHER. What use is a silk shawl to me, my dear, when I am going to die so soon?

FATHER. You believe what the doctor says?

MOTHER. What he says too, but most of all I believe the voice that speaks within me.

FATHER, *sorrowfully.* Then it really is grave . . . And you are thinking of your children, first and last.

MOTHER. They were my life, my justification, my happiness, and my sorrow.

FATHER. Kristina, forgive me . . . for everything.

MOTHER. For what? Ah, my dear, forgive *me!* We have both hurt each other. Why, we don't know. We could not do otherwise . . . However, here is the children's new linen. See that they change twice a week—on Wednesdays and Sundays, and that Louisa washes them—all over . . . Are you going out?

FATHER. I have to go to the school at eleven.

MOTHER. Before you go ask Alfred to come.

FATHER, *pointing to the* OFFICER. But, dear heart, he is here.

MOTHER. My sight must be going too . . . Yes, it's getting so dark. *Snuffs candle.* Alfred, come!

The FATHER goes out through the middle of the wall, nodding goodbye. The OFFICER moves forward to the MOTHER.

MOTHER. Who is that girl?

OFFICER, *whispering.* That's Agnes.

MOTHER. Oh, is it Agnes? Do you know what they are saying? That she is the daughter of the God Indra, who begged to come down to Earth so as to know what it is really like for human beings. But don't say anything.

OFFICER. She *is* a child of the Gods.

MOTHER, *raising her voice.* Alfred, my son, I shall soon be leaving you and your brothers and sisters. I want to say one thing—for you to remember all your life.

OFFICER, *sadly.* What is it, Mother?

MOTHER. Only one thing: never quarrel with God.

OFFICER. What do you mean, Mother?

MOTHER. You must not go on feeling you have been wronged by life.

OFFICER. But I've been treated so unjustly.

MOTHER. You're still harping on the time you were unjustly punished for taking that money which was afterwards found.

OFFICER. Yes. That piece of injustice gave a twist to the whole of my life.

MOTHER. I see. Well now, you just go over to that cupboard . . .

OFFICER, *ashamed.* So you know about that. The . . .

MOTHER. "The Swiss Family Robinson" which . . .

OFFICER. Don't say any more . . .

MOTHER. Which your brother was punished for . . . when it was *you* who had torn it to pieces and hidden it.

OFFICER. Think of that cupboard still being there after twenty years. We have moved so many times—and my mother died ten years ago.

MOTHER. Yes. What of it? You are always questioning everything, and so spoiling the best of life for yourself . . .
Ah, here's Lina!

Enter LINA.

LINA. Thank you very much all the same, Ma'am, but I can't
go to the christening.

MOTHER. Why not, child?

LINA. I've got nothing to wear.

MOTHER. You can borrow this shawl of mine.

LINA. Oh no, Ma'am, you're very kind, but that would never
do.

MOTHER. I can't see why not. I shan't be going to any more
parties.

OFFICER. What will Father say? After all, it's a present from
him.

MOTHER. What small minds!

FATHER, *putting his head in.* Are you going to lend my present
to the maid?

MOTHER. Don't talk like that! Remember I was in service
once myself. Why should you hurt an innocent girl?

FATHER. Why should you hurt me, your husband?

MOTHER. Ah, this life! If you do something good, someone
else is sure to think it bad; if you are kind to one person,
you're sure to harm another. Ah, this life!

*She snuffs the candle so that it goes out. The room grows
dark and the screen is drawn forward again.*

DAUGHTER. Human beings are to be pitied.

OFFICER. Do you think so?

DAUGHTER. Yes, life is hard. But love conquers everything.
Come and see.

They withdraw and the background disappears. The
OFFICER *vanishes and the* DAUGHTER *comes forward alone.*

*The new scene shows an old derelict wall. In the middle
of the wall a gate opens on an alley leading to a green
plot where a giant blue monkshood is growing. To the
left of the gate is the door-window of the Stage Door-*

keeper's lodge. The Stage Doorkeeper is sitting with a grey shawl over her head and shoulders, crocheting a star-patterned coverlet. On the right is an announcement-board which the BILLSTICKER *is washing. Near him is a fishnet with a green handle and a green fish box. Further right the cupboard [from the previous set] has become a door with an air-hole shaped like a four-leafed clover. To the left is a small lime tree with a coal-black stem and a few pale green leaves.*

The DAUGHTER *goes up to the* DOORKEEPER.

DAUGHTER. Isn't the star coverlet finished yet?

DOORKEEPER. No, my dear. Twenty-six years is nothing for such a piece of work.

DAUGHTER. And your sweetheart never came back?

DOORKEEPER. No, but it wasn't his fault. He *had* to take himself off, poor fellow. That was thirty years ago.

DAUGHTER, *to* BILLSTICKER. She was in the ballet, wasn't she? Here—at the Opera.

BILLSTICKER. She was the prima ballerina, but when *he* went away, it seems he took her dancing with him . . . so she never got any more parts.

DAUGHTER. All complain—with their eyes, and with their voices too.

BILLSTICKER. I haven't much to complain of—not now I've got my net and a green fish box.

DAUGHTER. Does that make you happy?

BILLSTICKER. Yes, very happy. That was my dream when I was little, and now it's come true. I'm all of fifty now, you know.

DAUGHTER. Fifty years for a fishnet and a box!

BILLSTICKER. A *green* box, a *green* one . . .

DAUGHTER, *to* DOORKEEPER. Let me have that shawl now, and I'll sit here and watch the children of men. But you must stand behind and tell me about them.

The DAUGHTER *puts on the shawl and sits down by the gate.*

DOORKEEPER. This is the last day of the Opera season. They hear now if they've been engaged for the next.

DAUGHTER. And those who have not?

DOORKEEPER. Lord Jesus, what a scene! I always pull my shawl over my head.

DAUGHTER. Poor things!

DOORKEEPER. Look, here's one coming. She's not been engaged. See how she's crying!

The SINGER *rushes in from the right and goes through the gate with her handkerchief to her eyes. She pauses a moment in the alley beyond and leans her head against the wall, then goes quickly out.*

DAUGHTER. Human beings are to be pitied.

DOORKEEPER. But here comes one who seems happy enough.

The OFFICER *comes down the alley, wearing a frock-coat and top hat. He carries a bouquet of roses and looks radiantly happy.*

DOORKEEPER. He's going to marry Miss Victoria.

OFFICER, *downstage, looks up and sings.* Victoria!

DOORKEEPER. The young lady will be down in a minute.

WOMAN'S VOICE, *from above, sings.* I am here!

OFFICER, *pacing.* Well, I am waiting.

DAUGHTER. Don't you know me?

OFFICER. No, I know only one woman—Victoria! Seven years I have come here to wait for her—at noon when the sun reaches the chimneys, and in the evening as darkness falls. Look at the paving. See? Worn by the steps of the faithful lover? Hurrah! She is mine. *Sings.* Victoria! *No answer.* Well, she's dressing now. *To the* BILLSTICKER. Ah, a fishnet I see! Everyone here at the Opera is crazy about fishnets—or rather about fish. Dumb fish—because they cannot sing . . . What does a thing like that cost?

BILLSTICKER. It's rather dear.

OFFICER, *sings.* Victoria! . . . *Shakes the lime tree.* Look, it's budding again! For the eighth time. *Sings.* Victoria!

. . . Now she's doing her hair . . . *To* DAUGHTER. Madam, kindly allow me to go up and fetch my bride.

DOORKEEPER. Nobody's to go on the stage.

OFFICER. Seven years I've walked up and down here. Seven times three hundred and sixty-five I make two thousand five hundred and fifty-five. *Stops and pokes the door with the clover-shaped hole.* Then this door I've seen two thousand five hundred and fifty-five times and I still don't know where it leads to. And this clover leaf to let in the light. Who does it let the light in for? Is anyone inside? Does anybody live there?

DOORKEEPER. I don't know. I've never seen it open.

OFFICER. It looks like a larder door I saw when I was four years old, when I went out one Sunday afternoon with the maid—to see another family and other maids. But I only got as far as the kitchen, where I sat between the water barrel and the salt tub. I've seen so many kitchens in my time, and the larders are always in the passage, with round holes and a clover leaf in the door. But the Opera can't have a larder as it hasn't got a kitchen. *Sings.* Victoria! *To* DAUGHTER. Excuse me, Madam, she can't leave by any other way, can she?

DOORKEEPER. No, there is no other way.

OFFICER. Good. Then I'm bound to meet her.

Members of the Opera Company swarm out of the building, scrutinised by the OFFICER. *They go out by the gate.*

She's sure to come. *To* DAUGHTER. Madam, that blue monkshood out there—I saw it when I was a child. Is it the same one? I remember it in a rectory garden when I was seven—with two doves, blue doves, under the hood. Then a bee came and went into the hood, and I thought: "Now I've got you," so I grabbed the flower, but the bee stung through it, and I burst into tears. However, the rector's wife came and put moist earth on it—and then we had wild strawberries and milk for supper . . . I believe it's growing dark already. Where are you off to, Billsticker?

BILLSTICKER. Home to my supper.

[*Exit with fishnet and box.*]

OFFICER, *rubbing his eyes*. Supper? At this time of day? . . .
To DAUGHTER. Excuse me, may I just step inside a moment and telephone to the Growing Castle?

DAUGHTER. What do you want to say to them?

OFFICER. I want to tell the glazier to put in the double windows. It will be winter soon and I'm so dreadfully cold.
The OFFICER *goes into the* DOORKEEPER's *Lodge.*

DAUGHTER. Who is Miss Victoria?

DOORKEEPER. She is his love.

DAUGHTER. A true answer. What she is to us or others doesn't
matter to him. Only what she is to *him*, that's what she *is*.
It grows dark suddenly.

DOORKEEPER, *lighting the lantern*. Dusk falls quickly today.

DAUGHTER. To the gods a year is as a minute.

DOORKEEPER. While to human beings a minute may be as long
as a year.
The OFFICER *comes out again. He looks shabbier, and
the roses are withered.*

OFFICER. Hasn't she come yet?

DOORKEEPER. No.

OFFICER. She's sure to come. She'll come. *Paces up and down.*
But all the same . . . perhaps it would be wiser to can-
cel that luncheon . . . as it's now evening. Yes, that's
what I'll do. *Goes in and telephones.*

DOORKEEPER. *To* DAUGHTER. May I have my shawl now?

DAUGHTER. No, my friend. You rest and I'll take your place,
because I want to know about human beings and life—
to find out if it really is as hard as they say.

DOORKEEPER. But you don't get any sleep on this job. Never
any sleep, night or day.

DAUGHTER. No sleep at night?

DOORKEEPER. Well, if you can get any with the bell wire on

your arm, because the night watchmen go up on the
stage and are changed every three hours . . .

DAUGHTER. That must be torture.

DOORKEEPER. So you think, but we others are glad enough
to get such a job. If you knew how much I'm envied.

DAUGHTER. Envied? Does one envy the tortured?

DOORKEEPER. Yes. But I'll tell you what's worse than night-
watching and drudgery and draughts and cold and damp.
That's having to listen, as I do, to all their tales of woe.
They all come to me. Why? Perhaps they read in my
wrinkles the runes of suffering, and that makes them talk.
In that shawl, my dear, thirty years of torment's hidden—
my own and others.

DAUGHTER. That's why it is so heavy and stings like nettles.

DOORKEEPER. Wear it if you like. When it gets too heavy,
call me and I'll come and relieve you of it.

DAUGHTER. Goodbye. What you can bear, surely I can.

DOORKEEPER. We shall see. But be kind to my young friends
and put up with their complaining.

The DOORKEEPER *disappears down the alley. The stage is
blacked out. When light returns, the lime tree is bare,
the blue monkshood withered, and the green plot at the
end of the alley has turned brown.*

The OFFICER *enters. His hair is grey and he has a grey
beard. His clothes are ragged; his collar soiled and limp.
He still carries the bouquet of roses, but the petals have
dropped.*

OFFICER, *wandering round.* By all the signs, summer is over
and autumn at hand. I can tell that by the lime tree—and
the monkshood. *Pacing.* But autumn is *my* spring, for then
the theatre opens again. And then she is bound to come.
To DAUGHTER. Dear lady, may I sit on this chair for a
while?

DAUGHTER. Do, my friend. I can stand.

OFFICER [*sitting*]. If only I could sleep a little it would be better.

He falls asleep for a moment, then starts up and begins

walking again. He stops by the clover-leaf door and pokes it.

OFFICER. This door—it gives me no peace. What is there behind it? Something must be. *Soft ballet music is heard from above.* Ah, the rehearsals have begun! *The lights come and go like a lighthouse beam.* What's this? *Speaking in time with the flashes.* Light and darkness; light and darkness.

DAUGHTER, *with the same timing.* Day and night; day and night. A merciful providence wants to shorten your waiting. And so the days fly, chasing the nights.

The light is now constant. The BILLSTICKER *enters with his net and his implements.*

OFFICER. Here's the Billsticker with his net. How was the fishing?

BILLSTICKER. Not too bad. The summer was hot and a bit long . . . the net was all right, but not quite what I had in mind.

OFFICER. "Not quite what I had in mind." Excellently put. Nothing ever is as one imagined it—because one's mind goes further than the act, goes beyond the object. *He walks up and down striking the bouquet against the walls until the last leaves fall.*

BILLSTICKER. Hasn't she come down yet?

OFFICER. No, not yet, but she'll come soon. Do you know what's behind that door, Billsticker?

BILLSTICKER. No, I've never seen it open.

OFFICER. I'm going to telephone to a locksmith to come and open it. *Goes into the Lodge. The* BILLSTICKER *pastes up a poster and moves away.*

DAUGHTER. What was wrong with the fishnet?

BILLSTICKER. Wrong? Well, there wasn't anything wrong exactly. But it wasn't what I'd had in mind, and so I didn't enjoy it *quite* as much . . .

DAUGHTER. How did you imagine the net?

BILLSTICKER. How? I can't quite tell you . . .

DAUGHTER. Let me tell you. In your imagination it was different—green but not *that* green.

BILLSTICKER. You understand, Madam. You understand everything. That's why they all come to you with their troubles.
Now if you'd only listen to me, just this once . . .

DAUGHTER. But I will, gladly. Come in here and pour out your
heart. *She goes into the Lodge. The* BILLSTICKER *stays
outside and talks to her through the window.*

*The stage is blacked out again, then gradually the lights
go up. The lime tree is in leaf; the monkshood in bloom;
the sun shines on the greenery at the end of the alley. The*
BILLSTICKER *is still at the window and the* DAUGHTER *can
be seen inside.*

The OFFICER *enters from the Lodge. He is old and
white-haired; his clothes and shoes are in rags. He carries
the stems of the bouquet. He totters backwards and for-
wards slowly like a very old man, and reads the poster.*

A BALLET GIRL [*comes out of the Theatre*].

OFFICER. Has Miss Victoria gone?

BALLET GIRL. No, she hasn't.

OFFICER. Then I'll wait. Will she come soon?

BALLET GIRL, *gravely*. Yes, she's sure to.

OFFICER. Don't go—then you'll be able to see what's behind
that door. I've sent for the locksmith.

BALLET GIRL. That will be really interesting to see this door
opened. The door and the Growing Castle. Do you know
the Growing Castle?

OFFICER. Do I? Wasn't I imprisoned there?

BALLET GIRL. Really, was that you? But why did they have
so many horses there?

OFFICER. It was a stable castle, you see.

BALLET GIRL, *distressed*. How silly of me not to have thought
of that.

[*Moves towards the Lodge. A* CHORUS GIRL *comes out of
the Theatre.*]

OFFICER. Has Miss Victoria gone?

CHORUS GIRL, *gravely.* No, she hasn't gone. She never goes.

OFFICER. That's because she loves me. No, you mustn't go before the locksmith comes. He's going to open this door.

CHORUS GIRL. Oh, is the door going to be opened? Really? What fun! I just want to ask the Doorkeeper something. [*She joins the* BILLSTICKER *at the window. The* PROMPTER *comes out of the Theatre.*]

OFFICER. Has Miss Victoria gone?

PROMPTER. Not so far as I know.

OFFICER. There you are! Didn't I say she was waiting for me? No, don't go. The door's going to be opened.

PROMPTER. Which door?

OFFICER. Is there more than one door?

PROMPTER. Oh, I see—the one with the clover-leaf! Of course I'll stay. I just want to have a few words with the Door-keeper.

[*He joins the group at the window. They all speak in turn to the* DAUGHTER.] *The* GLAZIER *comes through the gate.*

OFFICER. Are you the locksmith?

GLAZIER. No, the locksmith had company. But a glazier's just as good.

OFFICER. Yes, indeed . . . indeed. But . . . er . . . have you brought your diamond with you?

GLAZIER. Of course. A glazier without a diamond—what good would that be?

OFFICER. None. Let's get to work then. *He claps his hands. All group themselves in a circle round the door.* MALE CHORUS *in costumes of* Die Meistersinger, *and* GIRL DANCERS *from* Aïda *come out of the theatre and join them.* Locksmith—or Glazier—do your duty! *The* GLAZIER *goes towards the door holding out his diamond.* A moment such as this does not recur often in a lifetime. Therefore, my good friends, I beg you to reflect seriously upon . . .

[*During the last words the* POLICEMAN *has entered by the gate.*]

POLICEMAN. In the name of the law I forbid the opening of this door.

OFFICER. Oh God, what a fuss there is whenever one wants to do anything new and great! Well—we shall take proceedings . . . To the lawyer then, and we will see if the law holds good. To the lawyer!

Without any lowering of the curtain the scene changes to the LAWYER's *office. The gate has now become the gate in an office railing stretching across the stage. The* DOORKEEPER's *Lodge is a recess for the* LAWYER's *desk, the lime tree, leafless, a coat-and-hat stand. The announcement-board is covered with proclamations and Court decrees and the clover-door is a document cupboard.*

The LAWYER *in frock coat and white tie is sitting on the left inside the railing of the gate, at this high desk covered with papers. His appearance bears witness to unspeakable suffering. His face is chalk-white, furrowed and purple-shadowed. He is hideous; his face mirrors all the crime and vice with which, through his profession, he has been involved.*

Of his two clerks one has only one arm; the other a single eye.

The people, who had gathered to witness the opening of the door, are now clients waiting to see the LAWYER, *and look as if they have always been there.*

The DAUGHTER, *wearing the shawl, and the* OFFICER *are in front. The* OFFICER *looks curiously at the cupboard door and from time to time pokes it.*

The LAWYER *goes up to the* DAUGHTER.

LAWYER. If you let me have that shawl, my dear, I'll hang it here until the stove is lighted and then I'll burn it with all its griefs and miseries.

DAUGHTER. Not yet, my friend. I must let it get quite full first, and I want above all to gather *your* sufferings up in it, the crimes you have absorbed from others, the vices, swindles, slanders, libel . . .

LAWYER. My child, your shawl would not be big enough. Look at these walls! Isn't the wall-paper stained as if by every kind of sin? Look at these documents in which I write records of evil! Look at me! . . . Nobody who comes here ever smiles. Nothing but vile looks, bared teeth, clenched fists, and all of them squirt their malice, their envy, their suspicions over me. Look, my hands are black and can never be clean! See how cracked they are and bleeding! I can never wear my clothes for more than a few days because they stink of other people's crimes. Sometimes I have the place fumigated with sulphur, but that doesn't help. I sleep in the next room and dream of nothing but crime. I have a murder case in Court now— that's bad enough—but do you know what's worst of all? Separating husbands and wives. Then earth and heaven seem to cry aloud, to cry treason against primal power, the source of good, against love! And then, do you know, after reams of paper have been filled with mutual accusations, if some kindly person takes one or other of the couple aside and asks them in a friendly sort of way the simple question—"What have you really got against your husband—or your wife?"—then he, or she, stands speechless. They don't know. Oh, once it was something to do with a salad, another time about some word. Usually it's about nothing at all. But the suffering, the agony! All this I have to bear. Look at me! Do you think, marked as I am by crime, I can ever win a woman's love? Or that anyone wants to be the friend of a man who has to enforce payment of all the debts of the town? It's misery to be human.

DAUGHTER. Human life is pitiable!

LAWYER. It is indeed. And what people live on is a mystery to me. They marry with an income of two thousand crowns when they need four. They borrow, to be sure, they all borrow, and so scrape along somehow by the skin of their teeth until they die. Then the estate is always insolvent. Who has to pay up in the end? Tell me that.

DAUGHTER. He who feeds the birds.

LAWYER. Well, if He who feeds the birds would come down to earth and see the plight of the unfortunate children of men, perhaps He would have some compassion . . .

DAUGHTER. Human life is pitiful.

LAWYER. Yes, that's the truth. *To the* OFFICER. What do you want?

OFFICER. I only want to ask if Miss Victoria has gone.

LAWYER. No, she hasn't. You can rest assured of that. Why do you keep poking my cupboard?

OFFICER. I thought the door was so very like . . .

LAWYER. Oh, no, no, no!

Church bells ring.

OFFICER. Is there a funeral in the town?

LAWYER. No, it's Graduation—the conferring of Doctors' degrees. I myself am about to receive the degree of Doctor of Law. Perhaps you would like to graduate and receive a laurel wreath?

OFFICER. Why not? It would be a little distraction.

LAWYER. Then perhaps we should proceed at once to the solemn rites. But you must go and change.

Exit OFFICER.

The stage is blacked out and changes to the interior of the Church.
The barrier now serves as the chancel rail. The announcement-board shows the numbers of the hymns. The lime-tree hatstand has become a candelabra, the Lawyer's desk is the Chancellor's lectern, and the Clover-door leads to the vestry. The Chorus from Die Meistersinger are ushers with wands. The dancers carry the laurel wreaths. The rest of the people are the congregation.
The new background shows only a gigantic organ, with a mirror over the keyboard.
Music is heard. At the sides stand the four Deans of the Faculties—Philosophy, Theology, Medicine and Law. For a moment there is no movement, then:
The USHERS *come forward from the right.**

*This scene follows exactly the normal ceremony in a Swedish university when Doctors' degrees are conferred. As each Graduate has the wreath put on his head, a gun

The DANCERS *follow, holding laurel wreaths in their out-stretched hands.*

Three GRADUATES *come in from the left, are crowned in turn by the* DANCERS *and go out to the right.*

The LAWYER *advances to receive his wreath.*

The DANCERS *turn away, refusing to crown him, and go out.*

The LAWYER, *greatly agitated, leans against a pillar.*

Everyone disappears. The LAWYER *is alone.*

The DAUGHTER *enters with a white shawl over her head and shoulders.*

DAUGHTER. Look, I have washed the shawl. But what are you doing here? Didn't you get your laurels?

LAWYER. No. I was discredited.

DAUGHTER. Why? Because you have defended the poor, said a good word for the sinner, eased the burden of the guilty, obtained reprieve for the condemned? Woe to mankind! Men are not angels, but pitiable creatures.

LAWYER. Do not judge men harshly. It is my business to plead for them.

DAUGHTER, *leaning against the organ.* Why do they strike their friends in the face?

LAWYER. They know no better.

DAUGHTER. Let us enlighten them—you and I together. Will you?

LAWYER. There can be no enlightenment for them. Oh that the gods in heaven might hear our woe!

DAUGHTER. It shall reach the throne. *Sits at the organ.* Do you know what I see in this mirror? The world as it should be. For as it is it's wrong way up.

LAWYER. How did it come to be wrong way up?

DAUGHTER. When the copy was made.

---

outside is fired. The Chancellor and the Faculties bow. Then the new doctor bows to them.

One of the Graduates should be the Officer and another the Schoolmaster of the later scene.

LAWYER. Ah! You yourself have said it—the copy! I always
felt this must be a poor copy, and when I began to remember its origin nothing satisfied me. Then they said I
was cynical and had a jaundiced eye, and so forth.

DAUGHTER. It is a mad world. Consider these four Faculties.
Organized society subsidizes all four: Theology, the doc-
trine of Divinity, continually attacked and ridiculed by
Philosophy claiming wisdom for itself; and Medicine
always giving the lie to Philosophy and discounting
Theology as one of the sciences, calling it superstition.
And there they sit together on the Council, whose func-
tion is to teach young men respect for the University.
Yes, it's a madhouse. And woe to him who first recovers
his senses!

LAWYER. The first to discover it are the theologians. For their
preliminary studies they take Philosophy, which teaches
them that Theology is nonsense, and then they learn
from Theology that Philosophy is nonsense. Madness.

DAUGHTER. Then there's Law, serving all but its servants.

LAWYER. Justice, to the just unjust. Right so often wrong.

DAUGHTER. Thus you have made it, O Children of Men!
Child, come! You shall have a wreath from me . . . one
more fitting. *She puts a crown of thorns on his head.**
Now I will play to you. *She sits at the organ and plays a
Kyrie, but instead of the organ, voices are heard singing.
The last note of each phrase is sustained.*

CHILDREN'S VOICES. Lord! Lord!

WOMEN'S VOICES. Be merciful!

MEN'S VOICES (*Tenor*). Deliver us for Thy mercy's sake.

MEN'S VOICES (*Bass*). Save Thy children, O Lord, and be not
wrathful against us.

ALL. Be merciful! Hear us! Have compassion for mortals.
Are we so far from Thee? Out of the depths we call.
Grace, Lord! Let not the burden be too heavy for Thy
children. Hear us! Hear us!

*In Molander's production, as the Daughter put the
crown of thorns on the Lawyer's head he knelt, facing the
audience, his arms outstretched in the form of a crucifix.

The stage darkens as the DAUGHTER *rises and approaches the* LAWYER.

By means of lighting the organ is changed to the wall of a grotto. The sea seeps in between basalt pillars with a harmony of waves and wind.

LAWYER. Where are we?

DAUGHTER. What do you hear?

LAWYER. I hear drops falling.

DAUGHTER. Those are the tears of mankind weeping. What more do you hear?

LAWYER. A sighing . . . a moaning . . . a wailing.

DAUGHTER. The lamentation of mortals has reached so far, no further. But why this endless lamentation? Is there no joy in life?

LAWYER. Yes. The sweetest which is also the bitterest—love! Marriage and a home. The highest and the lowest.

DAUGHTER. Let me put it to the test.

LAWYER. With me?

DAUGHTER. With you. You know the rocks, the stumbling stones. Let us avoid them.

LAWYER. I am poor.

DAUGHTER. Does that matter if we love one another? And a little beauty costs nothing.

LAWYER. My antipathies may be your sympathies.

DAUGHTER. They can be balanced.

LAWYER. Supposing we tire?

DAUGHTER. Children will come, bringing ever new interests.

LAWYER. You? You will take me, poor, ugly, despised, discredited?

DAUGHTER. Yes. Let us join our destinies.

LAWYER. So be it.

The scene changes to a very simple room adjoining the LAWYER's *office. On the right is a large curtained double bed, close to it a window with double panes; on the left a stove and kitchen utensils.*

*At the back an open door leads to the office, where a
number of poor people can be seen awaiting admission.*
KRISTIN, *the maid, is pasting strips of paper along the
edges of the inner window.*
The DAUGHTER, *pale and worn, is at the stove.*

KRISTIN. I paste, I paste.

DAUGHTER. You are shutting out the air. I am suffocating.

KRISTIN. Now there's only one small crack left.

DAUGHTER. Air, air! I cannot breathe.

KRISTIN. I paste, I paste.

LAWYER, *from the office.* That's right, Kristin. Warmth is
precious.

KRISTIN *pastes the last crack.*

DAUGHTER. Oh, it's as if you are glueing up my mouth!

LAWYER, *coming to the doorway with a document in his hand.*
Is the child asleep?

DAUGHTER. Yes, at last.

LAWYER, *mildly.* That screaming frightens away my clients.

DAUGHTER, *gently.* What can be done about it?

LAWYER. Nothing.

DAUGHTER. We must take a bigger flat.

LAWYER. We have no money.

DAUGHTER. May I open the window, please? This bad air is
choking me.

LAWYER. Then the warmth would escape, and we should
freeze.

DAUGHTER. It's horrible! Can't we at least scrub the place?

LAWYER. You can't scrub—neither can I, and Kristin must go
on pasting. She must paste up the whole house, every
crack in floor and walls and ceiling.

[*Exit* KRISTIN, *delighted.*]

DAUGHTER. I was prepared for poverty, not dirt.

LAWYER. Poverty is always rather dirty.

DAUGHTER. This is worse than I dreamt.

LAWYER. We haven't had the worst. There's still food in the pot.

DAUGHTER. But what food!

LAWYER. Cabbage is cheap, nourishing and good.

DAUGHTER. For those who like cabbage. To me it's repulsive.

LAWYER. Why didn't you say so?

DAUGHTER. Because I loved you. I wanted to sacrifice my taste.

LAWYER. Now I must sacrifice my taste for cabbage. Sacrifices must be mutual.

DAUGHTER. Then what shall we eat? Fish? But you hate fish.

LAWYER. And it's dear.

DAUGHTER. This is harder than I believed.

LAWYER, *gently.* You see how hard it is. And the child which should be our bond and blessing is our undoing.

DAUGHTER. Dearest! I am dying in this air, in this room with its backyard view, with babies screaming through endless sleepless hours, and those people out there wailing and quarrelling and accusing . . . Here I can only die.

LAWYER. Poor little flower, without light, without air.

DAUGHTER. And you say there are others worse off.

LAWYER. I am one of the envied of the neighbourhood.

DAUGHTER. None of it would matter, if only I could have some beauty in our home.

LAWYER. I know what you're thinking of—a plant, a heliotrope to be exact; but that costs as much as six quarts of milk or half a bushel of potatoes.

DAUGHTER. I would gladly go without food to have my flower.

LAWYER. There is one kind of beauty that costs nothing. Not to have it in his home is sheer torture for a man with any sense of beauty.

DAUGHTER. What is that?

LAWYER. If I tell you, you will lose your temper.

DAUGHTER. We agreed never to lose our tempers.

LAWYER. We agreed. Yes. All will be well, Agnes, if we can avoid those sharp hard tones. You know them—no, not yet.

DAUGHTER. We shall never hear those.

LAWYER. Never, if it depends on me.

DAUGHTER. Now tell me.

LAWYER. Well, when I come into a house, first I look to see
how the curtains are hung. *Goes to the window and ad-
justs the curtain.* If they hang like a bit of string or rag,
I soon leave. Then I glance at the chairs. If they are in
their places, I stay. *Puts a chair straight against the wall.*
Next I look at the candlesticks. If the candles are crooked,
then the whole house is askew. *Straightens a candle on
the bureau.* That you see, my dear, is the beauty which
costs nothing.

DAUGHTER, *bowing her head.* Not that sharp tone, Axel!

LAWYER. It wasn't sharp.

DAUGHTER. Yes it was.

LAWYER. The devil take it!

DAUGHTER. What kind of language is that?

LAWYER. Forgive me, Agnes. But I have suffered as much
from your untidiness as you do from the dirt. And I
haven't dared straighten things myself, because you would
have been offended and thought I was reproaching you.
Oh, shall we stop this?

DAUGHTER. It is terribly hard to be married, harder than
anything. I think one has to be an angel.

LAWYER. I think one has.

DAUGHTER. I am beginning to hate you after all this.

LAWYER. Alas for us then! But let us prevent hatred. I promise never to mention untidiness again, although it is torture to me.

DAUGHTER. And I will eat cabbage, although that is torment
to me.

LAWYER. And so—life together is a torment. One's pleasure is
the other's pain.

DAUGHTER. Human beings are pitiful.

LAWYER. You see that now?

DAUGHTER. Yes. But in God's name let us avoid the rocks, now that we know them so well.

LAWYER. Let us do that. We are tolerant, enlightened people. Of course we can make allowances and forgive.

DAUGHTER. Of course we can smile at trifles.

LAWYER. We, only we can do it. Do you know, I read in the paper this morning . . . By the way, where is the paper?

DAUGHTER, *embarrassed*. Which paper?

LAWYER, *harshly*. Do I take more than one newspaper?

DAUGHTER. Smile—and don't speak harshly! I lit the fire with your newspaper.

LAWYER, *violently*. The devil you did!

DAUGHTER. Please smile. I burnt it because it mocked what to me is holy.

LAWYER. What to me is unholy! Huh! *Striking his hands together, beside himself.* I'll smile, I'll smile till my back teeth show. I'll be tolerant and swallow my opinions and say yes to everything and cant and cringe. So you've burnt my paper, have you? *Pulls the bed curtains.* Very well. Now I'm going to tidy up until you lose your temper . . . Agnes, this is quite impossible!

DAUGHTER. Indeed it is.

LAWYER. Yet we must stay together. Not for our vows' sake, but for the child's.

DAUGHTER. That's true—for the child's sake. Yes, yes, we must go on.

LAWYER. And now I must attend to my clients. Listen to them muttering. They can't wait to tear one another to pieces, to get each other fined and imprisoned. Benighted souls!

Enter KRISTIN *with pasting materials.*

DAUGHTER. Wretched, wretched beings! And all this pasting! *She bows her head in dumb despair.*

KRISTIN. I paste, I paste!

The LAWYER *standing by the door, nervously fingers the handle.*

DAUGHTER. Oh how that handle squeaks! It is as if you were twisting my heart-strings.

LAWYER. I twist, I twist!

DAUGHTER. Don't!

LAWYER. I twist . . .

DAUGHTER. No!

LAWYER. I . . .

The OFFICER *[now middle-aged] takes hold of the handle from inside the office.*

OFFICER. May I?

LAWYER, *letting go of the handle.* Certainly. As you have got your degree.

OFFICER, *entering.* The whole of life is now mine. All paths are open to me. I have set foot on Parnassus, the laurels are won. Immortality, fame, all are mine!

LAWYER. What are you going to live on?

OFFICER. Live on?

LAWYER. You'll need a roof surely, and clothes and food?

OFFICER. Those are always to be had, as long as there's someone who cares for you.

LAWYER. Fancy that now, fancy that! Paste, Kristin, paste! Until they cannot breathe. *Goes out backwards, nodding.*

KRISTIN. I paste, I paste! Until they cannot breathe.

OFFICER. Will you come now?

DAUGHTER. Oh quickly! But where to?

OFFICER. To Fairhaven, where it is summer and the sun is shining. Youth is there, children and flowers, singing and dancing, feasting and merrymaking.

[Exit KRISTIN.]

DAUGHTER. I would like to go there.

OFFICER. Come!

LAWYER, *entering.* Now I shall return to my first hell. This one was the second—and worst. The sweetest hell is the worst. Look, she's left hairpins all over the floor again! *Picks one up.*

OFFICER. So he has discovered the hairpins too.

LAWYER. Too? Look at this one. There are two prongs but one pin. Two and yet one. If I straighten it out, it becomes one single piece. If I bend it, it is two, without ceasing to be one. In other words the two are one. But if I break it—like this—*breaks it in half*—then the two are two. *He throws away the pieces.*

OFFICER. So much he has seen. But before one can break it, the prongs must diverge. If they converge, it holds.

LAWYER. And if they are parallel, they never meet. Then it neither holds nor breaks.

OFFICER. The hairpin is the most perfect of all created things. A straight line which is yet two parallel lines.

LAWYER. A lock that closes when open.

OFFICER. Closes open—a plait of hair loosed while bound.

LAWYER. Like this door. When I close it, I open the way out, for you, Agnes.

Goes out, closing the door.

DAUGHTER. And now?

The scene changes. The bed with its hangings is transformed into a tent, the stove remaining. The new background shows a beautiful wooded shore, with beflagged landing stages and white boats, some with sails set. Among the trees are little Italianesque villas, pavilions, kiosks and marble statues.
In the middle distance is a strait.
The foreground presents a sharp contrast with the background. Burnt hillsides, black and white tree stumps as after a forest fire, red heather, red pigsties and outhouses. On the right is an open-air establishment for remedial exercises, where people are being treated on machines resembling instruments of torture.
On the left is part of the Quarantine Station; open sheds with furnaces, boilers and pipes.
[The DAUGHTER and the OFFICER are standing as at the end of the previous scene.]
The QUARANTINE MASTER, dressed as a blackamoor, comes along the shore.

OFFICER, *going up and shaking hands with the* QUARANTINE MASTER. What? You here, old Gasbags?*

Q. MASTER. Yes, I'm here.

OFFICER. Is this place Fairhaven?

Q. MASTER. No, that's over there. [*Points across the strait.*] This is Foulstrand.

OFFICER. Then we've come wrong.

Q. MASTER. We! Aren't you going to introduce me?

OFFICER. It wouldn't do. *Low.* That is the Daughter of Indra.

Q. MASTER. Of Indra? I thought it must be Varuna himself. Well, aren't you surprised to find me black in the face?

OFFICER. My dear fellow, I am over fifty, at which age one ceases to be surprised. I assumed at once that you were going to a fancy dress ball this afternoon.

Q. MASTER. Quite correct. I hope you'll come with me.

OFFICER. Certainly, for there doesn't seem to be any attraction in this place. What kind of people live here?

Q. MASTER. The sick live here, and the healthy over there.

OFFICER. But surely only the poor here?

Q. MASTER. No, my boy, here you have the rich. [*Indicates the gymnasium.*] Look at that man on the rack. He's eaten too much pâté-de-foie-gras with truffles, and drunk so much Burgundy that his feet are knotted.

OFFICER. Knotted?

Q. MASTER. He's got knotted feet, and that one lying on the guillotine has drunk so much brandy that his backbone's got to be mangled.

OFFICER. That's not very pleasant either.

Q. MASTER. What's more here on this side live all those who have some misery to hide. Look at this one coming now, for instance.

An elderly fop is wheeled on to the stage in a bath chair, accompanied by a gaunt and hideous coquette of sixty, dressed in the latest fashion and attended by the "Friend," a man of forty.

*Original "Ordström," meaning "Stream of Words."

OFFICER. It's the Major! Our schoolfellow.

Q. MASTER. Don Juan! You see, he's still in love with the spectre at his side. He doesn't see that she has grown old, that she is ugly, faithless, cruel.

OFFICER. There's true love for you. I never would have thought that flighty fellow had it in him to love so deeply and ardently.

Q. MASTER. That's a nice way of looking at it.

OFFICER. I've been in love myself—with Victoria. As a matter of fact I still pace up and down the alley, waiting for her.

Q. MASTER. So you're the fellow who waits in the alley?

OFFICER. I am he.

Q. MASTER. Well, have you got that door open yet?

OFFICER. No, we're still fighting the case. The Billsticker is out with his fishnet, you see, which delays the taking of evidence. Meanwhile, the Glazier has put in window-panes at the castle, which has grown half a story. It has been an unusually good year this year—warm and damp.

Q. MASTER, *pointing to the sheds*. But you've certainly had nothing like the heat of my place there.

OFFICER. What's the temperature of your furnaces then?

Q. MASTER. When we're disinfecting cholera suspects, we keep them at sixty degrees.

OFFICER. But is there cholera about again?

Q. MASTER. Didn't you know?

OFFICER. Of course I know. But I so often forget what I know.

Q. MASTER. And I so often wish I could forget—especially my-self. That's why I go in for masquerades, fancy dress, theatricals.

OFFICER. Why. What's the matter with you?

Q. MASTER. If I talk, they say I'm bragging. If I hold my tongue they call me a hypocrite.

OFFICER. Is that why you blacked your face?

Q. MASTER. Yes. A shade blacker than I am.

OFFICER. Who's this coming?

Q. MASTER. Oh, he's a poet! He's going to have his mud bath. *The POET enters, looking at the sky and carrying a pail of mud.*

OFFICER. But, good heavens, he ought to bathe in light and air!

Q. MASTER. No, he lives so much in the higher spheres that he gets homesick for the mud. It hardens his skin to wallow in the mire, just as it does with pigs. After his bath he doesn't feel the gadflies stinging.

OFFICER. What a strange world of contradictions!

POET, *ecstatically.* Out of clay the god Ptah fashioned man on a potter's wheel, a lathe, *mockingly,* or some other damned thing . . . *Ecstatically.* Out of clay the sculptor fashions his more or less immortal masterpieces, *mockingly,* which are usually only rubbish. *Ecstatically.* Out of clay are formed those objects, so domestically essential bearing the generic name of pots and pans. *Mockingly.* Not that it matters in the least to me what they're called. *Ecstatically.* Such is clay! When clay is fluid, it is called mud. *C'est mon affaire! Calls.* Lina!

Enter LINA with a bucket.

POET. Lina, show yourself to Miss Agnes. She knew you ten years ago when you were a young, happy, and, let me add, pretty girl. *To DAUGHTER.* Look at her now! Five children, drudgery, squalling, hunger, blows. See how beauty has perished, how joy has vanished in the fulfilment of duties which should give that inner contentment which shows in the harmonious lines of a face, in the tranquil shining of the eyes . . .

Q. MASTER, *putting a hand to the POET's lips.* Shut up! Shut up!

POET. That's what they all say. But if you are silent, they tell you to talk. How inconsistent people are!

Distant dance music is heard.

DAUGHTER, *going up to LINA.* Tell me your troubles.

No, I daren't. I'd catch it all the worse if I did.

DAUGHTER. Who is so cruel?

LINA. I daren't talk about it. I'll be beaten.

POET. May be, but I shall talk about it even if the Blackamoor knocks my teeth out. I shall talk about all the injustice there is here. Agnes, Daughter of the Gods, do you
hear that music up on the hill? Well, that's a dance for
Lina's sister, who has come home from town—where she
went astray, you understand. Now they are killing the
fatted calf, while Lina, who stayed at home, has to carry
the swill pail and feed the pigs.

DAUGHTER. There is rejoicing in that home because the wan-
derer has forsaken the path of evil, not only because she
has come home. Remember that.

POET. Then give a ball and a supper every evening for this
blameless servant who has never gone astray. Do that for
her—they never do. On the contrary, when Lina is free,
she has to go to prayer meetings where she's reprimanded
for not being perfect. Is that justice?

DAUGHTER. Your questions are difficult to answer, because
there are so many unknown factors.

POET. The Caliph, Harun the Just, was of the same opinion.
Sitting quietly on his exalted throne he could never see
how those below were faring. Presently complaints
reached his lofty ear, so one fine day he stepped down
in disguise and walked unobserved among the crowd to
watch the workings of justice.

DAUGHTER. You do not think I am Harun the Just, do you?

OFFICER. Let's change the subject. Here are newcomers.

*A white boat, shaped like a dragon, glides into the Strait.
It has a light blue silken sail on a gilded yard, and a
golden mast with a rose-red pennon. At the helm, with
their arms round each other's waists, sit* HE *and* SHE.

There you see perfect happiness, utter bliss, the ecstasy of
young love.

The light grows stronger. HE *stands up in the boat and
sings.*

HE.   *Hail fairest bay!*
             Where I passed youth's spring tide,
             where I dreamed its first roses,
             I come now again,
             no longer alone.
             Forests and havens,
             heaven and sea,
             greet her!
             My love, my bride,
             my sun, my life!

The flags on Fairhaven dip in salute. White handkerchiefs wave from villas and shores. The music of harps and violins sound over the strait.

POET. See how light streams from them! And sound rings across the water! Eros!

OFFICER. It is Victoria.

Q. MASTER. Well, if it is . . .

OFFICER. It is his Victoria. I have my own, and mine no one will ever see. Now hoist the quarantine flag while I haul in the catch.

The QUARANTINE MASTER *waves a yellow flag. The* OFFICER *pulls on a line which causes the boat to turn in towards Foulstrand.*

Hold hard there!

HE *and* SHE *become aware of the dreadful landscape and show their horror.*

Q. MASTER. Yes, yes, it's hard lines, but everyone has to land here, everyone coming from infectious areas.

POET. Think of being able to speak like that—to behave like that when you see two human beings joined in love. Do not touch them! Do not lay hands on love—that is high treason. Alas, alas! All that is most lovely will now be dragged down, down into the mud.

HE *and* SHE *come ashore, shamed and sad.*

HE. What is it? What have we done?*

────────

Literally "woe to us."

Q. MASTER. You don't have to do anything in order to meet with life's little discomforts.

SHE. How brief are joy and happiness!

HE. How long must we stay here?

Q. MASTER. Forty days and forty nights.

SHE. We would rather throw ourselves into the sea.

HE. Live here—among burnt hills and pigsties?

POET. Love can overcome everything, even sulphur fumes and carbolic acid.*

The QUARANTINE MASTER *goes into a shed. Blue sulphurous vapour pours out.*

Q. MASTER [*coming out*]. I'm burning the sulphur. Will you kindly step inside.

SHE. Oh, my blue dress will lose its colour!

Q. MASTER. And turn white. Your red roses will turn white too.

HE. So will your cheeks, in forty days.

SHE, *to the* OFFICER. That will please you.

OFFICER. No, it won't. True, your happiness was the source of my misery, but . . . that's no matter. [HE *and* SHE *go into the shed.*] [*To* DAUGHTER.] I've got my degree now, and a job as tutor over there. [*Indicates Fairhaven.*] Heigho! And in the fall I'll get a post in a school, teaching the boys the same lessons I learnt myself, all through my childhood, all through my youth. Teach them the same lessons I learnt all through my manhood and finally all through my old age. The same lessons! What is twice two? How many times does two go into four without remainder? Until I get a pension and have nothing to do but wait for meals and the newspapers, until in the end I'm carried out to the crematorium and burnt to ashes.

To QUARANTINE MASTER *as he comes out of the shed.*

Have you no pensioners here? To be a pensioner is the worst fate after twice two is four, going to school again

*The Poet does not speak again and is not mentioned until the end of the later quayside scene, so perhaps here he goes out.

when one's taken one's degree, asking the same questions until one dies . . .

An elderly man walks past with his hands behind his back.

Look, there goes a pensioner waiting for his life to ebb. A Captain, probably, who failed to become a Major, or a Clerk to the Court who was never promoted. Many are called, but few are chosen. He's just walking about, waiting for breakfast.

PENSIONER. No, for the paper, the morning paper!

OFFICER. And he is only fifty-four. He may go on for another twenty-five years, waiting for meals and the newspaper. Isn't that dreadful?

PENSIONER. What is not dreadful? Tell me that. Tell me that.

OFFICER. Yes. Let him tell who can.

Exit PENSIONER.

Now I shall teach boys twice two is four. How many times does two go into four without remainder? *He clutches his head in despair.*

Enter HE *and* SHE *from the shed. Her dress and roses are white, her face pale. His clothes are also bleached.*

And Victoria whom I loved, for whom I desired the greatest happiness on earth, she has her happiness now, the greatest happiness she can know, while I suffer, suffer, suffer!

SHE. Do you think I can be happy, seeing your suffering? How can you believe that? Perhaps it comforts you to know that I shall be a prisoner here for forty days and forty nights. Tell me, does it comfort you?

OFFICER. Yes and no. I cannot have pleasure while you have pain. Oh!

HE. And do you think my happiness can be built on your agony?

OFFICER. We are all to be pitied—all of us.

All lift their hands to heaven. A discordant cry of anguish breaks from their lips.

!

DAUGHTER. O God, hear them! Life is evil! Mankind is to be pitied.

ALL, *as before.* Oh!

The stage is blacked out and the scene changes.

The whole landscape is in winter dress with snow on the ground and on the leafless trees. Foulstrand is in the background, in shadow.

The strait is still in the middle distance. On the near side is a landing stage with white boats and flags flying from flagstaffs. In the strait a white warship, a brig with gunports, is anchored.

The foreground presents Fairhaven, in full light.

On the right is a corner of the Assembly Rooms with open windows through which are seen couples dancing. On a box outside stand three MAIDS, *their arms round each other's waists, watching the dancing.*

On the steps is a bench on which UGLY EDITH *is sitting, bareheaded and sorrowful, with long dishevelled hair, before an open piano.*

On the left is a yellow wooden house outside which two children in summer dresses are playing ball.

The DAUGHTER *and* OFFICER *enter.*

DAUGHTER. Here is peace and happiness. Holiday time. Work over, every day a festival, everyone in holiday attire. Music and dancing even in the morning. *To the* MAIDS. Why don't you go in and dance, my dears?

SERVANTS. Us?

OFFICER. But they are servants.

DAUGHTER. True. But why is Edith sitting there instead of dancing?

EDITH *buries her face in her hands.*

OFFICER. Don't ask her! She has been sitting there for three hours without being invited to dance. *He goes into the yellow house.*

DAUGHTER. What cruel pleasure!

The MOTHER, *in a décolleté dress, comes out of the Assembly Rooms and goes up to* EDITH.

MOTHER. Why don't you go in as I told you?

EDITH. Because . . . because I can't be my own partner. I know I'm ugly and no one wants to dance with me, but I can avoid being reminded of it. *She begins to play Bach's Toccata con Fuga, No. 10.*

The waltz at the ball is heard too, first faintly, then growing louder as if in competition with the Toccata. Gradually EDITH *overcomes it and reduces it to silence. Dance couples appear in the doorway, and everyone stands reverently listening.*

A NAVAL OFFICER *seizes* ALICE, *one of the guests, by the waist.*

N. OFFICER. Come, quick! *He leads her down to the landing stage.* EDITH *breaks off, rises and watches them in despair. She remains standing as if turned to stone.*

The front wall of the yellow house vanishes. Boys are sitting on forms, among them the OFFICER *looking uncomfortable and worried. In front of them stands the* SCHOOLMASTER, *wearing spectacles and holding chalk and a cane.*

SCHOOLMASTER, *to the* OFFICER. Now, my boy, can you tell me what twice two is?

The OFFICER *remains seated, painfully searching his memory without finding an answer.*

You must stand up when you are asked a question.

OFFICER, *rising anxiously.* Twice two . . . let me see . . . That makes two twos.

S. MASTER. Aha! So you have not prepared your lesson.

OFFICER, *embarrassed.* Yes, I have, but . . . I know what it is, but I can't say it.

S. MASTER. You're quibbling. You know the answer, do you? But you can't say it. Perhaps I can assist you. *Pulls the* OFFICER's *hair.*

OFFICER. Oh, this is dreadful, really dreadful!

S. MASTER. Yes, it is dreadful that such a big boy should have no ambition.

OFFICER, *agonised.* A *big* boy. Yes, I certainly am big, much
bigger than these others. I am grown up, I have left
school . . . *As if waking.* I have even graduated. Why
am I sitting here then? Haven't I got my degree?

S. MASTER. Certainly. But you have got to stay here and
mature. Do you see? You must mature. Isn't that so?

OFFICER, *clasping his head.* Yes, that's so, one must mature
. . . Twice two—is two, and this I will demonstrate by
analogy, the highest form of proof. Listen! Once one is
one, therefore twice two is two. For that which applies
to the one must also apply to the other.

S. MASTER. The proof is perfectly in accord with the laws of
logic, but the answer is wrong.

OFFICER. What is in accord with the laws of logic cannot be
wrong. Let us put it to the test. One into one goes once,
therefore two into two goes twice.

S. MASTER. Quite correct according to analogy. But what then
is once three?

OFFICER. It is three.

S. MASTER. Consequently twice three is also three.

OFFICER, *pondering.* No, that can't be right . . . It can't be,
for if so . . . *Sits down in despair.* No, I am not mature
yet . . .

S. MASTER. No, you are not mature by a long way.

OFFICER, Then how long shall I have to stay here?

S. MASTER. How long? Here? You believe that time and space
exist? Assuming time does exist, you ought to be able to
say what time is. What is time?

OFFICER. Time . . . *Considers.* I can't say, although I know
what it is. Ergo, I may know what twice two is without
being able to say it. Can you yourself say what time is?

S. MASTER. Certainly I can.

ALL THE BOYS. Tell us then!

S. MASTER. Time? . . . Let me see. *Stands motionless with
his finger to his nose.* While we speak, time flies. Consequently time is something which flies while I am speaking.

BOY, *rising.* You're speaking now, sir, and while you're speaking, I fly. Consequently I am time. *Flies.*

S. MASTER. That is quite correct according to the laws of logic.

OFFICER. Then the laws of logic are absurd, for Nils, though he did fly, can't be time.

S. MASTER. That is also quite correct according to the laws of logic, although it is absurd.

OFFICER. Then logic is absurd.

S. MASTER. It really looks like it. But if logic is absurd, then the whole world is absurd . . . and I'll be damned if I stay here and teach you absurdities! If anyone will stand us a drink, we'll go and bathe.

OFFICER. That's a *posterus prius,* a world back to front, for it's customary to bathe first and have one's drink afterwards. You old fossil!

S. MASTER. Don't be so conceited, Doctor.

OFFICER. Captain, if you please. I am an officer, and I don't understand why I should sit here among a lot of schoolboys and be insulted.

S. MASTER, *wagging his finger.* We must mature!

Enter QUARANTINE MASTER.

Q. MASTER. The quarantine period has begun.

OFFICER. So there you are. Fancy this fellow making me sit here on a form, when I've taken my degree.

Q. MASTER. Well, why don't you go away?

OFFICER. Go away? That's easier said than done.

S. MASTER. So I should think. Try!

OFFICER, *to* QUARANTINE MASTER. Save me! Save me from his eyes!

Q. MASTER. Come on then! Come and help us dance. We must dance before the plague breaks out. We must.

OFFICER. Will the ship sail then?

Q. MASTER. The ship will sail first. A lot of tears will be shed of course.

OFFICER. Always tears; when she comes in and when she sails. Let's go.

They go out. The SCHOOLMASTER *continues to give his lesson in mime.*

The MAIDS, *who were standing at the window of the ballroom, walk sadly down to the quay.* EDITH, *until then motionless beside the piano, follows them.*

DAUGHTER, *to* OFFICER. Isn't there one happy person in this paradise?

OFFICER. Yes, here comes a newly wed couple. Listen to them.

The NEWLY WED COUPLE *enter.*

HUSBAND, *to* WIFE. My happiness is so complete that I wish to die.

WIFE. But why to die?

HUSBAND. In the midst of happiness grows a seed of unhappiness. Happiness consumes itself like a flame. It cannot burn for ever, it must go out, and the presentiment of its end destroys it at its very peak.

WIFE. Let us die together, now at once.

HUSBAND. Die! Yes, let us die. For I fear happiness, the deceiver.

They go towards the sea and disappear.

DAUGHTER, *to the* OFFICER. Life is evil. Human beings are to be pitied!

OFFICER. Look who's coming now. This is the most envied mortal in the place. *The* BLIND MAN *is led in.* He is the owner of these hundreds of Italian villas. He owns all these bays and creeks and shores and woods, the fish in the water, the birds in the air and the game in the woods. These thousands of people are his tenants, and the sun rises over his sea and sets over his lands.

DAUGHTER. And does he complain too?

OFFICER. Yes, with good cause, as he cannot see.

Q. MASTER. He is blind.

DAUGHTER. The most envied of all!

OFFICER. Now he's going to see the ship sail with his son aboard.

BLIND MAN. I do not see, but I hear. I hear the fluke of the anchor tearing the clay bed, just as when the hook is dragged out of a fish and the heart comes up too through the gullet. My son, my only child, is going to journey to strange lands across the great sea. Only my thoughts can go with him . . . Now I hear the chain clanking . . . and there's something flapping and lashing like washing on a clothes line . . . Wet handkerchiefs perhaps . . . And I hear a sound of sighing . . . or sobbing . . . like people crying . . . Maybe the plash of small waves against the hull, or maybe the girls on the quay, the abandoned, the inconsolable. I once asked a child why the sea was salt, and the child, whose father was on a long voyage, replied at once: "The sea is salt because sailors cry so much." "But why do sailors cry so much?" "Well," he said, "because they keep going away . . . And so they're always drying their handkerchiefs up on the masts." "And why do people cry when they're sad?" I asked. "Oh," said he, "that's because the eye window must be washed sometimes, so we can see better."

*The brig has set sail and glided away. The girls on the quay alternately wave their handkerchiefs and dry their eyes. Now on the topmast is hoisted the signal "*YES,*" a red ball on a white ground.* ALICE *waves a triumphant reply.*

DAUGHTER, *to* OFFICER. What does that flag mean?

OFFICER. It means "yes." It is the lieutenant's "yes" in red, red as heart's blood, written on the blue cloth of the sky.

DAUGHTER. Then what is "no" like?

OFFICER. Blue as tainted blood in blue veins. Look how elated Alice is.

DAUGHTER. And how Edith is weeping.

BLIND MAN. Meeting and parting, parting and meeting. That's life. I met his mother, then she went away. My son was left; now he has gone.

DAUGHTER. But he will come back.

BLIND MAN. Who is speaking to me? I have heard that voice before. In my dreams, in boyhood when summer holidays began, in early married life when my child was born. Whenever life smiled, I heard that voice, like the whisper of the South wind, like the sounds of a heavenly harp, like the angels' greeting, as I imagine it, on Christmas Eve. *The* LAWYER *enters, goes up to the* BLIND MAN *and whispers.*

Really?

LAWYER. Yes, it's a fact. *Goes across to the* DAUGHTER. You have seen most things now, but you have not yet experienced the worst thing of all.

DAUGHTER. What can that be?

LAWYER. Repetitions, reiterations. Going back. Doing one's lessons again . . . Come!

DAUGHTER. Where to?

LAWYER. To your duties.

DAUGHTER. What are they?

LAWYER. Everything you abominate. Everything you least want to do, and yet must. They are to abstain and renounce, to go without, to leave behind. They are everything that is disagreeable, repulsive, painful.

DAUGHTER. Are there no pleasant duties?

LAWYER. They become pleasant when they are done.

DAUGHTER. When they no longer exist. So duty is altogether unpleasant. What then can one enjoy?

LAWYER. What one enjoys is sin.

DAUGHTER. Sin?

LAWYER. Which is punished. Yes. If I enjoy myself one day, one evening, the next day I have a bad conscience and go through the torments of hell.

DAUGHTER. How strange!

LAWYER. I wake in the morning with a headache, and then the repetition begins, but it is a distorted repetition, so that everything which was charming and witty and beautiful the night before appears in memory ugly, stupid, repulsive. Pleasure stinks, and enjoyment falls to pieces. What people call success is always a step towards the next failure. The successes in my life have been my downfall. Men have an instinctive dread of another's good fortune. They feel it's unjust that fate should favour any one man, so try to restore the balance by rolling boulders across his path. To have talent is to be in danger of one's life—one may so easily starve to death. However, you must go back to your duties, or I shall take proceedings against you, and we shall go through all three Courts, first, second, third.

DAUGHTER. Go back? To the stove and the cabbage and the baby clothes?

LAWYER. Yes. And it's washing day—the big wash when all the handkerchiefs have to be done.

DAUGHTER. Oh, must I do that again?

LAWYER. The whole of life is only repetition. Look at the schoolmaster there. Yesterday he took his doctor's degree, was crowned with laurels, scaled Parnassus, was embraced by the monarch. Today he is back at school, asking what twice two is . . . and that's what he will go on doing until he dies. But come now, back to your home.

DAUGHTER. I would rather die.

LAWYER. Die? One can't do that. To begin with taking one's own life is so dishonourable that even one's corpse is dishonoured. And to add to that one is damned, for it is a mortal sin.

DAUGHTER. It is not easy to be human.

ALL. Hear, hear!

DAUGHTER. I will not go back with you to humiliation and dirt. I shall return to the place from which I came. But first the door must be opened, so that I may know the secret. I wish the door to be opened.

Enter the POET.

LAWYER. Then you must retrace your steps, go back the way you came, and put up with all the horrors of a lawsuit; the repetitions, the redraftings, the reiterations.

DAUGHTER. So be it. But first I shall seek solitude in the wilderness to find myself. We shall meet again. *To the* POET. Come with me.

A distant cry of lamentation rises.

VOICES. Oh! oh! oh!

DAUGHTER. What was that?

LAWYER. The doomed at Foulstrand.

DAUGHTER. Why do they wail so today?

LAWYER. Because here the sun is shining, here is music and dance and youth. This makes them suffer more.

DAUGHTER. We must set them free.

LAWYER. Try! Once a deliverer came, but he was hanged upon a cross.

DAUGHTER. By whom?

LAWYER. By all the righteous.

DAUGHTER. Who are they?

LAWYER. Don't you know the righteous? Well, you will.

DAUGHTER. Was it they who refused you your degree?

LAWYER. Yes.

DAUGHTER. Then I do know them.

The scene changes to a Mediterranean resort. In the background are villas, a Casino with a terrace, and a blue strip of sea. In the foreground is a white wall over which hang branches of orange trees in fruit. Below this to one side a huge heap of coal and two wheel barrows.

The DAUGHTER *and the* LAWYER *come on to the terrace.*

DAUGHTER. This is paradise.

1ST. COAL HEAVER. This is hell.

2ND. C. H. A hundred and twenty in the shade.

1ST. C. H. Shall we get into the sea?

2ND. C. H. Then the police'd come: "You mustn't bathe here!"

1ST. C. H. Can't we have a bit of fruit off that tree?

2ND. C. H. No. The police would come.

1ST. C. H. One can't work in this heat. I'm going to chuck it.

2ND. C. H. Then the police will come and take you up. *Pause.* Besides, you'll have nothing to eat.

1ST. C. H. Nothing to eat! We, who do the most work, get the least food. And the rich, who do nothing, get it all. Might one not, without taking liberties with the truth, call this unjust? What has the Daughter of the Gods up there to say about it?

DAUGHTER. I have no answer. But, tell me, what have you done to get so black and have so hard a lot?

1ST. C. H. What have we done? Got ourselves born of poor and pretty bad parents. Been sentenced a couple of times maybe.

DAUGHTER. Sentenced?

1ST. C. H. Yes. The ones that don't get caught sit up there in the Casino eating eight course dinners with wine.

DAUGHTER, *to* LAWYER. Can this be true?

LAWYER. More or less, yes.

DAUGHTER. Do you mean that everyone at some time or other deserves imprisonment?

LAWYER. Yes.

DAUGHTER. Even you?

LAWYER. Yes.

DAUGHTER. Is it true those poor men aren't allowed to bathe in that sea?

LAWYER. No, not even with their clothes on. Only those who try to drown themselves avoid paying. And they are more than likely to get beaten up at the police station.

DAUGHTER. Can't they go and bathe outside the town—in the country?

LAWYER. There is no country. It's all fenced in.

DAUGHTER. I mean where it is open and free.

LAWYER. Nothing is free. Everything is owned.

DAUGHTER. Even the sea, the vast, wide . . . ?

LAWYER. Everything. You can't go out in a boat, nor can you land, without it all being booked and paid for. It's marvellous.

DAUGHTER. This is not paradise.

LAWYER. I promise you that.

DAUGHTER. Why don't people do anything to improve conditions?

LAWYER. They certainly do. But all reformers end in prison or the madhouse.

DAUGHTER. Who puts them in prison?

LAWYER. All the righteous, all the respectable.

DAUGHTER. Who puts them in the madhouse?

LAWYER. Their own despair when they see the hopelessness of the struggle.

DAUGHTER. Has it occurred to anyone that there may be unknown reasons for this state of things?

LAWYER. Yes, the well-off always think that is so.

DAUGHTER. That there is nothing wrong with things as they are?

1ST. C. H. And yet we are the foundation of society. If there's no coal, the kitchen stove goes out and the fire on the hearth too. The machines in the factory stop working; the lights in streets and shops and homes all go out. Darkness and cold descend on you. That's why we sweat like hell carrying filthy coal. What do you give us in return?

LAWYER, *to* DAUGHTER. Help them. *Pause.* I know things can't be exactly the same for everybody, but why should there be such inequality?

The GENTLEMAN *and the* LADY *cross the terrace.*

LADY. Are you coming to play cards?

GENTLEMAN. No, I must go for a little walk to get an appetite for dinner.

Exeunt.

1ST. C. H. To *get* an appetite!

2ND. C. H. To *get* . . . !

Children enter. When they catch sight of the black workers they scream with terror [and run off].

1ST. C. H. They scream when they see us. They scream!

2ND. C. H. Curse it! We'd better get out the scaffolds soon and execute this rotten body.

1ST. C. H. Curse it, I say too!

LAWYER, *to* DAUGHTER. It's all wrong. It's not the people who are so bad, but . . .

DAUGHTER. But?

LAWYER. The system.

DAUGHTER, *hiding her face in her hands*. This is not paradise.

1ST. C. H. No. This is hell, pure hell.

The scene changes to [the earlier set of] Fingal's Cave. Long green billows roll gently into the cave. A red bell-buoy rocks upon the waves, but gives no sound until later. Music of the winds. Music of the waves.

The DAUGHTER *is with the* POET.

POET. Where have you brought me?

DAUGHTER. Far from the murmur and wailing of the children of men. To this grotto at the ends of the oceans to which we give the name *Indra's Ear*, for here, it is said, the King of Heaven listens to the lamentations of mortals.

POET. Why here?

DAUGHTER. Do you not see that this cave is shaped like a shell? Yes, you see it. Do you not know that your ear is shaped like a shell? You know, but you have given it no thought. *She picks up a shell.* As a child, did you never hold a shell to your ear and listen to the whisper of your heart's blood, to the humming of thoughts in your brain, to the parting of a thousand little worn-out tissues in the fabric of your body? All this you can hear in a small shell. Think then what may be heard in this great one.

POET, *listening*. I hear nothing but the sighing of the wind.

DAUGHTER. Then I will be its interpreter. Listen to the lamentation of the winds. *She speaks to soft music.*

> *Born under heaven's clouds,*
> *chased were we by Indra's fires*
> *down to the crust of earth.*
> *The mould of acres soiled our feet,*

> *we had to bear*
> *the dust of roads and city smoke,*
> *the kitchen's reek and fumes of wine.*
> *Out to these spacious seas we blew,*
> *to air our lungs,*
> *to shake our wings*
> *and bathe our feet.*
> *Indra, Lord of Heaven,*
> *hear us!*
> *Listen to our sighing!*
> *Earth is not clean,*
> *life is not just,*
> *men are not evil*
> *nor are they good.*
> *They live as best they may*
> *from one day to another,*
> *Sons of dust in dust they walk,*
> *born of the dust,*
> *dust they become.*
> *Feet they have to trudge,*
> *no wings.*
> *Dust-soiled they grow.*
> *Is the fault theirs*
> *or Thine?*

POET. So I heard once . . .

DAUGHTER. Hush! The winds are still singing.
   Continues to soft music.

> *We, the winds, the sons of air,*
> *bear man's lamentation.*
> *Thou hast heard us*
> *on autumn eves in the chimney stack,*
> *in the stove-pipe's vent,*
> *in the window cracks,*
> *as the rain wept on the tiles.*
> *Or on winter nights,*
> *mid the pine-wood's snows,*
> *or on the stormy ocean,*
> *hast heard the moaning and the whine,*

> *of rope and sail.*
> *That is us, the winds,*
> *the sons of air,*
> *who from human breasts*
> *we pierced ourselves,*
> *these sounds of suffering learnt.*
> *In sickroom, on the battlefield,*
> *and most where the newborn lie,*
> *screaming, complaining,*
> *of the pain of being alive.*
> *It is we, we, the winds*
> *who whine and whistle,*
> *woe! woe! woe!*

POET. It seems to me that once before . . .

DAUGHTER. Hush! The waves are singing.
Speaks to soft music.

> *It is we, we the waves,*
> *that rock the winds*
> *to rest.*
> *Green cradling waves,*
> *wet are we and salt.*
> *Like flames of fire,*
> *wet flames we are.*
> *Quenching, burning,*
> *cleansing, bathing,*
> *generating, multiplying.*
> *We, we the waves,*
> *that rock the winds*
> *to rest.*

False waves and faithless. Everything on earth that is not burned is drowned by those waves. Look there! *She points to the wreckage.* Look what the sea has stolen and destroyed! All that remains of those sunken ships is their figureheads . . . and the names—Justice, Friendship, Golden Peace, and Hope. That's all that's left of hope, treacherous hope. Spars, rowlocks, bailers. And see! The lifebuoy which saved itself, letting those in need perish.

POET, *searching the wreckage.* Here is the name of the ship
Justice. This is the ship which sailed from Fairhaven with
the Blind Man's son on board. So she sank. And Alice's
sweetheart was in her too, Edith's hopeless love.

DAUGHTER. The blind man? Fairhaven? Surely that I dreamt.
Alice's sweetheart, ugly Edith, Foulstrand and the quarantine, the sulphur and carbolic, graduation in the church,
the lawyer's office, the alley and Victoria. The Growing
Castle and the Officer . . . These things I dreamt.

POET. Of these things I once made poetry.

DAUGHTER. You know then what poetry is?

POET. I know what dreams are. What is poetry?

DAUGHTER. Not reality, but more than reality. Not dreams,
but waking dreams.

POET. Yet the children of men believe that poets merely play
—invent and fabricate.

DAUGHTER. It is just as well, my friend, or else the world
would be laid waste from lack of endeavour. All men
would lie upon their backs, gazing at the heavens; no
hand would be lifted to plough or spade, or plane or axe.

POET. Do you speak thus, Daughter of Indra? You, who are
half of heaven?

DAUGHTER. You are right to reproach me. I have lived too
long down here, and like you have bathed in mud. My
thoughts can no longer fly. Clay is on their wings and
soil about their feet. And I myself—*she raises her arms*—
I am sinking, sinking! Help me, Father, God of Heaven!
Silence. No longer can I hear His answer. The ether no
longer carries the sound of His lips to the shell of my ear
. . . the silver thread has snapped. Alas, I am earth-
bound!

POET. Do you mean then soon—to go?

DAUGHTER. As soon as I have burnt this earthly matter, for
the waters of the ocean cannot cleanse me. Why do you
ask?

POET. I have a prayer—a petition.

DAUGHTER. A petition?

POET. A petition from mankind to the ruler of the universe, drawn up by a dreamer.

DAUGHTER. Who is to present it?

POET. Indra's Daughter.

DAUGHTER. Can you speak the words?

POET. I can.

DAUGHTER. Speak them then.

POET. It is better that you should.

DAUGHTER. Where shall I read them?

POET. In my thoughts—or here. *He gives her a scroll.*

DAUGHTER. So be it. I will speak them. *She takes the scroll but does not read.*

> *"Why with anguish are you born?*
> *Why do you hurt your mother so,*
> *Child of man, when bringing her*
> *the joy of motherhood,*
> *joy beyond all other joys?*
> *Why wake to life,*
> *why greet the light*
> *with a cry of fury and of pain,*
> *Child of man, when to be glad*
> *should be the gift of life?*
> *Why are we born like animals?*
> *We who stem from God and man,*
> *whose souls are longing to be clothed*
> *in other than this blood and filth.*
> *Must God's own image cut its teeth?"*

Speaking her own thoughts.

Silence! No more! The work may not condemn the master.
Life's riddle still remains unsolved.

Continuing the POET's *bitter words.*

> *"And then the journey's course begins,*
> *over thistles, thorns and stones.*
> *If it should touch a beaten track,*
> *comes at once the cry: 'Keep off!'*

Pluck a flower, straight you'll find
the bloom you picked to be another's.
If cornfields lie across your path
and you must pursue your way,
trampling on another's crops,
others then will trample yours
that your loss may equal theirs.
Every pleasure you enjoy
brings to all your fellows sorrow,
yet your sorrow gives no gladness.
So sorrow, sorrow upon sorrow
on your way—until you're dead
and then, alas, give others bread.

Her own thought.

Is it thus, O son of dust,
You seek to win the ear of God?

POET. *How may son of dust find words,*
so pure, so light, so luminous,
that they can rise up from the earth?
Child of the Gods, translate for me,
this lamentation into speech
fit for Immortal ears.

DAUGHTER. I will.

POET, *pointing*. What is floating there—a buoy?

DAUGHTER. Yes.

POET. It is like a lung with a windpipe.

DAUGHTER. It is the watchman of the sea. When danger is
abroad, it sings.

POET. It seems to me that the sea is rising, and the waves beginning to . . .

DAUGHTER. You are not mistaken.

POET. Alas, what do I see? A ship—on the rocks.

DAUGHTER. What ship can it be?

POET. I believe it is the ghost-ship.

DAUGHTER. What is that?

POET. The Flying Dutchman.

DAUGHTER. He? Why is he punished so cruelly, and why does he not come ashore?

POET. Because he had seven unfaithful wives.

DAUGHTER. Shall he be punished for that?

POET. Yes. All righteous men condemned him.

DAUGHTER. Incomprehensible world! How can he be freed from this curse?

POET. Freed? One would beware of freeing him.

DAUGHTER. Why?

POET. Because . . . No, that is not the Dutchman. It is an ordinary ship in distress. Then why does the buoy not sound? Look how the sea is rising! The waves are towering, and soon we shall be imprisoned in this cave. Now the ship's bell is ringing. Soon there will be another figurehead in here. Cry out buoy! Watchman, do your duty!

The buoy sounds a four-part chord in fifths and sixths, like foghorns.

The crew is waving to us . . . but we ourselves perish.

DAUGHTER. Do you not want to be set free?

POET. Yes, yes I do! But not now . . . and not by water!

THE CREW, *singing four-part*. Christ Kyrie!

POET. They are calling and the sea is calling. But no one hears.

CREW, *singing as before*. Christ Kyrie!

DAUGHTER. Who is it coming there?

POET. Walking upon the water! Only One walks upon the water. It is not Peter, the rock, for he sank like a stone.

A white light appears over the sea.

CREW, *as before*. Christ Kyrie!

DAUGHTER. Is it He?

POET. It is He, the crucified.

DAUGHTER. Why, tell me why He was crucified.

POET. Because He wished to set men free.

DAUGHTER. Who—I have forgotten—who crucified Him?

The cave grows darker.

POET. All righteous men.

DAUGHTER. This incomprehensible world!

POET. The sea is rising. Darkness is falling on us. The storm is growing wilder.

The CREW *shriek.*

The crew are screaming with horror because they have seen their Saviour . . . and now . . . they are throwing themselves overboard in terror of the Redeemer.

The CREW *shriek again.*

Now they are screaming because they are going to die. They were born screaming and they die screaming.

The mounting waves threaten to drown them in the cave. The light begins to change.

DAUGHTER. If I were sure it was a ship . . .

POET. Indeed, I do not think it is a ship. It's a two storied house, with trees round it . . . and a telephone tower—a tower reaching to the skies. It's the modern Tower of Babel, sending up its wires to communicate with those above.

DAUGHTER. Child, man's thought needs no wires for its flight. The prayers of the devout penetrate all worlds. That is surely no Tower of Babel. If you wish to storm the heavens, storm them with your prayers.

POET. No, it's not a house . . . not a telephone tower. Do you see?

DAUGHTER. What do you see?

During the following speech, the scene changes to the alley of the Opera House.

POET. I see a snow-covered heath . . . a parade ground. The winter sun is shining behind a church on the hill, so that the tower casts its long shadow on the snow. Now a troop of soldiers comes marching over the heath. They march on the tower and up the spire . . . Now they are on the

cross, and I seem to know that the first to tread on the
weathercock must die . . . They are drawing near it. It's
the Corporal at their head who . . . Ah! A cloud is
sailing over the heath, across the sun . . . Now everything has gone. The moisture of the cloud has put out
the fire of the sun. The sunlight created a shadowy image
of the tower, but the shadow of the cloud smothered the
image of the tower.

[*It is springtime. The tree and the monkshood are in
bud. The* STAGE DOORKEEPER *sits in her old place. The*
DAUGHTER *enters, followed by the* POET.]

DAUGHTER, *to* DOORKEEPER. Has the Chancellor arrived yet?

DOORKEEPER. No.

DAUGHTER. Nor the Deans?

DOORKEEPER. No.

DAUGHTER. You must send for them at once. The door is going
to be opened.

DOORKEEPER. Is it so urgent?

DAUGHTER. Yes. It's thought that the answer to the riddle
of the universe is locked up in there. So send for the
Chancellor and the Deans of the four Faculties. *The*
DOORKEEPER *blows a whistle.* And don't forget the Glazier
and his diamond, or nothing can be done.

*The personnel of the Opera pour from the building as in
the earlier scene.*

The OFFICER [*young again*], *in morning coat and top
hat, comes through the gate, carrying a bouquet of roses
and looking radiantly happy.*

OFFICER, *singing.* Victoria!

DOORKEEPER. The young lady will be down in a minute.

OFFICER. Good. The carriage is waiting, the table is laid, the
champagne is on the ice . . . Let me embrace you,
Madam. *Embraces the* DOORKEEPER. Victoria!

WOMAN'S VOICE, *from above, singing.* I am here.

OFFICER, *pacing.* Well, I am waiting.

POET. I seem to have lived through all this before.

DAUGHTER. I too.

POET. Perhaps I dreamt it.

DAUGHTER. Or made a poem of it.

POET. Or made a poem.

DAUGHTER. You know then what poetry is.

POET. I know what dreaming is.

DAUGHTER. I feel that once before, somewhere else, we said these words.

POET. Then soon you will know what reality is.

DAUGHTER. Or dreaming.

POET. Or poetry.

Enter the CHANCELLOR *and the* DEANS OF THEOLOGY, PHILOSOPHY, MEDICINE *and* LAW, [*followed by the* GLAZIER *and a group of* RIGHTEOUS PEOPLE].

CHANCELLOR. It's all a question of the door, you understand. What does the Dean of Theology think about it?

DEAN OF THEOLOGY. I don't think—I believe. Credo.

DEAN OF PHILOSOPHY. I think.

DEAN OF MEDICINE. I know.

DEAN OF LAW. I doubt—until I have heard the evidence and witnesses.

CHANCELLOR. Now they will quarrel again. Well then, first what does Theology believe?

THEOLOGY. I believe that this door ought not to be opened, as it conceals dangerous truths.

PHILOSOPHY. The truth is never dangerous.

MEDICINE. What is truth?

LAW. Whatever can be proved by two witnesses.

THEOLOGY. Anything can be proved by two false witnesses— if you're a pettifogger.

PHILOSOPHY. Truth is wisdom, and wisdom and knowledge are philosophy itself. Philosophy is the science of sciences, the knowledge of knowledge. All other sciences are its servants.

MEDICINE. The only science is natural science. Philosophy is not science. It is mere empty speculation.

THEOLOGY. Bravo!

PHILOSOPHY, *to* DEAN OF THEOLOGY. You say bravo. And what, may I ask, are you? The arch enemy of knowledge, the antithesis of science. You are ignorance and darkness.

MEDICINE. Bravo!

THEOLOGY, *to* DEAN OF MEDICINE. And you say bravo—you who can't see further than the end of your own nose in a magnifying glass. You who believe in nothing but your deceptive senses—in your eyes, for instance, which may be long-sighted, short-sighted, blind, purblind, squinting, one-eyed, colour-blind, red-blind, green-blind . . .

MEDICINE. Blockhead!

THEOLOGY. Ass!

They fight.

CHANCELLOR. Enough! Birds of a feather shouldn't peck each other's eyes out.

PHILOSOPHY. Had I to choose between these two, Theology and Medicine, I should choose—neither.

LAW. And if I had to sit in judgment over you three, I should condemn—every one of you . . . You can't agree upon a single point, and never have been able to. Let's get back to the matter in hand. What's your opinion, Chancellor, of this door and the opening of it?

CHANCELLOR. Opinion? I don't have opinions. I am merely appointed by the Government to see you don't break each other's arms and legs in the Senate in the course of educating the young. Opinions? No, I take good care not to have any. I had a few once, but they were soon exploded. Opinions always are exploded—by opponents, of course. Perhaps we had better have the door opened now, even at the risk of it concealing dangerous truths.

LAW. What is truth? What is the truth?

THEOLOGY. I am the Truth and the Life . . .

PHILOSOPHY. I am the knowledge of knowledge.

MEDICINE. I am exact knowledge . . .

LAW. I doubt.

They fight.

DAUGHTER. Shame on you, teachers of youth!

LAW. Chancellor, as delegate of the Government and head of the teaching staff, denounce this woman. She has cried "shame on you" which is contumely, and she has ironically referred to you as "teachers of youth," which is slander.

DAUGHTER. Poor youth!

LAW. She pities youth, and that's tantamount to accusing us. Chancellor, denounce her!

DAUGHTER. Yes, I accuse you—all of you—of sowing the seeds of doubt and dissension in the minds of the young.

LAW. Listen to her! She herself is raising doubts in the young as to our authority, yet she is accusing us of raising doubts. I appeal to all righteous men. Is this not a criminal offence?

ALL THE RIGHTEOUS. Yes, it is criminal.

LAW. The righteous have condemned you. Go in peace with your gains. Otherwise . . .

DAUGHTER. My gains? Otherwise what?

LAW. Otherwise you will be stoned.

POET. Or crucified.

DAUGHTER [*to the* POET]. I am going. Come with me and learn the answer to the riddle.

POET. Which riddle?

DAUGHTER. What does he mean by my "gains"?

POET. Probably nothing at all. That's what we call idle chatter. He was just chattering.

DAUGHTER. But that hurt me more than anything else.

POET. That's why he said it. Human beings are like that.

The GLAZIER *opens the door and looks inside.*

ALL THE RIGHTEOUS. Hurrah! The door is open.

The DEANS *look inside.*

CHANCELLOR. What was concealed behind that door?

GLAZIER. I can't see anything.

CHANCELLOR. He can't see anything. Well, I'm not surprised. Deans! What was concealed behind that door?

THEOLOGY. Nothing. That is the solution of the riddle of the universe. Out of nothing in the beginning God created heaven and earth.

PHILOSOPHY. Out of nothing comes nothing.

MEDICINE. Bosh! That is nothing.

LAW. I doubt everything. And there's some swindle here. I appeal to all righteous men.

DAUGHTER, *to* POET. Who are these righteous?

POET. Let him tell you who can. All the righteous are often just one person. Today they are me and mine, tomorrow you and yours. One is nominated for the post, or rather, one nominates oneself.

ALL THE RIGHTEOUS. We have been swindled.

CHANCELLOR. Who has swindled you?

ALL THE RIGHTEOUS. The Daughter!

CHANCELLOR. Will the Daughter kindly inform us what her idea was in having the door opened.

DAUGHTER. No, my friends. If I told you, you would not believe it.

MEDICINE. But there's nothing there.

DAUGHTER. What you say is correct. But you have not understood it.

MEDICINE. What she says is bosh.

ALL. Bosh!

DAUGHTER, *to* POET. They are to be pitied.

POET. Do you mean that seriously?

DAUGHTER. Very seriously.

POET. Do you think the righteous are to be pitied too?

DAUGHTER. They most of all perhaps.

POET. And the four Faculties?

DAUGHTER. They too, and not least. Four heads and four minds with a single body. Who created such a monster?

ALL. She does not answer.

CHANCELLOR. Then stone her!

DAUGHTER. This is the answer.

CHANCELLOR. Listen! She is answering.

ALL. Stone her! She is answering.

Enter LAWYER.

DAUGHTER. If she answers, or if she does not answer, stone her! *To* POET. Come, you Seer, and I will answer the riddle, but far from here, out in the wilderness, where none can hear us, none can see us. For . . .

The LAWYER *interrupts by taking hold of her arm.*

LAWYER. Have you forgotten your duties?

DAUGHTER. God knows I have not. But I have higher duties.

LAWYER. But your child?

DAUGHTER. My child? Yes?

LAWYER. Your child is calling you.

DAUGHTER. My child! Alas, I am earthbound! And this anguish in my breast, this agony, what is it?

LAWYER. Don't you know?

DAUGHTER. No.

LAWYER. It is the pangs of conscience.

DAUGHTER. The pangs of conscience?

LAWYER. Yes. They come after every neglected duty, after every pleasure, however innocent—if there is such a thing as an innocent pleasure, which is doubtful. And they also come every time one causes pain to one's neighbour.

DAUGHTER. Is there no remedy?

LAWYER. Yes, but only one. To do one's duty instantly.

DAUGHTER. You look like a devil when you say the word "duty." But when one has, as I, two duties?

LAWYER. Fulfil first one and then the other.

DAUGHTER. The higher first. Therefore, you look after my child, and I will do my duty.

LAWYER. Your child is unhappy without you. Can you let another suffer on your account?

DAUGHTER. There is conflict in my soul. It is pulled this way and that until it is torn in two.

LAWYER. These, you see, are life's little trials.

DAUGHTER. Oh, how they tear one!

POET. You would have nothing to do with me, if you knew what misery I have caused through following my vocation—yes, my vocation, which is the highest duty of all.

DAUGHTER. What do you mean?

POET. I had a father, whose hopes were centred in me, his only son. I was to have carried on his business, but I ran away from the Commercial College. Worry brought my father to his grave. My mother wanted me to be religious. I couldn't be religious. She disowned me. I had a friend who helped me when I was desperate, but that friend turned out to be a tyrant to the very people whose cause I upheld. So to save my soul I had to strike down my friend and benefactor. Since that time I have had no peace. I am considered base, contemptible, the scum of the earth. Nor do I get any comfort from my conscience when it tells me I did right, for the next moment it assures me I did wrong. That is the way of life.

DAUGHTER. Come with me, out into the wilderness.

LAWYER. Your child!

DAUGHTER, *indicating all present*. These are my children. Each one of them is good, but as soon as they are together they fight and turn into devils. Farewell!

[*Blackout. When the lights go up the scene has changed to*] Outside the Castle.
The set is the same as the earlier one, except that now the ground is covered with blue monkshood, aconite and other flowers. The chrysanthemum bud at the top of the tower is on the point of bursting. The Castle windows are lit with candles. [*In the foreground is a fire.*]

DAUGHTER. The hour is at hand when with the aid of fire I shall ascend again into the ether. This is what you call death and approach with so much fear.

POET. Fear of the unknown.

DAUGHTER. Which yet you know.

POET. Who knows it?

DAUGHTER. Mankind. Why do you not believe your prophets?

POET. Prophets have never been believed. Why is that? If they truly speak with the voice of God, why then do men not believe? His power to convince should be irresistible.

DAUGHTER. Have you always doubted?

POET. No, I have had faith many times, but after a while it drifted away, like a dream when one awakens.

DAUGHTER. To be mortal is not easy.

POET. You understand this now?

DAUGHTER. Yes.

POET. Tell me, did not Indra once send his son down to earth to hear man's complaint?

DAUGHTER. He did. And how was he received?

POET. How did he fulfil his mission?—to answer with a question.

DAUGHTER. To answer with another—was not the state of mankind bettered by his visit to the earth? Answer truly.

POET. Bettered? Yes, a little, a very little. Now, instead of further questions, will you tell me the answer to the riddle?

DAUGHTER. What purpose would that serve? You would not believe me.

POET. I shall believe you, for I know who you are.

DAUGHTER. Then I will tell you. In the dawn of time, before your sun gave light, Brahma, the divine primal force let himself be seduced by Maya, the World Mother, that he might propagate. This mingling of the divine element with the earthly was the Fall from heaven. This world, its life and its inhabitants are therefore only a mirage, a reflection, a dream image.

POET. My dream!

DAUGHTER. A true dream. But, in order to be freed from the earthly element, the descendants of Brahma sought renunciation and suffering. And so you have suffering as the deliverer. But this yearning for suffering comes into conflict with the longing for joy, for love. Now you understand what love is; supreme joy in the greatest suffering, the sweetest is the most bitter. Do you understand now what woman is? Woman, through whom sin and death entered into life.

POET. I understand. And the outcome?

DAUGHTER. What you yourself know. Conflict between the pain of joy and the joy of pain, between the anguish of the penitent and the pleasure of the sensual.

POET. And the conflict?

DAUGHTER. The conflict of opposites generates power, as fire and water create the force of steam.

POET. But peace? Rest?

DAUGHTER. Hush! You must ask no more, nor may I answer. The altar is decked for the sacrifice, the flowers keep vigil, the candles are lighted, the white sheet hangs in the window, the threshold is strewn with pine.*

POET. How calmly you speak! As if suffering did not exist for you.

DAUGHTER. Not exist? I suffered all your sufferings a hundred fold because my sensibilities were finer.

POET. Tell me your sorrows.

DAUGHTER. Poet, could you tell your own with utter truth? Could your words ever once convey your thoughts?

POET. You are right. No. To myself I have always seemed a deaf mute, and while the crowd was acclaiming my song, to me it seemed a jangle. And so, you see, I was always ashamed when men paid me homage.

DAUGHTER. And yet you wish me to speak? Look into my eyes.

POET. I cannot endure your gaze.

DAUGHTER. How then will you endure my words, if I speak in my own language?

POET. Even so, before you go, tell me from what you suffered most down here.

*Signs of mourning in Sweden.

DAUGHTER. From living. From feeling my vision dimmed by having eyes, my hearing dulled by having ears, and my thought, my airy, luminous thought, bound down in a labyrinth of fat. You have seen a brain. What twisting channels, what creeping ways!

POET. Yes, and that is why the minds of the righteous are twisted.

DAUGHTER. Cruel, always cruel, each one of you.

POET. How can we be otherwise?

DAUGHTER. Now first I shake the dust from my feet, the earth, the clay. *She takes off her shoes and puts them in the fire.*

[*One after another the following characters come in, put their contributions on the fire, cross the stage and go out, while the* POET *and the* DAUGHTER *stand watching.*]

DOORKEEPER. Perhaps I may burn my shawl too?

OFFICER. And I my roses, of which only the thorns are left.

BILLSTICKER. The posters can go, but my fishnet never.

GLAZIER. Farewell to the diamond that opened the door.

LAWYER. The report of the proceedings in the High Court touching the Pope's beard or the diminishing water supply in the sources of the Ganges.

QUARANTINE MASTER. A small contribution in the shape of the black mask which turned me into a blackamoor against my will.

VICTORIA [SHE]. My beauty—my sorrow.

EDITH. My ugliness—my sorrow.

BLINDMAN, *putting his hand in the fire.* I give my hand which is my sight.

DON JUAN *is pushed in in the bathchair* [*accompanied by the* COQUETTE *and the* FRIEND].

DON JUAN. Make haste, make haste! Life is short.

POET. I have read that when a life is nearing its end, everything and everyone pass by in a single stream. Is this the end?

DAUGHTER. For me, yes. Farewell!

POET. Say a parting word!

DAUGHTER. No, I cannot. Do you think your language can express our thoughts?

Enter the DEAN OF THEOLOGY, *raging.*

THEOLOGY. I am disowned by God; I am persecuted by men; I am abandoned by the Government, and scorned by my colleagues. How can I have faith when no one else has faith? How can I defend a God who does not defend His own people? It's all bosh!

He throws a book on the fire and goes out. The POET *snatches the book from the flames.*

POET. Do you know what this is? A Book of Martyrs, a calendar with a martyr for each day of the year.

DAUGHTER. A martyr?

POET. Yes, one who was tortured and put to death for his faith. Tell me why. Do you believe all who are tortured suffer, all who are put to death feel pain? Surely suffering is redemption and death deliverance.

KRISTIN *enters with her paste and strips of paper.*

KRISTIN. I paste, I paste, till there is nothing left to paste.

POET. If heaven itself cracked open, you would try to paste it up. Go away!

KRISTIN. Are there no inner windows in the Castle?

POET. No, none there.

KRISTIN. I'll go then, I'll go.

Exit.

[*As the* DAUGHTER *speaks her last lines the flames rise until the Castle is on fire.*]

DAUGHTER. *The parting time has come; the end draws near.*
        Farewell, you child of man, dreamer,
        poet, who knows best the way to live.
        Above the earth on wings you hover,
        plunging at times to graze the dust,
        but not to be submerged.
        Now I am going, now the hour has come

to leave both friend and place,
how sharp the loss of all I loved,
how deep regret for all destroyed!
Ah, now I know the whole of living's pain!
This then it is to be a human being—
ever to miss the thing one never prized
and feel remorse for what one never did,
to yearn to go, yet long to stay.
And so the human heart is split in two,
emotions by wild horses torn—
conflict, discord and uncertainty.
Farewell! Tell all on earth I shall remember them.
Where I am going, and in your name
carry their lamentations to the throne.
Farewell!

*She goes into the Castle. Music is heard. The background
is lighted up by the burning Castle, and now shows a wall
of human faces, questioning, mourning, despairing. While
the Castle is burning, the flower-bud on the roof bursts
into a giant chrysanthemum.*

THE GHOST SONATA

by

AUGUST STRINDBERG

INTRODUCTION

I have called this most famous of Strindberg's Chamber
Plays, written for his own Intimate Theatre, THE GHOST
SONATA, in spite of the tempting alternative SPOOK sometimes used before, because I believe "ghost" is a truer
translation of the author's "spök" than "spook." The latter
word has, in English, a facetious flavour—one inevitably
thinks of "spooky"—which the Swedish word has not and,
fantastic in part even grotesque though the play is, it is
very far from being facetious.

Strindberg's original title was "Kama-Loka," reflecting
the influence on him at the time of Theosophy, and the
theme is merciless exposure of life's most shameful secrets.
He was now writing, in 1907, at enormous speed and
under great pressure. The Intimate Theatre was opening
with the usual vicissitudes of small theatres and A DREAM
PLAY was going into rehearsal at the Swedish Theatre.
Since the end of their brief married life his domestic
affairs had been all awry, and the whole situation was a
strain.

Nevertheless, in THE GHOST SONATA Strindberg produced a masterpiece, once again using the dream idiom,
in which everything was possible and probable, but adding to the vision of the poet the technique of the Naturalist. In THE GHOST SONATA there is no angelic child as in
EASTER to bring poor mortals peace, no goddess to pity
their woe. The weird mummy woman, who can stop time
and undo what was done, leaves the soul only one way
out of its hell—the way of retribution and death.

Strindberg's own obsession with "the labour of keeping
the dirt of life at a distance" breaks the tender idyll of
the Student and the Hyacinth Girl, and the huge, sinister,
vampire cook is a telling piece of Symbolism. The play
ends, oddly, with a view of one of Strindberg's favourite
pictures: Böcklin's *Isle of the Dead.* Rereading E. M.
Forster's novel *Howard's End,* I find he makes his half-
German heroine say:

"My blood boils . . . when I listen to the tasteful contempt of the average islander for things Teutonic . . . 'Oh, Böcklin,' they say; 'he strains after beauty, he peoples Nature with gods too consciously.' Of course Böcklin strains, because he wants something—beauty and all the other intangible gifts that are floating about the world . . ."

The same might be said of Strindberg.

E. S.

Characters

THE OLD MAN, *Hummel, a Company Director*
THE STUDENT, *Arkenholtz*
THE MILKMAID, *an apparition*
THE CARETAKER'S WIFE
THE CARETAKER
THE LADY IN BLACK, *the daughter of the Caretaker's Wife and the Dead Man. Also referred to as the Dark Lady*
THE COLONEL
THE MUMMY, *the Colonel's wife*
THE GIRL, *the Colonel's daughter, actually the daughter of the Old Man*
THE ARISTOCRAT, *Baron Skanskorg. Engaged to the Lady in Black*
JOHANSSON, *the Old Man's servant*
BENGTSSON, *the Colonel's servant*
THE FIANCÉE, *a white-haired old woman, once betrothed to the Old Man*
THE COOK
A MAIDSERVANT
BEGGARS

SCENE ONE

Outside the house. The corner of the façade of a modern house, showing the ground floor above, and the street in front. The ground floor terminates on the right in the Round Room, above which, on the first floor, is a balcony with a flagstaff. The windows of the Round Room face the street in front of the house, and at the corner look on to the suggestion of a side-street running towards the back. At the beginning of the scene the blinds of the Round Room are down. When, later, they are raised, the white marble statue of a young woman can be seen, surrounded with palms and brightly lighted by rays of sunshine.

To the left of the Round Room is the Hyacinth Room; its window filled with pots of hyacinths, blue, white and pink. Further left, at the back, is an imposing double front door with laurels in tubs on either side of it. The doors are wide open, showing a staircase of white marble with a banister of mahogany and brass. To the left of the front door is another ground-floor window, with a window-mirror.* On the balcony rail in the corner above the Round Room are a blue silk quilt and two white pillows. The windows to the left of this are hung with white sheets.†

In the foreground, in front of the house, is a green bench; to the right a street drinking-fountain, to the left an advertisement column.

It is a bright Sunday morning, and as the curtain rises the bells of several churches, some near, some far away, are ringing.

On the staircase the LADY IN BLACK *stands motionless.*

*Set at an angle inside the window, so as to show what is going on in the street.
†Sign of mourning.

The CARETAKER'S WIFE *sweeps the doorstep, then polishes the brass on the door and waters the laurels.*

In a wheel-chair by the advertisement column sits the OLD MAN, *reading a newspaper. His hair and beard are white and he wears spectacles.*

The MILKMAID *comes round the corner on the right, carrying milk bottles in a wire basket. She is wearing a summer dress with brown shoes, black stockings and a white cap. She takes off her cap and hangs it on the fountain, wipes the perspiration from her forehead, washes her hands and arranges her hair, using the water as a mirror.*

A steamship bell is heard, and now and then the silence is broken by the deep notes of an organ in a nearby church.

After a few moments, when all is silent and the MILK-MAID *has finished her toilet, the* STUDENT *enters from the left. He has had a sleepless night and is unshaven. He goes straight up to the fountain. There is a pause before he speaks.*

STUDENT. May I have the cup? *The* MILKMAID *clutches the cup to her.* Haven't you finished yet?

The MILKMAID *looks at him with horror.*

OLD MAN, *to himself.* Who's he talking to? I don't see anybody. Is he crazy?

He goes on watching them in great astonishment.

STUDENT, *to the* MILKMAID. What are you staring at? Do I look so terrible? Well, I've had no sleep, and of course you think I've been making a night of it . . . *The* MILKMAID *stays just as she is.* You think I've been drinking, eh? Do I smell of liquor? *The* MILKMAID *does not change.* I haven't shaved, I know. Give me a drink of water, girl. I've earned it. *Pause.* Oh well, I suppose I'll have to tell you. I spent the whole night dressing wounds and looking after the injured. You see, I was there when that house collapsed last night. Now you know. *The* MILKMAID *rinses the cup and gives him a drink.* Thanks. *The* MILKMAID *stands motionless. Slowly.* Will you do me a great favor?

Pause. The thing is, my eyes, as you can see, are inflamed, but my hands have been touching wounds and corpses, so it would be dangerous to put them near my eyes. Will you take my handkerchief—it's quite clean—and dip it in the fresh water and bathe my eyes? Will you do this? Will you play the good Samaritan? *The* MILKMAID *hesitates, but does as he bids.* Thank you, my dear. *He takes out his purse. She makes a gesture of refusal.* Forgive my stupidity, but I'm only half-awake. . . .

The MILKMAID *disappears.*

OLD MAN, *to the* STUDENT. Excuse me speaking to you, but I heard you say you were at the scene of the accident last night. I was just reading about it in the paper.

STUDENT. Is it in the paper already?

OLD MAN. The whole thing, including your portrait. But they regret that they have been unable to find out the name of the splendid young student. . . .

STUDENT. Really? *Glances at the paper.* Yes, that's me. Well I never!

OLD MAN. Who was it you were talking to just now?

STUDENT. Didn't you see? *Pause.*

OLD MAN. Would it be impertinent to inquire—what in fact your name is?

STUDENT. What would be the point? I don't care for publicity. If you get any praise, there's always disapproval too. The art of running people down has been developed to such a pitch. . . . Besides, I don't want any reward.

OLD MAN. You're well off, perhaps.

STUDENT. No, indeed. On the contrary, I'm very poor.

OLD MAN. Do you know, it seems to me I've heard your voice before. When I was young I had a friend who pronounced certain words just as you do. I've never met anyone else with quite that pronunciation. Only him—and you. Are you by any chance related to Mr. Arkenholtz, the merchant?

STUDENT. He was my father.

OLD MAN. Strange are the paths of fate. I saw you when you were an infant, under very painful circumstances.

STUDENT. Yes, I understand I came into the world in the middle of a bankruptcy.

OLD MAN. Just that.

STUDENT. Perhaps I might ask your name.

OLD MAN. I am Mr. Hummel.

STUDENT. Are you the? . . . I remember that . . .

OLD MAN. Have you often heard my name mentioned in your family?

STUDENT. Yes.

OLD MAN. And mentioned perhaps with a certain aversion? *The* STUDENT *is silent.* Yes, I can imagine it. You were told, I suppose, that I was the man who ruined your father? All who ruin themselves through foolish speculations consider they were ruined by those they couldn't fool. *Pause.* Now these are the facts. Your father robbed me of seventeen thousand crowns—the whole of my savings at that time.

STUDENT. It's queer that the same story can be told in two such different ways.

OLD MAN. You surely don't believe I'm telling you what isn't true?

STUDENT. What am I to believe?-My father didn't lie.

OLD MAN. That is so true. A father never lies. But I too am a father, and so it follows . . .

STUDENT. What are you driving at?

OLD MAN. I saved your father from disaster, and he repaid me with all the frightful hatred that is born of an obligation to be grateful. He taught his family to speak ill of me.

STUDENT. Perhaps you made him ungrateful by poisoning your help with unnecessary humiliation.

OLD MAN. All help is humiliating, sir.

STUDENT. What do you want from me?

OLD MAN. I'm not asking for the money, but if you will render me a few small services, I shall consider myself well paid.

You see that I am a cripple. Some say it is my own fault; others lay the blame on my parents. I prefer to blame life itself, with its pitfalls. For if you escape one snare, you fall headlong into another. In any case, I am unable to climb stairs or ring doorbells, and that is why I am asking you to help me.

STUDENT. What can I do?

OLD MAN. To begin with, push my chair so that I can read those playbills. I want to see what is on tonight.

STUDENT, *pushing the chair*. Haven't you got an attendant?

OLD MAN. Yes, but he has gone on an errand. He'll be back soon. Are you a medical student?

STUDENT. No, I am studying languages, but I don't know at all what I'm going to do.

OLD MAN. Aha! Are you good at mathematics?

STUDENT. Yes, fairly.

OLD MAN. Good. Perhaps you would like a job.

STUDENT. Yes, why not?

OLD MAN. Splendid. *He studies the playbills.* They are doing *The Valkyrie* for the matinée. That means the Colonel will be there with his daughter, and as he always sits at the end of the sixth row, I'll put you next to him. Go to that telephone kiosk please and order a ticket for seat eighty-two in the sixth row.

STUDENT. Am I to go to the Opera in the middle of the day?

OLD MAN. Yes. Do as I tell you and things will go well with you. I want to see you happy, rich and honored. Your début last night as the brave rescuer will make you famous by tomorrow and then your name will be worth something.

STUDENT, *going to the telephone kiosk*. What an odd adventure!

OLD MAN. Are you a gambler?

STUDENT. Yes, unfortunately.

OLD MAN. We'll make it fortunately. Go on now, telephone. *The* STUDENT *goes. The* OLD MAN *reads his paper. The*

LADY IN BLACK *comes out on to the pavement and talks to the* CARETAKER'S WIFE. *The* OLD MAN *listens, but the audience hears nothing. The* STUDENT *returns.* Did you fix it up?

STUDENT. It's done.

OLD MAN. You see that house?

STUDENT. Yes, I've been looking at it a lot. I passed it yesterday when the sun was shining on the windowpanes, and I imagined all the beauty and elegance there must be inside. I said to my companion: "Think of living up there in the top flat, with a beautiful young wife, two pretty little children and an income of twenty thousand crowns a year."

OLD MAN. So that's what you said. That's what you said. Well, well! I too am very fond of this house.

STUDENT. Do you speculate in houses?

OLD MAN. Mm—yes. But not in the way you mean.

STUDENT. Do you know the people who live here?

OLD MAN. Every one of them. At my age one knows everybody, and their parents and grandparents too, and one's always related to them in some way or other. I am just eighty, but no one knows me—not really. I take an interest in human destiny. *The blinds of the Round Room are drawn up. The* COLONEL *is seen, wearing mufti. He looks at the thermometer outside one of the windows, then turns back into the room and stands in front of the marble statue.* Look, that's the Colonel, whom you will sit next to this afternoon.

STUDENT. Is he—the Colonel? I don't understand any of this, but it's like a fairy story.

OLD MAN. My whole life's like a book of fairy stories, sir. And although the stories are different, they are held together by one thread, and the main theme constantly recurs.

STUDENT. Who is that marble statue of?

OLD MAN. That, naturally, is his wife.

STUDENT. Was she such a wonderful person?

OLD MAN. Er . . . yes.

STUDENT. Tell me.

OLD MAN. We can't judge people, young man. If I were to tell you that she left him, that he beat her, that she returned to him and married him a second time, and that now she is sitting inside there like a mummy, worshipping her own statue—then you would think me crazy.

STUDENT. I don't understand.

OLD MAN. I didn't think you would. Well, then we have the window with the hyacinths. His daughter lives there. She has gone out for a ride, but she will be home soon.

STUDENT. And who is the dark lady talking to the caretaker?

OLD MAN. Well, that's a bit complicated, but it is connected with the dead man, up there where you see the white sheets.

STUDENT. Why, who was he?

OLD MAN. A human being like you or me, but the most conspicuous thing about him was his vanity. If you were a Sunday child, you would see him presently come out of that door to look at the Consulate flag flying at half-mast. He was, you understand, a Consul, and he reveled in coronets and lions and plumed hats and colored ribbons.

STUDENT. Sunday child, you say? I'm told I was born on a Sunday.

OLD MAN. No, were you really? I might have known it. I saw it from the color of your eyes. Then you can see what others can't. Have you noticed that?

STUDENT. I don't know what others do see, but at times. . . . Oh, but one doesn't talk of such things!

OLD MAN. I was almost sure of it. But you can talk to me, because I understand such things.

STUDENT. Yesterday, for instance . . . I was drawn to that obscure little street where later on the house collapsed. I went there and stopped in front of that building which I had never seen before. Then I noticed a crack in the wall. . . . I heard the floor boards snapping. . . . I dashed over and picked up a child that was passing under

the wall. . . . The next moment the house collapsed. I
was saved, but in my arms, which I thought held the
child, was nothing at all.

OLD MAN. Yes, yes, just as I thought. Tell me something. Why
were you gesticulating that way just now by the fountain?
And why were you talking to yourself?

STUDENT. Didn't you see the milkmaid I was talking to?

OLD MAN, *in horror.* Milkmaid?

STUDENT. Surely. The girl who handed me the cup.

OLD MAN. Really? So that's what was going on. Ah well, I
haven't second sight, but there are things I can do. THE
FIANCÉE *is now seen to sit down by the window which has
the window-mirror.* Look at that old woman in the window. Do you see her? Well, she was my fiancée once,
sixty years ago. I was twenty. Don't be alarmed. She
doesn't recognize me. We see one another every day, and
it makes no impression on me, although once we vowed
to love one another eternally. Eternally!

STUDENT. How foolish you were in those days! We never talk
to our girls like that.

OLD MAN. Forgive us, young man. We didn't know any better. But can you see that that old woman was once young
and beautiful?

STUDENT. It doesn't show. And yet there's some charm in her
looks. I can't see her eyes.

The CARETAKER'S WIFE *comes out with a basket of
chopped fir branches.**

OLD MAN. Ah, the caretaker's wife! That dark lady is her
daughter by the dead man. That's why her husband was
given the job of caretaker. But the dark lady has a suitor,
who is an aristocrat with great expectations. He is in the
process of getting a divorce—from his present wife, you
understand. She's presenting him with a stone mansion in
order to be rid of him. This aristocratic suitor is the son-
in-law of the dead man, and you can see his bedclothes

*It was customary in Sweden to strew the ground with
these for a funeral.

being aired on the balcony upstairs. It is complicated, I must say.

STUDENT. It's fearfully complicated.

OLD MAN. Yes, that it is, internally and externally, although it looks quite simple.

STUDENT. But then who was the dead man?

OLD MAN. You asked me that just now, and I answered. If you were to look round the corner, where the tradesmen's entrance is, you would see a lot of poor people whom he used to help—when it suited him.

STUDENT. He was a kind man then.

OLD MAN. Yes—sometimes.

STUDENT. Not always?

OLD MAN. No-o. That's the way of people. Now, sir, will you push my chair a little, so that it gets into the sun. I'm horribly cold. When you're never able to move about, the blood congeals. I'm going to die soon, I know that, but I have a few things to do first. Take my hand and feel how cold I am.

STUDENT, *taking it.* Yes, inconceivably. *He shrinks back, trying in vain to free his hand.*

OLD MAN. Don't leave me. I am tired now and lonely, but I haven't always been like this, you know. I have an enormously long life behind me, enormously long. I have made people unhappy and people have made me unhappy—the one cancels out the other—but before I die I want to see you happy. Our fates are entwined through your father— and other things.

STUDENT. Let go of my hand. You are taking all my strength. You are freezing me. What do you want with me?

OLD MAN, *letting go.* Be patient and you shall see and understand. Here comes the young lady.

They watch the GIRL *approaching, though the audience cannot yet see her.*

STUDENT. The Colonel's daughter?

OLD MAN. His daughter—yes. Look at her. Have you ever seen such a masterpiece?

STUDENT. She is like the marble statue in there.

OLD MAN. That's her mother, you know.

STUDENT. You are right. Never have I seen such a woman of woman born. Happy the man who may lead her to the altar and his home.

OLD MAN. You can see it. Not everyone recognizes her beauty. So, then, it is written.

The GIRL *enters, wearing an English riding habit. Without noticing anyone she walks slowly to the door, where she stops to say a few words to the* CARETAKER'S WIFE. *Then she goes into the house.*

The STUDENT *covers his eyes with his hand.*

OLD MAN. Are you weeping?

STUDENT. In the face of what's hopeless there can be nothing but despair.

OLD MAN. I can open doors and hearts, if only I find an arm to do my will. Serve me and you shall have power.

STUDENT. Is it a bargain? Am I to sell my soul?

OLD MAN. Sell nothing. Listen. All my life I have *taken*. Now I have a craving to give—give. But no one will accept. I am rich, very rich, but I have no heirs, except for a good-for-nothing who torments the life out of me. Become my son. Inherit me while I am still alive. Enjoy life so that I can watch, at least from a distance.

STUDENT. What am I to do?

OLD MAN. First go to *The Valkyrie*.

STUDENT. That's settled. What else?

OLD MAN. This evening you must be in there—in the Round Room.

STUDENT. How am I to get there?

OLD MAN. By way of *The Valkyrie*.

STUDENT. Why have you chosen me as your medium? Did you know me before?

OLD MAN. Yes, of course. I have had my eye on you for a long

time. But now look up there at the balcony. The maid is
hoisting the flag to half-mast for the Consul. And now she
is turning the bedclothes. Do you see that blue quilt?
It was made for two to sleep under, but now it covers
only one. *The* GIRL, *having changed her dress, appears
in the window and waters the hyacinths.* There is my little
girl. Look at her, look! She is talking to the flowers. Is she
not like that blue hyacinth herself? She gives them drink
—nothing but pure water, and they transform the water
into color and fragrance. Now here comes the Colonel
with the newspaper. He is showing her the bit about the
house that collapsed. Now he's pointing to your portrait.
She's not indifferent. She's reading of your brave
deed. . . .

I believe it's clouding over. If it turns to rain I shall be
in a pretty fix, unless Johansson comes back soon. *It grows
cloudy and dark. The* FIANCÉE *at the window-mirror
closes her window.* Now my fiancée is closing the window.
Seventy-nine years old. The window-mirror is the only
mirror she uses, because in it she sees not herself, but the
world outside—in two directions. But the world can see
her; she hasn't thought of that. Anyhow she's a handsome
old woman.

Now the DEAD MAN, *wrapped in a winding sheet, comes
out of the door.*

STUDENT. Good God, what do I see?

OLD MAN. What do you see?

STUDENT. Don't *you* see? There, in the doorway, the dead
    man?

OLD MAN. I see nothing, but I expected this. Tell me.

STUDENT. He is coming out into the street. *Pause.* Now he is
    turning his head and looking up at the flag.

OLD MAN. What did I tell you? You may be sure he'll count
    the wreaths and read the visiting cards. Woe to him who's
    missing.

STUDENT. Now he's turning the corner.

OLD MAN. He's gone to count the poor at the back door. The

poor are in the nature of a decoration, you see. "Followed
by the blessings of many." Well, he's not going to have
my blessing. Between ourselves he was a great scoundrel.

STUDENT. But charitable.

OLD MAN. A charitable scoundrel, always thinking of his grand
funeral. When he knew his end was near, he cheated the
State out of fifty thousand crowns. Now his daughter has
relations with another woman's husband and is wondering
about the Will. Yes, the scoundrel can hear every word
we're saying, and he's welcome to it. Ah, here comes
Johansson! JOHANSSON *enters.* Report! JOHANSSON *speaks,
but the audience does not hear.* Not at home, eh? You are
an ass. And the telegram? Nothing? Go on. . . . At six
this evening? That's good. Special edition, you say? With
his name in full. Arkenholtz, a student, born . . . parents
. . . That's splendid. . . . I think it's beginning to rain.
. . . What did he say about it? So—so. He wouldn't?
Well, he must. Here comes the aristocrat. Push me round
the corner, Johansson, so I can hear what the poor are
saying. And, Arkenholtz, you wait for me here. Understand? *To* JOHANSSON. Hurry up now, hurry up.

JOHANSSON *wheels the chair round the corner. The*
STUDENT *remains watching the* GIRL, *who is now loosening
the earth round the hyacinths. The* ARISTOCRAT, *wearing
mourning, comes in and speaks to the* DARK LADY, *who
has been walking to and fro on the pavement.*

ARISTOCRAT. But what can we do about it? We shall have to
wait.

LADY. I can't wait.

ARISTOCRAT. You can't? Well then, go into the country.

LADY. I don't want to do that.

ARISTOCRAT. Come over here or they will hear what we are
saying.

*They move towards the advertisement column and con-
tinue their conversation inaudibly.* JOHANSSON *returns.*

JOHANSSON, *to the* STUDENT. My master asks you not to forget
that other thing, sir.

STUDENT, *hesitating.* Look here . . . first of all tell me . . . who is your master?

JOHANSSON. Well, he's so many things, and he has been everything.

STUDENT. Is he a wise man?

JOHANSSON. Depends what that is. He says all his life he's been looking for a Sunday child, but that may not be true.

STUDENT. What does he want? He's grasping, isn't he?

JOHANSSON. It's power he wants. The whole day long he rides round in his chariot like the god Thor himself. He looks at houses, pulls them down, opens up new streets, builds squares. . . . But he breaks into houses too, sneaks through windows, plays havoc with human destinies, kills his enemies—and never forgives. Can you imagine it, sir? This miserable cripple was once a Don Juan—although he always lost his women.

STUDENT. How do you account for that?

JOHANSSON. You see he's so cunning he makes the women leave him when he's tired of them. But what he's most like now is a horse-thief in the human market. He steals human beings in all sorts of different ways. He literally stole me out of the hands of the law. Well, as a matter of fact I'd made a slip—hm, yes—and only he knew about it. Instead of getting me put in gaol, he turned me into a slave. I slave—for my food alone, and that's none of the best.

STUDENT. Then what is it he means to do in this house?

JOHANSSON. I'm not going to talk about that. It's too complicated.

STUDENT. I think I'd better get away from it all.

The GIRL *drops a bracelet out the window.*

JOHANSSON. Look! The young lady has dropped her bracelet out of the window. *The* STUDENT *goes slowly over, picks up the bracelet and returns it to the* GIRL, *who thanks him stiffly. The* STUDENT *goes back to* JOHANSSON. So you mean to get away. That's not so easy as you think, once he's got you in his net. And he's afraid of nothing between heaven and earth—yes, of one thing he is—of one person rather. . . .

STUDENT. Don't tell me. I think perhaps I know.

JOHANSSON. How can you know?

STUDENT. I'm guessing. Is it a little milkmaid he's afraid of?

JOHANSSON. He turns his head the other way whenever he meets a milk cart. Besides, he talks in his sleep. It seems he was once in Hamburg. . . .

STUDENT. Can one trust this man?

JOHANSSON. You can trust him—to do anything.

STUDENT. What's he doing now round the corner?

JOHANSSON. Listening to the poor. Sowing a little word, loosening one stone at a time, till the house falls down—metaphorically speaking. You see I'm an educated man. I was once a book-seller. . . . Do you still mean to go away?

STUDENT. I don't like to be ungrateful. He saved my father once, and now he only asks a small service in return.

JOHANSSON. What is that?

STUDENT. I am to go to *The Valkyrie.*

JOHANSSON. That's beyond me. But he's always up to new tricks. Look at him now, talking to that policeman. He is always thick with the police. He uses them, gets them involved in his interests, holds them with false promises and expectations, while all the time he's pumping them. You'll see that before the day is over he'll be received in the Round Room.

STUDENT. What does he want there? What connection has he with the Colonel?

JOHANSSON. I think I can guess, but I'm not sure. You'll see for yourself once you're in there.

STUDENT. I shall never be in there.

JOHANSSON. That depends on yourself. Go to *The Valkyrie.*

STUDENT. Is that the way?

JOHANSSON. Yes, if he said so. Look. Look at him in his war

chariot, drawn in triumph by the beggars, who get nothing for their pains but the hint of a treat at his funeral.

The OLD MAN *appears standing up in his wheel-chair, drawn by one of the beggars and followed by the rest.*

OLD MAN. Hail the noble youth who, at the risk of his own life, saved so many others in yesterday's accident. Three cheers for Arkenholtz! *The* BEGGARS *bare their heads but do not cheer. The* GIRL *at the window waves her handkerchief. The* COLONEL *gazes from the window of the Round Room. The* OLD WOMAN *rises at her window. The* MAID *on the balcony hoists the flag to the top.* Clap your hands, citizens. True, it is Sunday, but the ass in the pit and the ear in the corn field will absolve us. And although I am not a Sunday child, I have the gift of prophecy and also that of healing. Once I brought a drowned person back to life. That was in Hamburg on a Sunday morning just like this. . . .

The MILKMAID *enters, seen only by the* STUDENT *and the* OLD MAN. *She raises her arms like one who is drowning and gazes fixedly at the* OLD MAN. *He sits down, then crumples up, stricken with horror.*

Johansson! Take me away! Quick! . . . Arkenholtz, don't forget *The Valkyrie.*

STUDENT. What is all this?

JOHANSSON. We shall see. We shall see.

SCENE TWO

Inside the Round Room. At the back is a white porcelain stove. On either side of it are a mirror, a pendulum clock and candelabra. On the right of the stove is the entrance to the hall beyond which is a glimpse of a room furnished in green and mahogany. On the left of the stove is the door to a cupboard, papered like the wall. The statue, shaded by palms has a curtain which can be drawn to conceal it.

A door on the left leads into the Hyacinth Room, where the GIRL *sits reading.*

The back of the COLONEL *can be seen, as he sits in the Green Room, writing.*

BENGTSSON, *the Colonel's servant, comes in from the hall. He is wearing livery, and is followed by* JOHANSSON, *dressed as a waiter.*

BENGTSSON. Now you'll have to serve the tea, Johansson, while I take the coats. Have you ever done it before?

JOHANSSON. It's true I push a war chariot in the daytime, as you know, but in the evenings I go as a waiter to receptions and so forth. It's always been my dream to get into this house. They're queer people here, aren't they?

BENGTSSON. Ye-es. A bit out of the ordinary anyhow.

JOHANSSON. Is it to be a musical party or what?

BENGTSSON. The usual ghost supper, as we call it. They drink tea and don't say a word—or else the Colonel does all the talking. And they crunch their biscuits, all at the same time. It sounds like rats in an attic.

JOHANSSON. Why do you call it the ghost supper?

BENGTSSON. They look like ghosts. And they've kept this up for twenty years, always the same people saying the same things or saying nothing at all for fear of being found out.

JOHANSSON. Isn't there a mistress of the house?

BENGTSSON. Oh yes, but she's crazy. She sits in a cupboard because her eyes can't bear the light. *He points to the papered door.* She sits in there.

JOHANSSON. In there?

BENGTSSON. Well, I told you they were a bit out of the ordinary.

JOHANSSON. But then—what does she look like?

BENGTSSON. Like a mummy. Do you want to have a look at her? *He opens the door.* There she is.

The figure of the COLONEL'S WIFE *is seen, white and shrivelled into a* MUMMY.

JOHANSSON. Oh my God!

MUMMY, *babbling*. Why do you open the door? Haven't I told you to keep it closed?

BENGTSSON, *in a wheedling tone*. Ta, ta, ta, ta. Be a good girl now, then you'll get something nice. Pretty Polly.

MUMMY, *parrot-like*. Pretty Polly. Are you there, Jacob? Currrr!

BENGTSSON. She thinks she's a parrot, and maybe she's right. *To the* MUMMY. Whistle for us, Polly.

The MUMMY *whistles*.

JOHANSSON. Well, I've seen a few things in my day, but this beats everything.

BENGTSSON. You see, when a house gets old, it grows moldy, and when people stay a long time together and torment each other they go mad. The mistress of the house—shut up, Polly!—that mummy there, has been living here for forty years—same husband, same furniture, same relatives, same friends. *He closes the papered door*. And the goings-on in this house—well, they're beyond me. Look at that statue—that's her when she was young.

JOHANSSON. Good Lord! Is that the mummy?

BENGTSSON. Yes. It's enough to make you weep. And somehow, carried away by her own imagination or something, she's got to be a bit like a parrot—the way she talks and the way she can't stand cripples or sick people. She can't stand the sight of her own daughter, because she's sick.

JOHANSSON. Is the young lady sick?

BENGTSSON. Didn't you know that?

JOHANSSON. No. And the Colonel, who is he?

BENGTSSON. You'll see.

JOHANSSON, *looking at the statue*. It's horrible to think that . . . How old is she now?

BENGTSSON. Nobody knows. But it's said that when she was thirty-five she looked nineteen, and that's what she made the Colonel believe she was—here in this very house. Do you know what that black Japanese screen by the couch is for? They call it the death-screen, and when someone's going to die, they put it round—same as in a hospital.

JOHANSSON. What a horrible house! And the student was longing to get in, as if it were paradise.

BENGTSSON. What student? Oh, I know. The one who's coming here this evening. The Colonel and the young lady happened to meet him at the Opera, and both of them took a fancy to him. Hm. Now it's my turn to ask questions. Who is your master—the man in the wheelchair?

JOHANSSON. Well, he er . . . Is he coming here too?

BENGTSSON. He hasn't been invited.

JOHANSSON. He'll come uninvited—if need be.

The OLD MAN *appears in the hall on crutches, wearing a frock-coat and top-hat. He steals forward and listens.*

BENGTSSON. He's a regular old devil, isn't he?

JOHANSSON. Up to the ears.

BENGTSSON. He looks like old Nick himself.

JOHANSSON. And he must be a wizard too, for he goes through locked doors.

The OLD MAN *comes forward and takes hold of* JOHANSSON *by the ear.*

OLD MAN. Rascal—take care! *To* BENGTSSON. Tell the Colonel I am here.

BENGTSSON. But we are expecting guests.

OLD MAN. I know. But my visit is as good as expected, if not exactly looked forward to.

BENGTSSON. I see. What name shall I say? Mr. Hummel?

OLD MAN. Exactly. Yes. BENGTSSON *crosses the hall to the Green Room, the door of which he closes behind him. To* JOHANSSON. Get out! JOHANSSON *hesitates.* Get out! JOHANSSON *disappears into the hall. The* OLD MAN *inspects the room and stops in front of the statue in much astonishment.* Amelia! It is she—she!

MUMMY, *from the cupboard.* Prrr-etty Polly. *The* OLD MAN *starts.*

OLD MAN. What was that? Is there a parrot in the room? I don't see it.

MUMMY. Are you there, Jacob?

OLD MAN. The house is haunted.

MUMMY. Jacob!

OLD MAN. I'm scared. So these are the kind of secrets they guard in this house. *With his back turned to the cupboard he stands looking at a portrait.* There he is—he!

The MUMMY *comes out behind the* OLD MAN *and gives a pull at his wig.*

MUMMY. Currrrr! Is it . . . ? Currrrr!

OLD MAN, *jumping out of his skin.* God in heaven! Who is it?

MUMMY, *in a natural voice.* Is it Jacob?

OLD MAN. Yes, my name is Jacob.

MUMMY, *with emotion.* And my name is Amelia.

OLD MAN. No, no, no . . . Oh my God!

MUMMY. That's how I look. Yes. *Pointing to the statue.* And that's how I *did* look. Life opens one's eyes, does it not? I live mostly in the cupboard to avoid seeing and being seen. . . . But, Jacob, what do you want here?

OLD MAN. My child. Our child.

MUMMY. There she is.

OLD MAN. Where?

MUMMY. There—in the Hyacinth Room.

OLD MAN, *looking at the* GIRL. Yes, that is she. *Pause.* And what about her father—the Colonel, I mean—your husband?

MUMMY. Once, when I was angry with him, I told him everything.

OLD MAN. Well. . . . ?

MUMMY. He didn't believe me. He just said: "That's what all wives say when they want to murder their husbands." It was a terrible crime none the less. It has falsified his whole life—his family tree too. Sometimes I take a look in the Peerage, and then I say to myself: Here she is, going about with a false birth certificate like some servant girl, and for such things people are sent to the reformatory.

OLD MAN. Many do it. I seem to remember your own date of birth was given incorrectly.

MUMMY. My mother made me do that. I was not to blame. And in our crime, *you* played the biggest part.

OLD MAN. No. Your husband caused that crime, when he took my fiancée from me. I was born one who cannot forgive until he has punished. That was to me an imperative duty—and is so still.

MUMMY. What are you expecting to find in this house? What do you want? How did you get in? Is it to do with my daughter? If you touch her, you shall die.

OLD MAN. I mean well by her.

MUMMY. Then you must spare her father.

OLD MAN. No.

MUMMY. Then you shall die. In this room, behind that screen.

OLD MAN. That may be. But I can't let go once I've got my teeth into a thing.

MUMMY. You want to marry her to that student. Why? He is nothing and has nothing.

OLD MAN. He will be rich, through me.

MUMMY. Have you been invited here tonight?

OLD MAN. No, but I propose to get myself an invitation to this ghost supper.

MUMMY. Do you know who is coming?

OLD MAN. Not exactly.

MUMMY. The Baron. The man who lives up above—whose father-in-law was buried this afternoon.

OLD MAN. The man who is getting a divorce in order to marry the daughter of the Caretaker's wife . . . The man who used to be—your lover.

MUMMY. Another guest will be your former fiancée, who was seduced by my husband.

OLD MAN. A select gathering.

MUMMY. Oh God, if only we might die, might die!

OLD MAN. Then why have you stayed together?

MUMMY. Crime and secrets and guilt bind us together. We have broken our bonds and gone our own ways, times without number, but we are always drawn together again.

OLD MAN. I think the Colonel is coming.

MUMMY. Then I will go in to Adèle. *Pause.* Jacob, mind what you do. Spare him. *Pause. She goes into the Hyacinth Room and disappears.*

The COLONEL *enters, cold and reserved, with a letter in his hand.*

COLONEL. Be seated, please. *Slowly the* OLD MAN *sits down. Pause. The* COLONEL *stares at him.* You wrote this letter, sir?

OLD MAN. I did.

COLONEL. Your name is Hummel?

OLD MAN. It is. *Pause.*

COLONEL. As I understand, you have bought in all my unpaid promissory notes. I can only conclude that I am in your hands. What do you want?

OLD MAN. I want payment, in one way or another.

COLONEL. In what way?

OLD MAN. A very simple one. Let us not mention the money. Just bear with me in your house as a guest.

COLONEL. If so little will satisfy you . . .

OLD MAN. Thank you.

COLONEL. What else?

OLD MAN. Dismiss Bengtsson.

COLONEL. Why should I do that? My devoted servant, who has been with me a lifetime, who has the national medal for long and faithful service—why should I do that?

OLD MAN. That's how you see him—full of excellent qualities. He is not the man he appears to be.

COLONEL. Who is?

OLD MAN, *taken aback.* True. But Bengtsson must go.

COLONEL. Are you going to run my house?

OLD MAN. Yes. Since everything here belongs to me—furniture, curtains, dinner service, linen . . . and more too.

COLONEL. How do you mean—more?

OLD MAN. Everything. I own everything here. It is mine.

COLONEL. Very well, it is yours. But my family escutcheon and my good name remain my own.

OLD MAN. No, not even those. *Pause.* You are not a nobleman.

COLONEL. How dare you!

OLD MAN, *producing a document.* If you read this extract from *The Armorial Gazette,* you will see that the family whose name you are using has been extinct for a hundred years.

COLONEL. I have heard rumors to this effect, but I inherited the name from my father. *Reads.* It is true. You are right. I am not a nobleman. Then I must take off my signet ring. It is true, it belongs to you. *Gives it to him.* There you are.

OLD MAN, *pocketing the ring.* Now we will continue. You are not a Colonel either.

COLONEL. I am not . . . ?

OLD MAN. No. You once held the temporary rank of Colonel in the American Volunteer Force, but after the war in Cuba and the reorganization of the Army, all such titles were abolished.

COLONEL. Is this true?

OLD MAN, *indicating his pocket.* Do you want to read it?

COLONEL. No, that's not necessary. Who are you, and what right have you to sit there stripping me in this fashion?

OLD MAN. You will see. But as far as stripping you goes . . . do you know who you are?

COLONEL. How dare you?

OLD MAN. Take off that wig and have a look at yourself in the mirror. But take your teeth out at the same time and shave off your moustache. Let Bengtsson unlace your metal stays and perhaps a certain X.Y.Z., a lackey, will recognize himself. The fellow who was a cupboard lover in a certain kitchen . . . *The* COLONEL *reaches for the bell on the table, but* HUMMEL *checks him.* Don't touch that bell, and don't call Bengtsson. If you do, I'll have him arrested. *Pause.* And now the guests are beginning to arrive. Keep your composure and we will continue to play our old parts for a while.

COLONEL. Who are you? I recognize your voice and eyes.

OLD MAN. Don't try to find out. Keep silent and obey.

The STUDENT *enters and bows to the* COLONEL.

STUDENT. How do you do, sir.

COLONEL. Welcome to my house, young man. Your splendid behavior at that great disaster has brought your name to everybody's lips, and I count it an honor to receive you in my home.

STUDENT. My humble descent, sir . . . Your illustrious name and noble birth. . . .

COLONEL. May I introduce Mr. Arkenholtz—Mr. Hummel. If you will join the ladies in here, Mr. Arkenholtz—I must conclude my conversation with Mr. Hummel. *He shows the* STUDENT *into the Hyacinth Room, where he remains visible, talking shyly to the* GIRL. A splendid young man, musical, sings, writes poetry. If he only had blue blood in him, if he were of the same station, I don't think I should object . . .

OLD MAN. To what?

COLONEL. To my daughter . . .

OLD MAN. *Your* daughter! But apropos of that, why does she spend all her time in there?

COLONEL. She insists on being in the Hyacinth Room except when she is out-of-doors. It's a peculiarity of hers. Ah, here comes Miss Beatrice von Holsteinkrona—a charming woman, a pillar of the Church, with just enough money of her own to suit her birth and position.

OLD MAN, *to himself.* My fiancée.

The FIANCÉE *enters, looking a little crazy.*

COLONEL. Miss Holsteinkrona—Mr. Hummel. *The* FIANCÉE *curtseys and takes a seat. The* ARISTOCRAT *enters and seats himself. He wears mourning and looks mysterious.* Baron Skanskorg . . .

OLD MAN, *aside, without rising.* That's the jewel-thief, I think. *To the* COLONEL. If you bring in the Mummy, the party will be complete.

COLONEL, *at the door of the Hyacinth Room.* Polly!

MUMMY, *entering.* Currrrr . . . !

COLONEL. Are the young people to come in too?

OLD MAN. No, not the young people. They shall be spared. *They all sit silent in a circle.*

COLONEL. Shall we have the tea brought in?

OLD MAN. What's the use? No one wants tea. Why should we pretend about it?

COLONEL. Then shall we talk?

OLD MAN. Talk of the weather, which we know? Inquire about each other's health, which we know just as well. I prefer silence—then one can hear thoughts and see the past. Silence cannot hide anything—but words can. I read the other day that differences of language originated among savages for the purpose of keeping one tribe's secrets hidden from another. Every language therefore is a code, and he who finds the key can understand every language in the world. But this does not prevent secrets from being exposed without a key, specially when there is a question of paternity to be proved. Proof in a Court of Law is another matter. Two false witnesses suffice to prove anything about which they are agreed, but one does not take witnesses along on the kind of explorations I have in mind. Nature herself has instilled in human beings a sense of modesty which tries to hide what should be hidden, but we slip into situations unintentionally, and by chance sometimes the deepest secret is divulged—the mask torn from the impostor, the villain exposed. . . . *Pause. All look at each other in silence.* What a silence there is now! *Long silence.* Here, for instance, in this honorable house, in this elegant home, where beauty, wealth and culture are united. . . . *Long silence.* All of

us now sitting here know who we are—do we not? There's
no need for me to tell you. And you know me, although
you pretend ignorance. *He indicates the Hyacinth Room.*
In there is my daughter. *Mine*—you know that too. She had
lost the desire to live, without knowing why. The fact is
she was withering away in this air charged with crime
and deceit and falseness of every kind. That is why I
looked for a friend for her in whose company she might
enjoy the light and warmth of noble deeds. *Long silence.*
That was my mission in this house: to pull up the weeds,
to expose the crimes, to settle all accounts, so that those
young people might start afresh in this home, which is
my gift to them. *Long silence.* Now I am going to grant
safe-conduct, to each of you in his and her proper time
and turn. Whoever stays I shall have arrested. *Long
silence.* Do you hear the clock ticking like a death-watch
beetle in the wall? Do you hear what it says? "It's time,
it's time, it's time." When it strikes, in a few moments,
your time will be up. Then you can go, but not before.
It's raising its arm against you before it strikes. Listen!
It is warning you. "The clock can strike." And I can
strike too. *He strikes the table with one of his crutches.*
Do you hear?

Silence. The MUMMY *goes up to the clock and stops it,
then speaks in a normal and serious voice.*

MUMMY. But I can stop time in its course. I can wipe out the
past and undo what is done. But not with bribes, not with
threats—only through suffering and repentance. *She goes
up to the* OLD MAN. We are miserable human beings, that
we know. We have erred and we have sinned, we like
all the rest. We are not what we seem, because at bottom
we are better than ourselves, since we detest our sins.
But when you, Jacob Hummel, with your false name,
choose to sit in judgment over us, you prove yourself
worse than us miserable sinners. For you are not the one
you appear to be. You are a thief of human souls. You
stole me once with false promises. You murdered the
Consul who was buried today; you strangled him with

debts. You have stolen the student, binding him by the
pretence of a claim on his father, who never owed you a
farthing. *Having tried to rise and speak, the* OLD MAN
*sinks back in his chair and crumples up more and more as
she goes on.* But there is one dark spot in your life which
I am not quite sure about, although I have my suspicions.
I think Bengtsson knows. *She rings the bell on the table.*

OLD MAN. No, not Bengtsson, not him.

MUMMY. So he does know. *She rings again. The* MILKMAID
appears in the hallway door, unseen by all but the OLD
MAN, *who shrinks back in horror. The* MILKMAID *vanishes
as* BENGTSSON *enters.* Do you know this man, Bengtsson?

BENGTSSON. Yes, I know him and he knows me. Life, as you
are aware, has its ups and downs. I have been in his
service; another time he was in mine. For two whole years
he was a sponger in my kitchen. As he had to be away
by three, the dinner was got ready at two, and the family
had to eat the warmed-up leavings of that brute. He
drank the soup stock, which the cook then filled up with
water. He sat out there like a vampire, sucking the marrow out of the house, so that we became like skeletons.
And he nearly got us put in prison when we called the
cook a thief. Later I met this man in Hamburg under
another name. He was a usurer then, a blood-sucker. But
while he was there he was charged with having lured a
young girl out on to the ice so as to drown her, because
she had seen him commit a crime he was afraid would be
discovered. . . .

The MUMMY *passes her hand over the* OLD MAN'S *face.*

MUMMY. *This* is you. Now give up the notes and the Will.
JOHANSSON *appears in the hallway door and watches the
scene with great interest, knowing he is now to be freed
from slavery. The* OLD MAN *produces a bundle of papers
and throws it on the table. The* MUMMY *goes over and
strokes his back.* Parrot. Are you there, Jacob?

OLD MAN, *like a parrot.* Jacob is here. Pretty Polly. Currrrr!

MUMMY. May the clock strike?

OLD MAN, *with a clucking sound.* The clock may strike. *Imitating a cuckoo clock.* Cuckoo, cuckoo, cuckoo. . . .

The MUMMY *opens the cupboard door.*

MUMMY. Now the clock has struck. Rise, and enter the cupboard where I have spent twenty years repenting our crime. A rope is hanging there, which you can take as the one with which you strangled the Consul, and with which you meant to strangle your benefactor. . . . Go! *The* OLD MAN *goes in to the cupboard. The* MUMMY *closes the door.* Bengtsson! Put up the screen—the death-screen. BENGTSSON *places the screen in front of the door.* It is finished. God have mercy on his soul.

ALL. Amen. *Long silence.*

The GIRL *and the* STUDENT *appear in the Hyacinth Room. She has a harp, on which he plays a prelude, and then accompanies the* STUDENT's *recitation.*

STUDENT.   *I saw the sun. To me it seemed*
        that I beheld the Hidden.
        Men must reap what they have sown;
        blest is he whose deeds are good.
        Deeds which you have wrought in fury,
        cannot in evil find redress.
        Comfort him you have distressed
        with loving-kindness—this will heal.
        No fear has he who does no ill.
        Sweet is innocence.

SCENE THREE

Inside the Hyacinth Room. The general effect of the room is exotic and oriental. There are hyacinths everywhere, of every color, some in pots, some with the bulbs in glass vases and the roots going down into the water.

On top of the tiled stove is a large seated Buddha, in

whose lap rests a bulb from which rises the stem of a
shallot (Allium ascalonicum), bearing its globular cluster
of white, starlike flowers.
On the right is an open door, leading into the Round
Room, where the COLONEL *and the* MUMMY *are seated,*
inactive and silent. A part of the death-screen is also
visible.
On the left is a door to the pantry and kitchen.
The STUDENT *and the* GIRL *(Adèle) are beside the table;*
he standing, she seated with her harp.

GIRL. Now sing to my flowers.

STUDENT. Is this the flower of your soul?

GIRL. The one and only. Do you too love the hyacinth?

STUDENT. I love it above all other flowers—its virginal shape
rising straight and slender out of the bulb, resting on the
water and sending its pure white roots down into the
colorless fluid. I love its colors: the snow-white, pure as
innocence, the yellow honey-sweet, the youthful pink, the
ripe red, but best of all the blue—the dewy blue, deep-
eyed and full of faith. I love them all, more than gold or
pearls. I have loved them ever since I was a child, have
worshipped them because they have all the fine qualities
I lack. . . . And yet . . .

GIRL. Go on.

STUDENT. My love is not returned, for these beautiful blossoms hate me.

GIRL. How do you mean?

STUDENT. Their fragrance, strong and pure as the early winds
of spring which have passed over melting snows, confuses
my senses, deafens me, blinds me, thrusts me out of the
room, bombards me with poisoned arrows that wound
my heart and set my head on fire. Do you know the legend
of that flower?

GIRL. Tell it to me.

STUDENT. First its meaning. The bulb is the earth, resting on
the water or buried in the soil. Then the stalk rises,

straight as the axis of the world, and at the top are the six-pointed star-flowers.

GIRL. Above the earth—the stars. Oh, that is wonderful! Where did you learn this? How did you find it out?

STUDENT. Let me think . . . In your eyes. And so, you see, it is an image of the Cosmos. This is why Buddha sits holding the earth-bulb, his eyes brooding as he watches it grow, outward and upward, transforming itself into a heaven. This poor earth will become a heaven. It is for this that Buddha waits.

GIRL. I see it now. Is not the snowflake six-pointed too like the hyacinth flower?

STUDENT. You are right. The snowflakes must be falling stars.

GIRL. And the snowdrop is a snow-star, grown out of snow.

STUDENT. But the largest and most beautiful of all the stars in the firmament, the golden-red Sirius, is the narcissus with its gold and red chalice and its six white rays.

GIRL. Have you seen the shallot in bloom?

STUDENT. Indeed I have. It bears its blossoms within a ball, a globe like the celestial one, strewn with white stars.

GIRL. Oh how glorious! Whose thought was that?

STUDENT. Yours.

GIRL. Yours.

STUDENT. Ours. We have given birth to it together. We are wedded.

GIRL. Not yet.

STUDENT. What's still to do?

GIRL. Waiting, ordeals, patience.

STUDENT. Very well. Put me to the test. *Pause.* Tell me. Why do your parents sit in there so silently, not saying a single word?

GIRL. Because they have nothing to say to each other, and because neither believes what the other says. This is how my father puts it: What's the point of talking, when neither of us can fool the other?

STUDENT. What a horrible thing to hear!

GIRL. Here comes the Cook. Look at her, how big and fat she is. *They watch the* COOK, *although the audience cannot yet see her.*

STUDENT. What does she want?

GIRL. To ask me about the dinner. I have to do the house-keeping as my mother's ill.

STUDENT. What have we to do with the kitchen?

GIRL. We must eat. Look at the Cook. I can't bear the sight of her.

STUDENT. Who is that ogress?

GIRL. She belongs to the Hummel family of vampires. She is eating us.

STUDENT. Why don't you dismiss her?

GIRL. She won't go. We have no control over her. We've got her for our sins. Can't you see that we are pining and wasting away?

STUDENT. Don't you get enough to eat?

GIRL. Yes, we get many dishes, but all the strength has gone. She boils the nourishment out of the meat and gives us the fibre and water, while she drinks the stock herself. And when there's a roast, she first boils out the marrow, eats the gravy and drinks the juices herself. Everything she touches loses its savor. It's as if she sucked with her eyes. We get the grounds when she has drunk the coffee. She drinks the wine and fills the bottles up with water.

STUDENT. Send her packing.

GIRL. We can't.

STUDENT. Why not?

GIRL. We don't know. She won't go. No one has any control over her. She has taken all our strength from us.

STUDENT. May I get rid of her?

GIRL. No. It must be as it is. Here she is. She will ask me what is to be for dinner. I shall tell her. She will make objections and get her own way.

STUDENT. Let her do the ordering herself then.

GIRL. She won't do that.

STUDENT. What an extraordinary house! It is bewitched.

GIRL. Yes. But now she is turning back, because she has seen you.

THE COOK, *in the doorway*. No, that wasn't the reason. *She grins, showing all her teeth.*

STUDENT. Get out!

COOK. When it suits me. *Pause.* It does suit me now. *She disappears.*

GIRL. Don't lose your temper. Practise patience. She is one of the ordeals we have to go through in this house. You see, we have a housemaid too, whom we have to clean up after.

STUDENT. I am done for. *Cor in æthere.* Music!

GIRL. Wait.

STUDENT. Music!

GIRL. Patience. This room is called the room of ordeals. It looks beautiful, but it is full of defects.

STUDENT. Really? Well, such things must be seen to. It is very beautiful, but a little cold. Why don't you have a fire?

GIRL. Because it smokes.

STUDENT. Can't you have the chimney swept?

GIRL. It doesn't help. You see that writing-desk there?

STUDENT. An unusually fine piece.

GIRL. But it wobbles. Every day I put a piece of cork under that leg, and every day the housemaid takes it away when she sweeps and I have to cut a new piece. The penholder is covered with ink every morning and so is the inkstand. I have to clean them up every morning after that woman, as sure as the sun rises. *Pause.* What's the worst job you can think of?

STUDENT. To count the washing. Ugh!

GIRL. That I have to do. Ugh!

STUDENT. What else?

GIRL. To be waked in the middle of the night and have to get up and see to the window, which the housemaid has left banging.

STUDENT. What else?

GIRL. To get up on a ladder and tie the cord on the damper*
which the housemaid has torn off.

STUDENT. What else?

GIRL. To sweep after her, to dust after her, to light the fire in
the stove when all she's done is throw in some wood. To
see to the damper, to wipe the glasses, to lay the table
over again, to open the bottles, to see that the rooms are
aired, to remake my bed, to rinse the water-bottle when
it's green with sediment, to buy matches and soap which
are always lacking, to wipe the chimneys and trim the
wicks to keep the lamps from smoking—and so that they
don't go out when we have company, I have to fill them
myself. . . .

STUDENT. Music!

GIRL. Wait. The labor comes first. The labor of keeping the
dirt of life at a distance.

STUDENT. But you are wealthy and have two servants.

GIRL. It doesn't help. Even if we had three. Living is hard
work, and sometimes I grow tired. *Pause.* Think then if
there were a nursery as well.

STUDENT. The greatest of joys.

GIRL. And the costliest. Is life worth so much hardship?

STUDENT. That must depend on the reward you expect for
your labors. I would not shrink from anything to win your
hand.

GIRL. Don't say that. You can never have me.

STUDENT. Why not?

GIRL. You mustn't ask. *Pause.*

STUDENT. You dropped your bracelet out of the window. . . .

GIRL. Because my hand has grown so thin. *Pause.*

The COOK *appears with a Japanese bottle in her hand.*

There she is—the one who devours me and all of us.

STUDENT. What has she in her hand?

*Damper to the big stove.

GIRL. It is the bottle of coloring matter that has letters like
scorpions on it. It is the soy which turns water into soup
and takes the place of gravy. She makes cabbage soup
with it—and mock-turtle soup too.

STUDENT, *to* COOK. Get out!

COOK. You drain us of sap, and we drain you. We take the
blood and leave you the water, but colored . . . colored.
I am going now, but all the same I shall stay, as long as
I please.

She goes out.

STUDENT. Why did Bengtsson get a medal?

GIRL. For his great merits.

STUDENT. Has he no defects?

GIRL. Yes, great ones. But you don't get a medal for them.
They smile.

STUDENT. You have many secrets in this house.

GIRL. As in all others. Permit us to keep ours.

STUDENT. Don't you approve of candor?

GIRL. Yes—within reason.

STUDENT. Sometimes I'm seized with a raging desire to say
all I think. But I know the world would go to pieces if
one were completely candid. *Pause.* I went to a funeral
the other day . . . in church. It was very solemn and
beautiful.

GIRL. Was it Mr. Hummel's?

STUDENT. My false benefactor's—yes. At the head of the coffin
stood an old friend of the deceased. He carried the mace.
I was deeply impressed by the dignified manner and moving words of the clergyman. I cried. We all cried. Afterwards we went to a tavern, and there I learned that the
man with the mace had been in love with the dead man's
son. . . . *The* GIRL *stares at him, trying to understand.*
And that the dead man had borrowed money from his
son's admirer. *Pause.* Next day the clergyman was arrested
for embezzling the church funds. A pretty story.

GIRL. Oh . . . ! *Pause.*

STUDENT. Do you know how I am thinking about you now?

GIRL. Don't tell me, or I shall die.

STUDENT. I must, or I shall die.

GIRL. It is in asylums that people say everything they think.

STUDENT. Exactly. My father finished up in an asylum.

GIRL. Was he ill?

STUDENT. No, he was well, but he was mad. You see, he broke out once—in these circumstances. Like all of us, he was surrounded with a circle of acquaintances; he called them friends for short. They were a lot of rotters, of course, as most people are, but he had to have some society—he couldn't get on all alone. Well, as you know, in everyday life no one tells people what he thinks of them, and he didn't either. He knew perfectly well what frauds they were—he'd sounded the depths of their deceit —but as he was a wise and well-bred man, he was always courteous to them. Then one day he gave a big party. It was in the evening and he was tired by the day's work and by the strain of holding his tongue and at the same time talking rubbish with his guests. . . . *The* GIRL *is frightened.* Well, at the dinner table he rapped for silence, raised his glass, and began to speak. Then something loosed the trigger. He made an enormous speech in which he stripped the whole company naked, one after the other, and told them of all their treachery. Then, tired out, he sat down on the table and told them all to go to hell.

GIRL. Oh!

STUDENT. I was there, and I shall never forget what happened then. Father and Mother came to blows, the guests rushed for the door . . . and my father was taken to a mad-house, where he died. *Pause.* Water that is still too long stagnates, and so it is in this house too. There is something stagnating here. And yet I thought it was paradise itself that first time I saw you coming in here. There I stood that Sunday morning, gazing in. I saw a Colonel who was no Colonel. I had a benefactor who was a thief and had to hang himself. I saw a mummy who was not a mummy and an old maid—what of the maidenhood, by the way?

Where is beauty to be found? In nature, and in my own mind, when it is in its Sunday clothes. Where are honor and faith? In fairy-tales and children's fancies. Where is anything that fulfills its promise? In my imagination. Now your flowers have poisoned me and I have given the poison back to you. I asked you to become my wife in a home full of poetry and song and music. Then the Cook came. . . . *Sursum Corda!* Try once more to strike fire and glory out of the golden harp. Try, I beg you, I implore you on my knees. *Pause.* Then I will do it myself. *He picks up the harp, but the strings give no sound.* It is dumb and deaf. To think that the most beautiful flowers are so poisonous, are the most poisonous. The curse lies over the whole of creation, over life itself. Why will you not be my bride? Because the very life-spring within you is sick . . . now I can feel that vampire in the kitchen beginning to suck me. I believe she is a Lamia, one of those that suck the blood of children. It is always in the kitchen quarters that the seed-leaves of the children are nipped, if it has not already happened in the bedroom. There are poisons that destroy the sight and poisons that open the eyes. I seem to have been born with the latter kind, for I cannot see what is ugly as beautiful, nor call evil good. I cannot. Jesus Christ descended into hell. That was His pilgrimage on earth—to this madhouse, this prison, this charnel-house, this earth. And the madmen killed Him when He wanted to set them free; but the robber they let go. The robber always gets the sympathy. Woe! Woe to us all. Saviour of the world, save us! We perish.

And now the GIRL *has drooped, and it is seen that she is dying. She rings.*

BENGTSSON *enters.*

GIRL. Bring the screen. Quick. I am dying.

BENGTSSON *comes back with the screen, opens it and arranges it in front of the* GIRL.

STUDENT. The Liberator is coming. Welcome, pale and gentle one. Sleep, you lovely, innocent, doomed creature, suffering for no fault of your own. Sleep without dreaming, and when you wake again . . . may you be greeted by a sun that does not burn, in a home without dust, by friends without stain, by a love without flaw. You wise and gentle Buddha, sitting there waiting for a Heaven to sprout from the earth, grant us patience in our ordeal and purity of will, so that this hope may not be confounded.

The strings of the harp hum softly and a white light fills the room.

> I saw the sun. To me it seemed
> that I beheld the Hidden.
> Men must reap what they have sown,
> blest is he whose deeds are good.
> Deeds which you have wrought in fury,
> cannot in evil find redress.
> Comfort him you have distressed
> with loving-kindness—this will heal.
> No fear has he who does no ill.
> Sweet is innocence.

A faint moaning is heard behind the screen. You poor little child, child of this world of illusion, guilt, suffering and death, this world of endless change, disappointment, and pain. May the Lord of Heaven be merciful to you upon your journey.

The room disappears. Böcklin's picture The Island of the Dead *is seen in the distance, and from the island comes music, soft, sweet, and melancholy.*

ANCHOR BOOKS

for the permanent library of the serious reader

These ANCHOR BOOKS are available at your bookseller's at prices ranging from 65¢ to $1.25.

A21   THREE GREEK ROMANCES. Hadas. New translations of *Daphnis and Chloe*, *An Ephesian Tale*, and *The Hunters of Euboea*.

A22a   HISTORY OF ENGLAND. Trevelyan. The work of the great
A22b   English historian in three volumes.
A22c

A23   MAGIC, SCIENCE AND RELIGION. Malinowski. A renowned study of primitive man's relation to nature and the supernatural.

A24   MOZART. Turner. A critical biography.

A25   TEACHER IN AMERICA. Barzun. The famous commentary on modern American higher education.

A26   THE COUNTRY OF THE POINTED FIRS. Jewett. An American classic.

A27   THE MIND OF THE SOUTH. Cash. A thoughtful and timely study of the South, its people, and their outlook.

A28   THE TWO SOURCES OF MORALITY AND RELIGION. Bergson. The ultimate adaptation of creative evolution to morality and religion.

A29   A COLLECTION OF ESSAYS. Orwell. The major literary, social, and political writings of England's great modern essayist.

A30   FEAR AND TREMBLING and THE SICKNESS UNTO DEATH. Kierkegaard. Two of the great religious thinker's most important works.

A31   HAMLET AND OEDIPUS. Jones. The classic example of the psychoanalytical approach to literature.

A32   MEDIEVAL PEOPLE. Power. A classic of social history picturing life in the Middle Ages.

A33   THE ARCHITECTURE OF HUMANISM. Scott. A study in the history of taste.

A34   THE HUMAN USE OF HUMAN BEINGS. Wiener. A lucid exposition of the new science of Cybernetics.

A35   VICTORIAN ENGLAND: PORTRAIT OF AN AGE. Young.

A36   AESTHETICS AND HISTORY. Berenson. The substance of his theory of art.

A37   EIGHT ESSAYS. Wilson. Essays on history and literature.

A38   GREEK TRAGEDY. Kitto. A detailed study of the plays of the Greek dramatists.

A39   SEA AND SARDINIA and Selections from TWILIGHT IN ITALY. D. H. Lawrence. A revelation of the Italian character and the author's personal philosophy.

A40   THE GREAT TRADITION. Leavis. A study of the English novel.